Cybercriminology and Digital Investigation

Cybercriminology and Digital Investigation

Kyung-shick Choi

LFB Scholarly Publishing LLC
El Paso 2015

Library of Congress Cataloging-in-Publication Data

Choi, Kyung-shick, 1973- author.
Cybercriminology and digital investigation / Kyung-shick Choi.
pages cm
Includes bibliographical references and index.
ISBN 978-1-59332-770-5 (pbk. : alk. paper)
1. Computer crimes--Investigation. I. Title.
HV6773.C47777 2015
363.25'968--dc23
2015035244

ISBN 978-1-59332-770-5

Manufactured in the United States of America.

This book is dedicated to my daughter Clair, with love.

Table of Contents

Preface

I would like to address a brief statement prior to the main book contents. Although cybercrime substantially impacts our lives, such crime seemed to be less frequently studied by criminologists and criminal justice scholars. While it is a fact that our criminal justice system is slowly beginning to focus on cybercrime, it does not seem to adequately address the issues of cybercrime as a whole.

My interest in this area while pursuing my criminology studies led me to take a scholarly journey into a new crime area, "cybercrime." This book will discuss the broad category of cybercrime as well as specific computer crimes by addressing the wide range of crime victimization, criminological theories, research, legal issues, practices, and prevention strategies. The intended audience for this book includes anyone who is interested in learning details regarding cybercrime, the causes of individual computer crime/cybercrime victimization, its related empirical research, and practices.

This book also demonstrates empirical assessment of cybercrime victimizations via the application of Routine Activity Theory (RAT). The concept of three main risk factors, i) Motivated Offenders, ii) Suitable Target, and iii) Capable Guardianship, which contribute to computer crime/cybercrime, was used to assess the new theoretical model advanced in my research by providing an overall picture of the relationship among the causal factors and computer-crime/ cybercrime victimization. My integrated theory, which I call 'Cyber-Routine Activities Theory (2008),' has been applied to various cybercrime victimizations among cybercriminologists and received positive reviews. I personally look forward to seeing how Cyber-Routine Activities Theory can be expanded and tested within the realm of cybercriminology.

As an introduction, PART I lays the foundation of understanding cyberspace and cybercrime, which enables students to clearly recognize distinctions between the physical world and traditional crime. PARTS II and III focus on i) MOTIVATED OFFENDER as the first tenet of RAT. The chapters engage in discussions regarding cybercriminals' motivations using various theoretical perspectives and empirical research. As the second tenet of RAT, PART IV focuses on ii) TARGTET SUITABLITY OF CYBERCRIME VICTIMS by examining the criminology literature. PARTS V, VI, and VII examine the issues of law enforcement, legal procedures in crime investigation, forensic investigation, cyber-laws, and sanctions as a Section of iii) FORMAL CAPABLE GUARDIANSHIP. In addition, this book provides a framework for developing effective cybercrime prevention strategies.

This book aims to build a bridge between criminological perspective and cybercrime related disciplines and I hope it will provide potential benefits to researchers and practitioners of crossing disciplinary boundaries to minimize cybercrime issues via an application of criminological science. I also hope to see that the global community acknowledges the importance of utilizing a coordinated multi-disciplinary action to combatting cybercrime issues.

Acknowledgments

I would like to thank Dean Tanya Zlateva and Associate Dean Lou Chitkushev of Boston University for their kind support and encouragement. I also wish to thank, Dr. Daniel LeClair, at Boston University, for his mentorship, continuous emotional support and helpful advice for my life and academic career. Finally, I would like to extend a special thanks to Dr. Kyungseok Choo, who offered constant encouragement and guided me to build a strong scholarship.

PART I

Introduction and Overview of Cybercrime

Chapter 1 - Definition of Cybercrime and Computer Crime

Everyday aspects of our lives are performed at the leading edge of technology. Society depends heavily on computer technology for almost everything in life. The rapid development of technology is also increasing our dependency on computer systems. Perhaps we are currently living in two separate worlds: the physical world and the cyber-world. Even the level of connectedness people can achieve via high-speed Internet has altered the way we socialize. Individuals receive services, search for information, exchange customized text messages, and pay bills with a mobile phone browser. People are connected and socialize with others, visiting video-chatrooms and online games sites in cyberspace.

Thus, cybercrime has the potential to affect everyone's daily activities. Today, computer criminals are using this increased dependency on technology as a prime opportunity to engage in illicit or delinquent behaviors. It is almost impossible to have precise statistics on the number of computer crimes and the monetary loss to victims because computer crimes are rarely detected by victims or reported to authorities (Standler, 2002). In addition, policing in cyberspace is very minimal at best (Britz, 2004). Moreover, computer criminals are becoming more sophisticated in their criminal behavior. Cybercrime has become a real threat to the quality of life. Few people have recognized the overall impact of computer crime. More importantly, people do not realize how they are constructing their online lifestyles through the constant use of computer technology.

Today, we often hear about cybercrime topics such as Hacking, Internet Fraud, Identity Theft, Voice Fishing, Cyber-harassments,

Cyber-bullying, Cyber-stalking, Cyber-terrorism, Online gaming addiction, Cyber-piracy, etc. Are they all cybercrimes? What are computer crimes? To begin answering these questions, we need to understand basic terms and make clear distinctions between cybercrime and computer crime. Millions of people every day work, socialize, or consume entertainment on the Internet – in cyberspace. How would you define "cyberspace?" We will discuss the concept of cyberspace based on empirical reviews and explore jurisdiction issues associated with cyberspace. Moreover, we will be learning more about Cohen and Felson's Routine Activities Theory, which is a predominant theory that explains the patterns of crime victimization in both cyberspace and the physical world.

DEFINITIONS OF CYBERCRIME

The definition of cybercrime is somewhat imprecise since it covers some very broad concepts. Most people are confused about the difference between cybercrime and computer crime. In fact, some cybercrime authors do not appropriately separate the terms. Therefore, before looking into the details of computer-crime victimization, it is necessary to define the difference between cybercrime and computer crime.

Casey (2001) defines cybercrime as "any crime that involves computers and networks, including crimes that do not rely heavily on computers" (p. 8). Thomas and Loader (2000) also note that cybercrime is "computer-mediated activities which are either illegal or considered illicit by certain parties and which can be conducted through global electronic networks" (p. 3). Basically, cybercrimes cover wide categories of crime in cyberspace or on the World Wide Web, including "computer-assisted crimes" and "computer-focused crimes" (Furnell, 2002, p. 22).

In general, special computer operating skills are not required to commit cybercrimes. For example, a suspect and a victim may communicate via Web-based chatrooms, Microsoft Network messenger (MSN), or e-mail. Once the criminal gains the potential victim's trust, the criminal is in the position to commit a crime against the victim. In this case, even though the Internet probably assisted the suspect in communicating with the victim, it does not mean that the technology or the Internet caused the crime (Casey, 2000). Indeed, in computer-assisted crimes, a computer does not have to play a major role in the crime. It can merely be the tool that is used by the suspect that assists in facilitating the eventual offense such as in the case of fraud or in a confidence scam.

According to Casey (2000) the more general term cybercrime can be contrasted with computer crime or computer-focused crime, special types of cybercrime. These refer to

> a limited set of crimes that are specially defined in laws such as the US Computer Fraud and Abuse Act and the UK Computer Abuse Act. These crimes include theft of computer services; unauthorized access to protected computers [1]; software piracy and the alteration or theft of electronically stored information; extortion committed with the assistance of computers; obtaining unauthorized access to records from banks, credit card issuers, or customer reporting agencies; traffic in stolen passwords and transmission of destructive viruses or commands. (pp. 9-10)

The National White-collar Crime Center (2003) defines computer crime as a violation of law involving a computer. They assert that "true" computer crimes target the content of computer operating systems, programs, or networks (hereinafter referred to as "computer systems") and typically involve one or more of the following:

- Accessing computer systems without permission (unauthorized access)
- Damaging computer systems (sabotage)
- Acquiring information stored on computer systems—without permission (theft of data)

---

[1] The concept of "protected computers" was introduced by an amendment enacted in 1996; until then, section 1030 only reached conduct targeting "the U.S. federal interest computers." As a result of the 1996 amendment, the statute reaches conduct directed at any computer connected to the Internet, regardless of whether the computers involved are located in the same state. It also confers international jurisdiction (Clifford, 2006).

- Acquiring services from computer systems—without permission (theft of services)
  (National White-collar Crime Center, 2003)

Wall (2001) also established 4 legal categories of cybercrime:

1. Cyber-trespassing: crossing boundaries into other people's property and/or causing damage (e.g., hacking, defacement, viruses).
2. Cyber-deception and theft: stealing money, property, etc. (e.g., credit card fraud, intellectual property violations, etc. (a.k.a., piracy).
3. Cyber-pornography: activities that breach laws on obscenity and decency.
4. Cyber-violence: doing psychological harm to, or inciting physical harm against others, thereby breaching laws pertaining to the protection of the person (e.g., hate speech, stalking, etc.).

In fact, some general cybercrime categories overlap with computer crime activities, but computer crime is different than general cybercrime. Here is my definition clarifying Wall's 4 legal categories of cybercrime: computer crime is a component of cybercrime, but computer crime is not necessarily cybercrime. In other words, cybercrime is a bigger umbrella that encompasses computer crime, and computer crimes require more than a basic level of operating skills for offenders to commit them successfully against the victims. In addition, manipulation of digital data should be considered one of the key ingredients in computer crime. In fact, offenders who commit a cybercrime or a computer crime are both conducting their business in this new place, cyber-space, which is a realm different from the physical world that has different jurisdictions and different laws that we can apply.

Category	Data Manipulation	Types of Crime
Cybercrime	N/A	*Cyber-pornography –activities that breach laws on obscenity and decency.* *Cyber-violence–doing psychological harm to, or inciting physical harm against others, thereby breaching laws pertaining to the protection of the person, e.g. hate speech, stalking.*
Computer Crime	Yes	*Cyber-trespass-crossing boundaries into other people's property and/or causing damage, e.g. hacking, defacement, viruses.* *Cyber-deceptions and theft – stealing (money, property), e.g. credit card fraud, intellectual property violations (a.k.a. 'piracy').*

DISCUSSION:

What is the difference between computer crime and cybercrime? Provide examples of computer crime and cybercrime and define your own terms of computer crime and cybercrime.

Chapter 2 - Routine Activities Theory: Understanding Jurisdiction over Cybercrime

Prior to discussing major issues in cyberspace, I would like to introduce the concept of Routine Activity Theory, which may help you better understand the overall issues of cybercrime. As previously mentioned, our primary lessons in this book are strongly relevant to the theoretical components the Routine Activity theorists' posit.

In 1979, Cohen and Felson proposed their Routine Activity Theory, which focused mainly on opportunities for criminal events. Cohen and Felson posited that there are three major tenets that primarily affect criminal victimization. The main tenets are (a) motivated offenders, (b) suitable targets, and (c) the absence of capable guardians against a violation (Cohen and Felson, 1979; Cohen, Felson, and Land, 1981; Felson, 1986, 1988; Kennedy and Forde, 1990; Massey, Krohn, and Bonati, 1989; Miethe, Stafford, and Long, 1987; Roneck and Maier, 1991; Sherman, Gartin, and Buerger, 1989). The researchers argued that crime is likely to occur via the convergence of the three tenets. In other words, lack of any of the suggested tenets would most likely result in the prevention of a crime occurrence (Cohen and Felson). Other criminologists, namely Akers (1997) and Osgood, et al. (1996) noted that Routine Activity Theory suggests that most crimes are associated with the nature of an individual's daily routines based on sociological interrelationships, thus illustrating that crime is based on situational factors which enable the criminal opportunities.

Yar (2005) applied the Routine Activities Theory core concepts and "aetiological schema" to computer crime in cyberspace (p. 1). Even though Yar's study does not provide an empirical assessment, this chapter guides you to understand an optimum measurement strategy by clearly defining new conceptual definitions in computer crime and traits of cyberspace that reflect the core concepts of Routine Activities Theory. Therefore, this chapter will focus on two phases that reflect Yar's (2005) research. In the first phase, spatiality and temporality in cyberspace are presented, while comparing these items to crimes in the physical world. In the second phase, the major tenets of Routine Activities are presented via the application of computer crime.

Spatiality and Temporality in Cyberspace

Cohen and Felson (1979) emphasized the importance of "the spatial and temporal structure of routine legal activities" that facilitates an interpretation of how criminals take opportunities to transfer their criminal inclinations into criminal acts (p. 592). In other words, an individual's daily activities in a social situation produce certain conditions or opportunities for motivated offenders to commit criminal acts. Utilizing burglary as an example, frequent social activities away from home can facilitate increasing criminal opportunity, as the absence of a capable guardian at home is likely to make household property a suitable target (Garofalo, 1987).

Indeed, many studies support the likelihood of property crime victimization as being associated with frequent absences from the home (Corrado et al., 1980; Gottfredson, 1984; Sampson & Wooldredge, 1987; Smith, 1982). Routine Activities theorists also argue that crime victimization can be determined by a "proximity to high concentrations of potential offenders" (p. 596; see Lynch 1987; Cohen et al., 1981; Miethe & Meier, 1990). However, the important question is how to link these concepts in the physical world to computer-crime victimization in cyberspace.

Spatiality in Cyberspace

In order to apply the concept of routine activities to computer crime, cyber-spatial and cyber-temporal structures need to be defined. The Defense Department developed the Internet in the late 1960s.The

ARPA office of the Defense Department initially developed the idea of creating the Internet in 1966, and early components were constructed beginning in 1969 and became practical by equipping four computer peripherals known as 'nodes' that are connected to a network. In the early 1970s, a simple email system was operated via linking multiple networks by adding many more nodes, which is the main concept of the "Internet." The National Science Foundation and private carriers facilitated establishing the backbone of the Internet in the late 1980s and the Internet rapidly accelerated in 1990 right after the development of the World Wide Web. Since the early 1990s, the Internet has been widely available to private and commercial parties (Clifford, 2006). Cyberspace or online activities consist of Web sites hosted by digital communities ("bolgs," "chatrooms," "classrooms," "cafes," etc.) that link together via the World Wide Web (Adams, 1998, p. 88-89).

The significant difference between physical-space and cyberspace is that, unlike a physical location, cyberspace is not limited to distance, proximity, and physical separation (Yar, 2005). Mitchell (1995) referred to cyberspace and its environment as "antispatial" (p. 8). Stalder (1998) also asserted that the cyber environment is composed of a zero-distance dimension. Clicking a digital icon in cyberspace takes an online user everywhere and anywhere. Thus, the mobility of offenders in cyberspace far exceeds the mobility of offenders in the physical world. Although it has been proposed that the mobility rules of the physical world would not apply in the world of cyberspace (Yar, 2005), this would only necessarily apply in dealing with the weight or physical bulk of the target.

Examining social context factors in both physical and cyber-spatial structures is crucial because social environments interact with the traits of spatiality, and this association can provide criminal opportunities. In the physical world, numerous studies suggest that social context factors have a substantial influence on crime victimization. The National Crime Survey and British Crime Survey have consistently indicated that demographic factors such as age, race, and marital status are associated with general crime victimization (Cohen et al., 1981; Gottfredson, 1984, 1986; Laub, 1990). Cohen and Cantor (1980) specifically found that the demographic characteristics associated with typical larceny victimization include "a family income of $20,000 or more a year, sixteen through twenty-nine year olds, people who live alone, and persons who are unemployed" (p. 140). Mustaine and

Tewksbury (1998) examined minor and major theft victimization among college students and found that the victims' demographic factors, types of social activities, level of self-protective efforts, neighborhood environments (level of noise), and the participation in illegitimate behaviors (threats with a weapon) have a strong influence on the level of both minor and major theft victimization risk.

Bernburg and Thorlindsson (2001) expanded Routine Activity Theory, referring to it as "differential social relations," by mainly focusing on social context that addresses situational motivation and opportunity. The study was based on cross-sectional data from a national survey of Icelandic adolescents. Bernburg and Thorlindsson (2001) found that a routine activities indicator, "unstructured peer interaction in the absence of authority figures," is positively associated with deviant behaviors (violent behavior and property offense), and the association between the Routine Activities indicator and deviant behavior is significantly accounted for by social contextual factors (pp. 546-547).

Cyberspace also shares a common social environment with the physical world. Castells (2002) asserted that the composition of cyberspace is based on the social and international environment in our society and reflects the "real world" of socioeconomic and cultural dimensions (p. 203). In other words, cyberspace is "real space"' that is closely correlated to the physical world. Internet users can view diverse webpages every day as a Section of their routine activities in relation to their different needs. Online users with different demographic backgrounds may visit different types of websites based on their different interests and, thus, the compilation of a cyber-community can be distinguished by its members' interests in cyberspace (Castells, 2002).

In addition, even though there are no limitations on physical distance in order to connect another place in cyberspace, Internet users usually find a popular web site (i.e., Facebook, Tweeter, Pinterest, Amazon, Ebay, MSN, AOL, Myspace, etc.) that has a higher density of Internet connections than other domains via a search engine (i.e., Google, Bing, Yahoo, etc.). Therefore, a higher density of Internet connection may indicate the proximity of computer criminals and computer crime victims (Yar, 2005). In fact, computer victimization occurrences can be seen in many social networking web sites.

Temporality in Cyberspace

In terms of the concept of temporality, Routine Activities Theory assumes that a crime event occurs in a particular place *at a particular time*, which indicates the importance of a clear temporal sequence and order for a crime to occur. Cohen and Felson (1979) asserted that "the coordination of an offender's rhythms with those of a victim" facilitates a convergence of a potential offender and a target (p. 590). In Cohen and Felson's proposition, crime occurrences in particular places may be applicable to a study of computer-crime victimization because computer criminals often search suitable targets in certain social networking sites where online users are populated (Piazza, 2006). However, their proposition of a particular time does not seem to match with the temporal structure of cyberspace. The uniqueness of the temporal structure of cyberspace is that computer users and crime offenders are globally populated because the World Wide Web does not limit time zones and access to it is fully available to anyone at anytime (Yar, 2005). Thus, it is almost impossible to estimate the number of computer criminals that are engaging in crimes at any specific point in time. However, just as is noted in Routine Activities Theory, it is assumed that there is always a motivated offender waiting for the opportunity to commit a criminal act.

THREE CORE CONCEPTS: ROUTINE ACTIVITIES THEORY

Motivated Offender – Computer/Cyber Criminal

The Routine Activity theoretical perspective suggests that there will always be a sufficient supply of crime motivation: motivated offenders are a given situational factor (Cohen & Felson, 1979). This assertion implies an acceptance of Cohen and Felson's assumption that there will always be motivated offenders. Therefore, a few studies have tested this specific element of cybercrime victimization research, but it is important to explain computer criminals' motivations and why the existence of motivated offenders in cyberspace is a given situation.

The Internet has allowed certain people to find new and innovative ways to commit traditional crimes. These people are called "hackers." The term "hacker" originates from a tradition of creating attention-seeking pranks (called "hacks") at the Massachusetts Institute for Technology (MIT) in the 1950s and 1960s (Wark, 2010). Hacking was performed among computer enthusiasts for recognition via improvements or modifications to each other's programming code (Wark, 2010). Hackers form computer clubs and user groups, circulate newsletters, attend trade shows, and even have their own conventions. More recently, the term has changed to include negative connotations, referring to those who use computers for illegal, unauthorized, or disruptive activities (Knetzger and Muraski, 2009). In order to emphasize this difference, some use the term "cracker" to refer to the latter and "hacker" as it originally was used (Wark, 2010).

Britz (2004) described hackers as people who view and use computers as toolkits of exploration and exploitation. In fact, there has been very little research on how they truly operate in cyberspace. Holt (2009) argues that hackers have become engaged in various criminal activities such as cyber terrorism and organized crime, but the prevalence of these criminal groups within hacker subculture is unknown.

Hoffer and Straub's (1989) study of the motivations of computer abusers indicated that 34.1% of hackers abuse computer systems for their personal gain, 26% of hackers do so for fun and entertainment purposes, 11.4% of hackers intentionally attack computer systems, and 28.4% of hackers misuse computer systems due to ethical ignorance. According to the 2004 Australian Computer Crime and Security Survey (2005), 52% of respondents surveyed believed that the primary motive of the computer criminals was "unsolicited malicious damage" against their organization, while other respondents believed that the computer criminals were motivated by "the possibility of illicit financial gains or commercially motivated sabotage" (pp. 14-15).

Computer criminals use computers and telecommunications links, as a potentially dangerous and costly deviant behavior, partially for the purpose of breaking into various computer systems (Britz, 2004). They also steal valuable information, software, phone services, credit card numbers, and digital cash. They pass along and even sell their services and techniques to others, including organized crime organizations (Britz, 2004). In cyberspace, motivated computer criminals are online to find suitable targets (online users) who connect to the Internet without taking precautions or using computer security software (Britz, 2004).

Thus, in cyberspace, motivated offenders and suitable targets collide frequently. Grabosky (2000) lists the most evident motivations of computer criminals as "greed, lust, power, revenge, adventure, and the desire to taste 'forbidden fruit'" (p. 2). After an Internet Technology employee is fired from a company, the angered employee may retaliate by shutting down the company's computer systems. Computer criminals, like "cyber-punks," want to try hacking to have fun and they like to feel in control over others' computer systems (Britz, 2004). After getting caught by authorities, they often claim that they were just curious. In addition, "crackers" may implant a malicious virus into a computer system, or take valuable files that may contain customer information such as credit card numbers or social security numbers (Britz, 2004). They can then sell or illegally use the information, thus posing a threat to corporate security and personal privacy (Rosenblatt, 1996).

Parker (1998) also describes computer criminals' motives as greed, need, and the inability to recognize the harm caused to computer crime victims. In addition, Parker (1998) asserts that computer criminals tend to utilize "the Robin Hood syndrome" as their justification for committing crimes. Therefore, following Cohen and Felson's (1979) theoretical assumption in terms of motivated offenders, research also speculates that motivated offenders are a given situational factor. This is due to the fact that cybercriminals with various motivations exist in cyberspace. Thus, one of Routine Activity Theory's tenets, motivated offenders, nicely matches with motivated cybercriminals.

Suitable Target in Cyberspace

The second tenet, a "suitable target" refers to a person or item that may influence the criminal's propensity to commit a crime (Cohen, Kluegel, and Land, 1981; Felson, 1998). So, theoretically, the desirability of any given person or any given item could be the subject of a potential perpetrator (Cohen et al.; Felson, 1998). However, crime victimization is mostly determined by the accessibility dimension, which links to the level of capable guardianship, regardless of the target desirability (Cohen et al.; Yar, 2005).

Value

First, the evaluation of targets becomes complicated in computer crime because of the complexity associated with the offender's motivation or purpose to commit computer crime (Yar, 2005). Even though Hoffer and Straub's research (1989) and the 2004 Australian Computer Crime and Security Survey briefly delineate a computer criminal's motivation (for malicious intent, personal pleasure, personal gain, etc.) toward computer crime victims, it is difficult to conclude that the research reflects the true estimate of the computer criminal's motivation. This is due to the fact that the survey respondents, company employees, do not represent the pool of the computer criminal population. In fact, many criticisms of computer crime related quantitative and qualitative research point out the lack of "generalizable data" that exists on computer crime incidents against private victims in quantitative research frameworks and small sample sizes in qualitative research that may draw biased outcomes (Moitra, 2005).

However, research indicates that one of the clearest cybercriminal targets is an individual or an organization from whom they seek to obtain digital property. This is because cyberspace is formed by digital codes that contain digital information and digital property (Yar, 2005). Digital property such as business websites and personal websites can also be vandalized by computer criminals, or the criminals can steal important personal information such as social security numbers or credit card numbers (Yar). Thus, the targets in cyberspace can experience a wide range of offenses committed against them, including trespassing, theft, cyber stalking, or vandalism based on the potential offender's intent (See Birkbeck and LaFree, 1993; Bernburg and Thorlindsson, 2001; Yar).

Inertia

The second measure of VIVA, the inertia of crime targets, is an important criterion in target suitability. Inertia and suitability have an inverse relationship; a higher level of inertial resistance is likely to weaken the level of target suitability (Yar, 2005). In human-to-human confrontations, it may be more difficult for the offender to commit a violent crime against a physically stronger target (M. Felson 1998). Comparatively, in cyberspace, the level of inertia of crime targets may be affected by "the volume of data" if the computer criminals have limited computer systems, such as a very low capacity in their hard drive, their memories, or their CPUs (Yar).

However, overall, the inertia of a crime target in cyberspace is relatively weaker than in the physical world because the cost of computers is becoming more affordable and the development of technology constantly helps computer criminals equip themselves with more efficient tools, such as high-speed Internet and external hard drives, to commit computer crimes.

Visibility

The third measure of VIVA, the visibility of crime targets, has a positive association with target suitability (Bennett, 1991; Felson, 1998; Yar 2005). That is, the level of target visibility increases the suitability of the crime target. Since most computer-crime targets in cyberspace are intangible, consisting of digital information, it would be difficult to conceptualize its visibility (Yar, 2005). However, computer criminals gain the digital information from online users through various toolkits they can use in cyberspace, such as I.P. Trackers or Password Sniffers. Therefore, the gained valuable digital information such as credit card information, personal documentation, or passwords, is observable via a computer monitor. Such information can then be transformed to a hard copy via a printer. Thus, computer-crime targets are "globally visible" to computer criminals in cyberspace (Yar, 2005).

Accessibility

The fourth measure of VIVA, accessibility, has a positive correlation with target suitability. Felson (1998) defines accessibility as the "ability of an offender to get to the target and then get away from the scene of crime" (p. 58). The IC3 2004 Internet Crime Report (2005) indicated that one of the most significant problems in investigating and prosecuting computer crime is that "the offender and victim may be located anywhere worldwide" (p. 13). In fact, the Internet provides criminals with vast opportunities to locate an abundance of victims at a minimal cost, because computer criminals use computers to cross national and international boundaries electronically to victimize online users (Kubic, 2001).

In addition, the sophistication of computer criminal acts, such as utilizing anonymous “re-mailers,” encryption devices, and accessing third-party systems to commit an offense on the original target makes it difficult for law enforcement agencies to apprehend and prosecute the offenders (Grabosky, 2000; Grabosky & Smith, 2001; Furnell, 2002; Yar, 2005). Thus, anonymity and sophistication of computer criminal techniques in cyberspace strengthens the level of accessibility that provides computer criminals with the ability to get away in cyberspace.

In sum, the application of VIVA to cyberspace indicates that target suitability in cyberspace is a fully given situation. When an online user accesses the Internet, personal information in his or her computer naturally carries valuable information into cyberspace that attracts computer criminals. In addition, if computer criminals have sufficiently capable computer systems, the inertia of the crime target becomes almost non-existent in cyberspace. The nature of visibility and accessibility within the cyber-environment also allows the motivated cyber-offenders to detect crime targets and commit offenses from anywhere in the world.

Capable Guardianship in Cyberspace

In the third tenet of Routine Activities Theory, an absence of capable guardianship, a guardian can simply be a person who is able to protect the suitable target (Eck and Weisburd, 1995). Guardianship can be defined in three categories: formal social control, informal social control, and target-hardening activities (Cohen, Kluegel, and Land, 1981). First, formal social control agents would be the criminal justice system, which plays an important role in reducing crime (Cohen, Kluegel, and Land, 1981). Examples of these formal social controls would be the police, the courts, and the correctional system.

In cyberspace, computer crime is likely to occur when online users have an absence of formal capable guardians. Law enforcement agencies contribute formal social control against criminals to protect prospective victims (Grabosky, 2000). Tiernan (2000) argued that primary difficulties in prosecuting computer criminals arise because much of the property involved is intangible and does not match well with traditional criminal statutes such as larceny or theft. This problem weakens the reliability of formal social control agents and is compounded by the increasing number of computer criminals who have been able to access both private and public computer systems, sometimes with disastrous results (Tieran, 2000).

As stated earlier, formal social control agencies have increasingly acknowledged the need to stress new priorities and promote innovative crime prevention strategies designed to counter the advent and continued growth of cybercrimes (Taylor, et. al, 2006). Even though federal agencies have guided law enforcement efforts against cybercrime, most state and local law enforcement officers still lack knowledge concerning the processing of digital data and related evidence which would be necessary for effective cybercrime investigations (Taylor, et. al, 2006). Hinduja (2009) argues that the lack of resources and failure of dissimilation of updated technology and training within local and state enforcement agencies are significant impediments to combat against the catalyst of new forms of computer-related crime. Specialized forces to patrol cyberspace are very limited, and they seem to face an extreme difficulty in building a strong formal guardianship for online users (Grabosky, 2000; Grabosky & Smith, 2001). In addition, computer criminals are able to commit crime from any geographic location, and they target victims from all over the world (Kowalski, 2002). Furthermore, the rapid development of technology allows a computer criminal's identity to be concealed by using various computer programs, some of which are mentioned above, which make it very difficult to identify a suspect (Grabosky, 2000).

The 2005 FBI Computer Crime Survey (2006) revealed that computer crime victims tend not to report incidents to law enforcement agencies for various reasons. The survey found that 23% of the respondents believed that law enforcement would not take any action against the crime and an equal percentage of respondents believed that law enforcement does not have the ability to help prevent computer crime. The findings also indicate that the computer crime victims are less likely to contact law enforcement agencies for assistance because of a lack of faith in the criminal justice system.

In the physical world, examples of informal social control agents would be parents, teachers, friends, and security personnel (e.g., see Eck, 1995; Felson, 1986). Informal social control involves groups of citizens and individuals who can increase the surveillance and protection function (Cohen, Kluegel, and Land, 1981). In cyberspace, informal social guardians range from "private network administrators and systems security staff" to "ordinary online citizens" (Yar, 2005, p. 423). Even though criminal justice policies have started to be geared toward computer crime initiatives to increase public awareness, by relying upon "self-regulation, codes-of-conduct or etiquettes, monitoring groups (against child pornography, for example), and cooperative measures by private and semi-public groups" in order to minimize computer crime, these initiatives are not yet fully viable (Moitra, 2005).

In other words, similar to formal social control, informal social control agents are not actively operative in our cyber society. In addition, it is almost impossible for both formal and informal social control agents to maintain existing effective guardianship since computer criminals have acquired "the ease of offender mobility and the temporal irregularity of cyber-spatial activities" (Yar, 2005, p. 423). Thus, the current study posits that both formal and informal social control agents have little impact on computer-crime victimization.

The last category of capable guardianship, target hardening, is associated with physical security such as lighting areas, using locks, alarms, and barriers which are good ways to reduce the incidence of property crime in the physical world (Tseloni et al., 2004). Various empirical studies support the assumption that increasing the level of target-hardening activities via physical security is likely to decrease victimization risk (Chatterton and Frenz, 1994; Clarke, 1992, 1995; Clarke and Homel, 1997; Laycock, 1985, 1991; Poyner, 1991; Tilley, 1993; Webb & Laycock, 1992). In cyberspace, physical security can be equivalent to computer security with a digital-capable guardian being the most crucial component to protect the computer systems from cybercriminals.

Even though technology has generated many serious cybercrimes, it has also created defense systems – so-called computer security – to reduce the opportunity to commit computer-related crimes. The failure of an individual to equip their personal computer with computer security, which can enhance the level of capable guardianship in cyberspace, can potentially lead to online victimization. Indeed, the absence of computer security significantly weakens the guardianship and facilitates the committing of crimes by computer criminals. Thus, this digital guardian, installed computer security, is likely to be one of the most crucial elements of a viable capable guardianship in cyberspace.

When computers are tied to modems or cables, a whole new avenue to potential attack is opened. Simple password protections become insufficient for users demanding tight security (Denning, 1999). Computer security programs, such as anti-hacking software programs, protect the systems against an online attack. The threat is reduced on the mainframe computer because of software incorporated to prevent one user from harming another user's computer by accidental or illegal access. Thus, today many corporations and computer users install software such as firewalls, antivirus, and antispyware programs, to protect computer systems against hackers. In addition, biometric devices such as fingerprint or voice recognition technology and retinal imaging enhance the protection against unauthorized access to information systems (Denning, 1999).

Unfortunately, computer security is never absolute and the only secure computer is one that has no contact with the outside world (Denning, 1999). In other words, the computer system will never be completely secured, so it is impossible to remove the opportunity for computer criminals to commit crimes. However, computer users can minimize the criminal opportunity by installing computer security, so they can hinder criminals from penetrating their computer systems.

DISCUSSION 1:

Describe the social circumstances surrounding how you learned to use a computer or other electronic device. Explain acculturation factors that significantly influenced your attitudes about using the technology in certain ways. Please link the factors to the routine activities theoretical components.

DISCUSSION 2:

Think about the importance of protecting information and assets in cyberspace. Please pick one of the important digital assets and utilize VIVA assessment to demonstrate the level of vulnerability based on your choice of asset.

PART II

Hacking and Internet Fraud/Identity Theft

In Part II, we will explore the world of hackers. There is a persistent popular image of hackers as stylish and sophisticated, even brilliant. But hackers post a real threat to individuals' personal privacy, and can cause real, tangible damage. We have learned the three major tenets of Routine Activities Theory in the previous chapter: Motivated Offender, Suitable Target, and Lack of Capable Guardianship. The theory simply posits that the convergence of the suggested three tenets contributes to crime victimization. As mentioned in the book overview, we will now examine the first tenet of Routine Activities Theory, Motivated Offender, in order to understand cybercriminals' mind-set and motivations.

Computer crime continues to pose a problem for Internet users and electronic transactions. It is nearly impossible to collect accurate statistical information on the number of computer crimes and their impact on monetary loss to victims (Standler, 2002). Policing in cyberspace is very scarce, and few computer crimes are detected by victims or reported to authorities (Britz, 2004; Standler, 2002). Consequently, the number of people victimized each year continues to increase (Gordon, Loef, Lucyshyn, and Richardson, 2004). Unfortunately, the general population has not yet acknowledged the overall impact of computer crime.

Moreover, cybercrime research is very limited when compared to traditional crimes. It is extremely difficult to build a solid crime equation to resolve computer crime problems since we have a lack of empirical evidence. In other words, there are significant gaps between what we know and what we don't know about computer criminals. In chapter 3 and 4, we will also discuss what cybercriminals can do and how they defraud people in cyberspace. We will specifically focus on hacking and Internet fraud as major computer crime categories.

Chapter 3 - Hackers

Hacking Statistics

Cybercrimes are on the rise, and the number of Internet crime victims is increasing every year. It is important to examine known information from our criminology literature based on crime victimization statistics below.

Flanagan and McMenamin (1992) explain that newer-generation criminals could cost computer crime victims anywhere from $500 million to $5 billion annually. In fact, a study conducted in 2001 through a collective summary of studies and surveys of computer crime estimated that losses to victims through virus infections peaked at upwards of $7.6 billion in just the first half of 1999 (Kabay, 2001). Moreover, according to the 2005 CSI/FBI Computer Crime and Security Survey, virus attacks continue to incur the most substantial financial losses and, compared to the year 2004, monetary losses significantly escalated due to "unauthorized access to information" and the "theft of proprietary information" (Gordon et al., 2004, p. 15). The 2008 Computer Security Institute (CSI) survey indicated that the average monetary loss per respondent (organization) based on computer security incidents decreased from $345,005 in 2007 to $288,618 in 2008. However, the monetary loss is still high compared to the loss of $167,713 in 2006 in light of the fact that 49% of the respondent organizations reported virus incidents.

The 2008 Internet Crime Complaint Center (IC3) also reported that the total dollar loss based on the total of 275,284 complaints of crime linked to Internet fraud cases was $265 million, as compared to $239.09 million in total reported losses in 2007. Also on the increase is the number of networks of remotely controlled computers, called bot nets, used by malicious hackers and conmen to carry out many different cybercrimes.

The 2009 IC3 indicated that the total monetary loss was $559.7 million based on 336,655 complaints, which was a 22.3 percent increase when compared to 275,284 complaints in 2008. In 2010, the IC3 received over 3 million complaints, with an average of 25,317 complaints per month. Non-delivery of payment and FBI related scams were the most common types of complaints in 2010. The IC3 reported that the total of 289,874 complaints were received in 2012, and the total monetary loss was $525.44 million, which is an 8.3 percent increase in reported losses when compared to 2011.

According to the 2014 IC3 report, the total dollar loss based on the total of 269, 422 complaints of crimes linked to Internet fraud cases was $800.49 million, as compared to $781.84 million in total reported losses in 2013. Also, the increased use of social media has largely influenced the number of Internet fraud crime via various social engineering skills used by cybercriminals. In addition, the usage of virtual currency, which is almost impossible to track in regard to transactions, has become popular among hackers.

Due to the nature of the Internet, once a hacker connects to a computer, the hacker can often connect to any other computer in the network. Another vulnerability of the computer system is "back doors". These are holes in security left open within a program that can be used by criminals to gain unauthorized access to the system. Viruses, Trojan Horses, and Worms all constitute threats to computer systems and most computer systems are not fully immune to them. The antivirus firm Kaspersky Lab claims that they are detecting 315,000 new malicious files every day (Kaspersky Virus News, 2013). Spyware and antivirus software cannot fully protect computers from new viruses, worms, or spyware because this software is usually developed as a countermeasure after malicious wares have been spread over the Internet.

Many computer users may think that their systems and their networks are safe. Unfortunately, computers that are connected to the Internet are never safe. If one has a computer and a modem or wireless device connected to the Internet, it is just like jumping into a high-crime neighborhood. The problem is that Internet connections are also shared by cybercriminals to gain access to one's computer system. Due to the nature of the Internet, once a cybercriminal connects to a computer, the cybercriminal can often connect to any other computer in the network. Another vulnerability of the computer system is "back doors." These are holes in security left open within a program that can be used by cybercriminals to gain unauthorized access to the system.

Consumer Reports conducted a survey of online consumers in 2014. Using a nationally representative sample of 3,110 households with Internet access, they found that:

1. 62 percent of the respondents took no measure to protect their privacy online;
2. about 29 percent of the respondents reported that their home computers were infected by malicious software;
3. 1 in 7 respondents experienced a personal data breach incident in 2013, which was a 56 percent increase when compared to 2012 (Consumer Reports, 2014).

Based on the evidence presented above, it is clear that more attention should be directed towards this growing issue. However, it is also important to consider that the actual number of cybercrime incidences against private and public sectors is still unknown. This is because many businesses do not want to publicize when their company has become the victim of a cybercrime attack. Businesses can lose hundreds of millions of dollars of value, brand equity, and corporate reputation when they fall prey to a cybercriminal (Goodman and Brenner, 2002). As a result, most system administers do not contact law enforcement officers when their computer systems are invaded, preferring instead to fix the damage and take action to keep cybercriminals from gaining access again with as little public attention as possible (Morris, 2005).

Twelve Cybercriminal Profiles

Profiling delineates distinctive behavior patterns to narrow the range of suspects in a certain crime and is commonly used in the criminal justice field. Although cybercriminal profiling is not widely available, cybercriminologists have been gradually building up cybercriminal profiling.

Shoemaker and Kennedy (2009) indicated 12 profiles of cybercriminals, which might be regularly encountered by law enforcement agencies and information assurance corporations.

Types of Criminal Groups	Intent	Motivation	Offender Description	Attack Tools	Level of Destruction
Kiddies	Trespass	Ego	Any Age/ Technologically Inept/ New to Crime	Preprogramed Tool Kits	*
Cyberpunk Hackers	Trespass or Invasion	Ego or Exposure	Young/ Technically Proficient/ Outsider	Virus, Application Layer, and DOS attacks	**
Old-timer Hackers	Proving their art by trespassing	Ego	Middle Age/ The Most Technically Proficient/ Professional History	Website defacement	_
Code Warriors	Theft or Sabotage	Ego or Revenge or Monetary Gain	Age range between 30 to 50/Technically superb/A degree in Tech.but unemployed/ Socially inept	Application Layer and Trojan horse	***
Cyber-thieves	Illegal possession of valuable information or outright theft	Monetary Gain	Any Age (usually younger than code warriors)/Most are organizational insiders/Use social engineering techniques	Surreptitious network attacks via sniffing or spoofing/ Simple programing exploits such as Trojans and malware	N/A

Types of Criminal Groups	Intent	Motivation	Offender Description	Attack Tools	Level of Destruction
Cyber-hucksters	Commercialization	Monetary Gain	Older (business types)/Use social engineering techniques	Tracking cookies, spyware, and legal data mining to find victims	N/A
Unhappy Insider	Theft, Sabotage, or harm items of value to the company	Revenge or Monetary Gain	Any age/ Employed/ Unhappy with company	Extortion or Exposure of company secrets via destructive logic bombs or malicious applications	*****
Ex-insider	Theft, Sabotage, or harm items of value to the company	Extortion, revenge, sabotage, or disinformation	Any age/ Terminated former employee/ Unhappy with company	Extortion or Exposure of company secrets via destructive logic bombs or malicious applications	****
Cyber-stalker	Invasion of Privacy	Ego and Deviance	Any age/ Psychological issue	Key-logger, Trojan horse or sniffers	N/A
Con Man	Theft or illicit commercialization	Monetary Gain	Any age/ Difficult to catch due to anonymity	Spoofing, the Nigerian scam, or phishing	N/A

Types of Criminal Groups	Intent	Motivation	Offender Description	Attack Tools	Level of Destruction
The Mafia Soldier	Theft, extortion, and invasion of privacy for the purposes of blackmail	Monetary Gain	Any age/ Organized crime group member/Active in the Far East and Eastern Europe	All types with the best technology	N/A
Warfighter	Protection for friends and harm to the enemy	Infowar	Any age/ Technically superb/ Non-criminal type/ if on the other side against law, violence can increase/ Members of an elite government agency	Application layer, logic bombs, DOS attacks	***** Or -

Source: Shoemaker, D. and Kennedy, D. (2009). Criminal profiling and cyber-criminal investigations. In F. Schmalleger, & M. Pittaro (Eds.), Crimes of the Internet (pp. 456-476). Upper Saddle River, NJ: Prentice Hall

Motive of Electronic Vandalism

We can consider the suggested 12 cybercriminal profiles as good candidates that can commit electronic vandalism. The motive of electronic vandalism can be summarized by 6 main reasons.

- Revenge: Anger (Destructive Desire)
- Exposure: An individual or a group shows off skills
- Hacktivism (Political Purpose)
- Ego: Challenges and Thrill
- Monetary Gain
- Entertainment, boredom, etc.

Revenge: Anger (Destructive Desire)

The first reason is anger; people attempt a destructive behavior to reveal their anger towards another person or group in order to achieve their own satisfaction. The Unhappy Insider and Ex-Insider would be classified within this category.

The Unhappy Insider: Of the twelve cybercriminal profiles, the unhappy insider is one of the most menacing. They have inside access behind security defenses to the organization they are attacking. This type of perpetrator can be at any level within the organization and be of any age. The motivation of this cybercriminal is usually monetary gain or revenge. The unhappy insider will usually expose company secrets or will extort in order to sabotage or commit theft against the company. They can set logic bombs, steal information, or conduct other vindictive acts against the computer system of the organization. The only way to guard against the unhappy insider cybercriminal is to watch for signs of employee unhappiness and monitor those individuals' behaviors, because a distinct characteristic of this type of criminal is unhappiness with the organization.

The Ex-Insider: The ex-insider is a former employee of any age that could have been employed at any level within the organization that was fired by the organization. They are motivated by sabotage, revenge, disinformation, or extortion and aim to hurt the organization they used to work for. Sometimes, the perpetrator may have been able to foresee the termination from the company and will have had the chance to carry out destructive acts, such as setting logic bombs. If not, the ex-insider will discredit or damage the company from the outside by using insider information. One way to tell that an ex-insider committed a cyberattack is if the attack was on organization vulnerabilities that were not known to the public. The only way for an organization to protect itself from cyberattacks from the ex-insider cybercriminal is to dismiss the employee cleanly and without hurt feelings.

Exposure

An individual or a group, especially a hacker group, may commit a crime to show off their expertise. To show off expertise, an individual invades well-secured companies or government organization systems and leaves one's own signature. Kiddies can be considered to be in this category.

Kiddies: Kiddies can be any age, they are outsiders and they are technologically unskilled. They commonly intend to trespass, are motivated by their ego, and use preprogramed toolkits. Kiddies that are more developed will invade privacy and exploit a vulnerability of a computer system. This type of cybercriminal is commonly new to crime and they can be caught by investigators by attaching the crime to a suspect that has downloaded a fitting toolkit from a hacker website.

Cyberpunks: The cyberpunk tends to be a young outsider that is proficient with technology. They intend to invade or trespass and are driven by their ego. If the intent is to invade, the cyberpunk's motive is exposure. This type of cybercriminal has been behind many application layers, viruses, and DOS attacks on companies and products. Cyberpunks will selectively commit acts of theft and sabotage.

Old-Timer Hackers: Within the hacker community, old-timer hackers are some of the most technology savvy. They are middle-aged or older and have a long professional and/or personal history in technology and perhaps, even hacking. Old-timers are ego driven. They are the last of the Old Guard, who only intend to show off their skills by trespassing. Old-timers are comparatively harmless in that they have nonthreatening motives and know what they are doing. Though they are seen as harmless, they usually specialize in website defacement, so when they deface websites, they can be seen as harmful.

Hacktivism (Political Purpose)

"Hacktivism" is the portmanteau of "hack" and "activism." Warfighters can be considered in this area. Warfighters are typically not a criminal type when they are fighting on your side. However, when the warfighter is on the other side of the law, his actions would be viewed as destructive.

Example:

In August 2009, the Melbourne international film festival's website was shut down all at once. The website was attacked via D.O.S. ("denial of service") by Chinese vandals because it was showing a film which contained anti-China contents. This example shows how some electronic vandalism occurs to appeal to the vandal's political opinions. What was a destructive attack against Melbourne was probably seen as a positive act by supporters/patriots of China.

Warfighters: Warfighters can be any age, highly organized, the cream of the crop in their country, and have great technology skills. They are usually Infowar or politically motivated. Warfighters are immensely dangerous due to their great technology skills; they can attack a country's electronic foundations to devastate its physical infrastructure. Due to the fact that "Warfighters" characterizes members within a government agency, the best way to defend against this type of cyberattacker is to seek out the help of friendly warfighters.

Monetary Gain

Last, but not least, electronic vandalism can be used for blackmailing for money and goods. After electronic vandalism, such as defacing a business's webserver, stealing essential data, or denial of service, an offender blackmails the victim for stopping the attack or returning data. These types of crimes have significantly increased since E-business has grown.

The Mafia Soldier: Of the cybercriminal types, the mafia soldier is motivated the most by monetary gain. They utilize acts of extortion, theft, invasion of privacy, and blackmail. Mafia soldier cybercriminals have the best technology support and work in organized groups. It is easy to imagine that organized crime groups, worldwide, will increasingly utilize technology to take advantage of the ease of use and profitability the Internet provides.

Cyber-Thieves: Cyber-thieves can be any age; they do not have to have an extended technology background, and are solely motivated by money. They usually utilize simple programming exploits and network tools like malware and Trojans. Cyber-thieves tend not to use sophisticated targeted code. They practice spoofing and social engineering, which is akin to how the con man cybercriminal uses con games like phishing and the Nigerian prince scam. Cyber-thieves are commonly insiders of an organization, which is dissimilar to the conman cybercriminal, who is not easy to catch because of the anonymity provided to them by the Internet. Structured internal control in the organization is the best way to defend against the cyber-thief cybercriminal type.

Types of Cybercriminal Exploits and Profiling

If we were to classify major cybercriminal exploits, there would be two general categories: 1) forms of malicious code injection or 2) technological exploit for a specific target.

Malicious Code Category

There are 4 major categories of malicious code: viruses, logic bombs, Trojan Horses, and malware.

1. Virus

    - The term "virus" was first used to refer to any unwanted computer code, but the term now generally refers to a segment of machine code that will copy its code into one or larger host programs when it is activated.
    - When these infected programs are run, the viral code is executed and the virus spreads further. This form of computer crime can be included in the class of crimes called system infection programs.

Viruses are the most common forms of malicious code and often cause denials of service. One of the most aggressive types of virus is the worm attack. Worms are computer programs designed to make copies of themselves automatically. A worm is self-executing, largely invisible to computer users, and spreads from computer to computer over a network without any user action.

The Slammer worm that spread during the weekend of January 25, 2003, attacked a known flaw in systems of several organizations, including American Express and the Seattle, WA police and fire 911 center. Believed to be the fastest-spreading Internet worm on record by infecting 90 percent of vulnerable computers nationwide, it challenged popular opinions that vital services were largely immune to such attacks (Wilson, 2005).

Worms are increasingly used for purposes of extortion and sabotage. The motivation behind worm attacks is destructive and aggressive. Thus, we should consider an organized type of perpetrator as a main suspect.

2. Time Bombs/ Logic Bombs (AKA "Slag Code")

   - Time bombs are known as pieces of illicit software that are activated by computer clocks to initiate a fraud, a disruption, or some other sort of vicious activity.
   - Logic bombs are similar to time bombs but they are activated by a combination of events rather than by the computer clock.

Since they are programs set in a host machine, the attacks are only activated based on parameters. Unless the perpetrator uses a Trojan horse, hands-on access is usually required to set a logic bomb. In other words, the main suspect would be a person who can physically access the machine to set the logic bombs. In the case of using a Trojan horse, the only way to track down a person who wrote the Trojan horse is by building a profile to identify a limited set of suspects in a narrow physical location.

3. Trojan Horses

   - The term "Trojan horse" refers to an apparently useful program such as a game program, a survey question, or media files, containing hidden code that either executes malicious acts when triggered by some external event or provides a trap door through which an intruder can secretly access the system.

4. Malware

    - If an online user visits a website embedded in malware, a malicious code is transferred to the visitor's computer. Malware can also deliver home page hijackers and key-loggers, and adware.

Since the victim can be anyone who visits the site, the site tends to be associated with "fringe" types of commerce such as pornography sites. In terms of the investigation, it is difficult to profile because the victims are almost self-selected by visiting unknown websites.

Targeted Attacks Category

Targeted attacks are very similar to organized criminal activity and the motivation is associated with a specific victimology. According to Shoemaker and Kennedy (2009), there are 8 generic types of targeted attacks: 1) insider, 2) password, 3) sniffing, 4) spoofing, 5) man-in-the-middle, 6) application layer, 7) denial of service, and 8) social engineering.

1. Insider Attacks

    - The insider attack has always been the most prevalent threat. An insider who knows the security system can easily steal valuable information by loading it on a flash-drive and walking out the door with it.

The characteristics of the perpetrator almost always fit the organized type, and the best policy is monitoring a potential attacker to prevent the acts before they occur.

2. Password Attacks

    - Password attacks can be committed by either guessing a password or obtaining it via social engineering. Access to the system can also lead to theft and sabotage.

- According to the CSI 2004 report, 90 percent of password attacks are associated with social engineering. Social engineering is the act of manipulating people to trick them into sharing sensitive information by using personal contact information. The primary suspect in this case would be an insider or client who is in close physical proximity to where the attack originated.

Password attacks are often driven from social engineering exploits but they can also originate from Trojan horses, network sniffing, or dictionary attacks that are software programs such as Word Password Recovery 1.0j. Dictionary attacks can randomly apply all letters of the alphabet to a targeted password until it figures out the correct password to open the application. Using strong passwords consisting of a combination of numbers, letters, and characters can help prevent a successful dictionary attack.

If the attack causes very little harm, the basic hacker profiles for kiddies, cyberpunks, or old-timers apply. If the attack aims are sabotage, extortion, or theft; code warriors, cyber-thieves, or the mafia soldier can fit the profile.

3. Sniffer-Based Attacks

- Sniffing involves detecting all data traveling through a network, enabling hackers to search for passwords that will allow for information access such as acquiring account or social security information, which can support ID theft or sabotage.

This type of attack is a carefully planned and executed exploit that requires technical proficiency. The suitable suspect would be found among the profile types of cyberpunks, cyber-thieves, and cyber-stalkers for just gaining access to the system. If the main aim of sniffing is theft or sabotage, the code warrior, mafia soldier, or warfighter fits the profile. In addition, if the purpose of the sniffing exploit is the invasion of privacy, the perpetrator almost always has some form of direct relationship to the victim, or the victim fulfills some type of fantasy for the perpetrator.

4. Spoofing-Based Attacks

- Spoofing is an organized type of crime because the attack is designed to convince others that the sender of an Internet message is legitimate.

These attacks typically involve spoofing an IP address by changing the packet-header information, which can entail phishing scams or spamming using familiar email addresses. The Nigerian Scam and the Lottery Scam would be a typical exploit.

In advanced exploit cases, cybercriminals create a false or shadow copy of a legitimate website that looks like the real one, with all the same pages and links. All network traffic between the victim's browser and the spoofed site is funneled through the perpetrator's machine. The perpetrator can acquire private information, such as passwords, credit card numbers, and account numbers.

5 & 6. Man-in-the-Middle and Application Layer Attacks

- Man-in-the-Middle (MITM) and application layer attacks are a type of eavesdropping attack that intercepts, sends, and receives data never meant for the victims.
- MITM involves inserting a malicious code such as a Trojan horse entity into a two-party conversation as a third party.
- Application layer attacks come at a specific application through a defect or vulnerability in the code such as a buffer overflow.

These exploits mainly target theft, extortion, sabotage, and Infowar (CSI, 2004). The mafia soldier, cyber-thief, and the code warrior would fit into the profile if the purpose of the attack was profit. If the target is a major corporation like Microsoft, the cyberpunk can also fit into this typology. Since the perpetrator is almost always unknown, law enforcement encounters extreme difficulty with these attacks.

7. Denial of Service (DoS)

- A DoS attack floods a server with phony authentication methods to prevent people from accessing the server and ultimately shutting it down.

The explicit attack can be a simple form of vandalizing the server. However, worm-based DoS attacks can create broad-spectrum damages. Single DoS exploits such as MyDoom cost corporations up to $250 million in lost productivity; Microsoft offered a $250,000 reward for the capture of the attackers (Stein, 2004).

If the attacks were done for profit, a code warrior or a mafia soldier would be the main suspect. If the attack is strategic, a warfighter fits into this typology. A cyberpunk could be considered as the culprit of a DoS attack in the sense that major corporations are frequently the intended victims.

8. Social Engineering

- Social engineering scams can be a sophisticated form of the dumpster diving criminal approach to steal a password or account information for profit.

Social engineering can be also used for all other purposes such as political, disinformation, Inforwar and strategic purposes. However, this technique is part of the art of the cyberthief, the cyberpunk, and the cyber-stalker.

RESEARCH ON HACKERS

In order to find common causation factors among computer criminals such as hackers and "crackers," cyber-criminologists tend to recruit and communicate with participants entirely in cyberspace through instant-messaging and email. However, this has posed a problem in gaining a participant's trust and willingness to participate in computer crime research. Major concerns associated with computer crime research on hackers are discussed in my research article (2011) titled *"Qualitative Analysis of Motivated Offender and Suitable Target: Methodological*

Challenges on Hacker Study." In order to show the intricate nature of researching hackers, my research will now be discussed.

Background of the Research

Computer crimes typically require more than a basic level of computer skills for offenders to be successful at victimizing targets (Choi, 2008). In this study, participants were classified by the specific type of computer crime he/she has committed. There were two specific types of computer crime used in this research, one of which was *hacking*. Historically, the term "hacking" referred to individuals who loved to explore the inter-workings of computer systems and networks to identify problems or vulnerabilities (Jordan & Taylor, 2004). However, over time, the public perception has evolved and the media have come to publicize hackers as those who gain unauthorized access to computer systems to vandalize victims by modifying computer settings or changing computer files, or causing various technical problems in that system (Barber, 2001; Jordan & Taylor, 1998).

The second type of computer crime utilized in this study is closely related to hacking – known as *cracking*. As Barber (2001) describes, the term "cracking" has similar methods for victimization – gaining unauthorized access to computer systems. However, the fundamental difference is that "essentially a hacker [evolves into] a cracker when his or her motivations become criminal" (Barber, 2001, p. 16). An act of cracking is much worse, because the intent of the offender may involve more than just the act of hacking (i.e. he/she may wish to cause further harm through fraud, identity theft, piracy, cyber-stalking, spamming, etc.).

Further, several classifications were used in this research to categorize hackers/crackers, which include: *white hat*, *black hat*, and *cyberpunks* (script kiddies). These definitions are identified as follows:

White hat – Synonymous with the heroes or "good guys" in western movies, a white hat hacker refers to an individual who commits hacking/cracking offenses for *non-malicious* reasons to research the technologies, methodologies, techniques, and practices of hackers in an effort to defend information assets and also detect, prevent and track hackers (Barber, 2001).

Black hat – Synonymous with the villains or "bad guys" in western movies, a black hat hacker refers to an individual who commits an act of hacking and/or cracking with the intent to modify computer settings or change computer files, cause various technical problems in a computer system, or obtain private information.

Cyberpunk/Script kiddie – An individual who has little to no understanding of hacking/cracking, and commits an act of hacking/cracking by using pre-packaged software tools written by others (Barber, 2001).

These definitions and terms were utilized primarily to address concerns over whether participants would deliberately or mistakenly misidentify themselves in the research process. It was used as a means of verification toward their stories and experiences in the world of cybercrime, as well as provided statistical data in regards to the sample collected.

A qualitative approach was taken for two reasons: to collect more in-depth and individualistic responses from participants and to address the absence of an analysis on the motivated offender in Choi's (2008) research. The study sought to estimate patterns of computer crime victimization through Routine Activity Theory; however, the quantitative victim-focused survey proved difficult to determine motivational factors among offenders (Choi, 2008). By utilizing a much more flexible interview process with computer crime offenders, this study provided valuable in-depth knowledge in this regard.

Information pertaining to how participants would be selected and interviewed was taken into consideration. Previous researchers who also conducted interviews with former and/or current hackers did not communicate, collect data, and recruit participants exclusively through cyber space (Denning, 1990; Taylor, 1999; Turgeman-Goldschmidt, 2008). Due to limitations with travel, our research sought to locate cyber criminals through cheaper means – directly through the Internet. It became much more convenient through this method and allowed us to locate participants potentially from anywhere in the world. Also, because the Internet is where cybercrime occurs, it made logical sense to look there for potential participants.

Other research on cyber criminals strongly supported and engaged in the practice of snowball sampling (Taylor, 1999; Turgeman-Goldschmidt, 2008). Maxfield and Babbie (2008) explain that snowball sampling can be defined in simple terms as "identifying a single subject or small number of subjects and then ask[ing] the subject(s) to identify others like him or her who might be willing to participate in a study" (p. 238). Because this study involved the active recruiting of criminals, it was advantageous for previous interview participants to vouch for our credibility and neutrality as academic researchers.

Findings Based on Theoretical Perspective

The findings are broken down into two sections: classification of participants and Routine Activity Theory. The former will discuss general demographic information concerning participants as well as common factors shared among them. The latter will analyze data obtained during the interview process and cross-reference the information with Cohen and Felson's Routine Activity Theory.

Classification of Participants

In order to control validity issues as well as collect general statistics from participants, a small 12 question "pre-interview questionnaire" was given to participants prior to their interview, which will be discussed in more detail later.

Data from the pre-interview questionnaire revealed that all participants identified themselves as male, with ages ranging from early to late twenties. Three out of the five participants were Caucasian and the remaining two identified themselves as Hispanic. Further, two participants' highest level of education was an undergraduate degree, two other participants achieved a high school diploma, and one completed their General Equivalency/Education Diploma (GED). Four participants identified the United States as their current country of residence, while one participant identified Mexico as their country of residence. Three out of the five were currently employed (as an NOC Engineer, Salesman, and Assistant Manager) and two were (at the time of their interview) unemployed. All of the participants' legitimate income was under $75,000 per year, and three out of five participants identified their income within the range of $0 - $24,000 per year. Illegitimate income varied among participants, ranging from $2,000 to

Figure 3-1. Classification of participants

	Age	Type of hacker: Self-identification	Type of hacker: Research-identified	Type of hacker: Mis-identified	Legitimate Income Per Year	Estimated Illegitimate Income Per Year	Hours of Daily Computer Usage
Participant 1	28	Black hat cracker	Black hat cracker		$50,000 - $74,999	$20,000	12
Participant 2	21	Black hat cyberpunk	Black hat cyberpunk		$0 - $24,999	$2,000	12
Participant 3	22	White hat cracker	Black hat hacker	X	$0 - $24,999	$4,000	1-5
Participant 4	21	White hat cracker	Black hat cracker	X	$0 - $24,999	$6,000	8
Participant 5	24	White hat hacker	Black hat cyberp	X	$25,000 - $49,999	$2,000	3-4

an upwards of $20,000 per year.

Additionally, participants revealed that they spend an average of 7 hours on the computer per day. Each individual also identified that he had some knowledge or experience with computer programming (60% - Java/Visual Basic/Other, 40% - C/C++/C#, 20% - VB.NET). Four out of the five participants admitted to committing a hacking offense in the past and three out of the five admitted to committing a cracking offense. Only one participant admitted to committing an offense (hacking or cracking) within the last six months.

Three participants identified themselves as white hat hackers, one identified himself as a cyberpunk, and one as a black hat hacker/cracker. However, when cross-referencing this information to our definitions mentioned previously, three individuals falsely/incorrectly identified themselves. Each of those three participants self-identified as white hat hackers; however, according to their testimonies during the interview process, their activities contradicted what Barber defined as a white hat hacker. Instead, all three participants were re-classified as black hat and their type of hacking-related activities were re-classified as well. One out of the three self-identified as a cracker, but he was re-classified – according to Barber – as a hacker and another was re-classified as a cyberpunk.

While the goal of this classification was to search potential patterns or commonalities among participants, the resulting small sample size threatened the integrity of the data as being a representative sample to the general population. This issue will be further discussed later when addressing methodological challenges.

Revisiting Routine Activity Theory

Expanding upon Cornish and Clarke's (2004) Rational Choice Theory, Cohen and Felson's Routine Activity Theory (RAT) attempts to look more specifically at factors that influence the range of choices available to an individual. They argue that three elemental factors affect whether or not a crime will occur: there must be motivated offenders, suitable targets, and absence of capable guardianship against a violation (Cohen and Felson, 2004). If any one of these factors is changed or missing in the convergence of time and space then it is likely the crime rate for particular offenses will change (Cohen and Felson, 2004). For example, if the proportion of motivated offenders to suitable targets increased within a community, Cohen and Felson (2004) argue that crime rates against those suitable targets will increase as well. Thus, controlling one or more of those factors might actually reduce the likelihood of that crime.

Specifically, in this research, each elemental factor in RAT was analyzed and referenced during the interview process to explore whether this theory is a useful tool in reducing future computer criminality. These are explored in depth below.

Motivated Offenders

As Akers and Sellers (2004) explain, the concept of the motivated offender in Routine Activity Theory can refer to an individual with a "pre-existing set of crime-prone motivations" or could include "anyone who is enticed by the opportunity for a quick gain...even though he or she may not have any previously existing criminal intentions." In computer crime, the former and the latter could be applied, as some individuals with advanced knowledge who voluntarily learn computer exploitation methods may have pre-existing motivations; and in opposition, those with no pre-existing intent to commit a computer crime may find themselves in possession of pre-packaged software tools, readily and easily available to be utilized at any given time. But, rather than analyzing one versus the other, this research explores both options as a rational choice, regardless of an individual's predisposition.

As explained by Cornish and Clarke (2004) in their Rational Choice Theory (RCT), an offender's commission of a crime is based on the principle of expected utility, which is an integral part of Economic Theory. Expected utility explains "...that people will make rational decisions based on the extent to which they expect the choice to maximize their profits or benefits and minimize costs or losses" (Akers & Sellers, 2004, p. 26). In other words, individuals may choose to commit crimes because they see it as an opportunity to maximize their profits and minimize their costs. For example, a hacker might rationalize that they can steal a victim's credit card information, which would minimize their costs (the information is free), and maximize their profits (selling or using that valuable information).

After conducting interviews with five hackers, their testimonials both support and oppose this tenet of rational choice. When questioned specifically about their motivation for hacking/cracking, participants generally produced different responses:

Participant 1: "...I am driven to challenge my mind. It seems like I am always in need of something to keep my mind going and without it I just seem unhappy. There have been cracking projects for monetary reasons as well..."

Participant 3: "One motivation was collecting everything I could collect in the game [Diablo II[2]]...basically becoming rich within [the] game..."

Participant 4: "...at first it was [for] fun, then [I hacked for] money"

In addition, the data collected from all participants showed that there were monetary gains, which each individual collected. In a few instances, participants admitted to stealing cd-keys for popular computer games, which retail $20 per licensed copy in most stores. One participant admitted to click fraud[3] while another admitted to stealing AOL[4] Internet service for several years.

Participant 1: "It was not uncommon for me to have lists of 5000+ AOL usernames and passwords...I went several years without paying for Internet service from 1997 until 2000 at least."

Participant 2: "It all depended, sometimes somebody would have something I wanted, like items for a game or cd-keys..."

---

[2] Diablo II is a fantasy role-playing game created by Blizzard Entertainment in the year 2000, and features online play with other Internet users through Battle.net.

[3] Click fraud is a type of fraudulent attack which happens when an advertiser or service provider generates clicks on an ad with the sole intent of increasing the payment of the advertiser (Immorlica, Jain, Mahdian, & Talwar, 2005).

[4] AOL (formerly America Online) which is owned by Time Warner, Inc. is an American Internet service provider and media company.

Participant 3: "[I] collected information [such as] account names, passwords, and cd-keys for the login process required for this online community."

Participant 4: "I wrote a small application and disguised it so I could get cd-keys and proxies."

Participant 4: "There was a contest on a website...and first place would win $2,000...and they based the winner on [the number of video] views...I wrote software to increase views [on my video] using proxies."

Participant 5: "I used to phish[5] people on Battle.net[6] and get them to give me their cd-keys and passwords."

Thus, these responses could be classified under RCT's premise that individuals choose to commit crimes based on expected utility as each individual sought to maximize benefits while minimizing losses.

After interviewing each participant, other motivations (more narrowly tailored) were revealed throughout the many responses and information gathered. These included such responses as:

---

5 "Phishing is a term that was coined in 1996 by US hackers who were stealing America Online ("AOL") accounts by scamming passwords from AOL users. The use of "ph" in the terminology traces back in the 70's to early hackers who were involved in "phreaking," the hacking of telephone systems. Phishing is today generally described as a luring method that thieves use to fish for unsuspecting Internet users' personal identifying information through e-mails and mirror-websites which look like those coming from legitimate businesses, including financial institutions, or government agencies" (Acoca, 2008, p. 17).

6 Battle.net is an online gaming service provided by Blizzard Entertainment. It is the official host in online gaming for Starcraft, Starcraft II, Warcraft II, Warcraft III, Diablo, and Diablo II.

Participant 1: "In my teenage years, I spent a lot of time on the AOL service. My focus there was not only programming, but also phishing. I used common phishing techniques such as instant message and e-mail, but also [wrote] trojans[7] whose job it was to email me the login [and] password of the person's AOL account... I went several years without paying for Internet service from 1997 until 2000 at least."

Participant 2: "[I hack] because I think it's an unbelievable [thing] to be able to gain access to a system without permission using the silly mistakes of some developer like an open doorway; and this is information I want to know, as I said earlier, I want to know all things computer related."

Participant 4: "I wrote a keylogger[8] to retrieve my school teacher's passwords...[which] I'm not proud of [but used it] to modify my grades."

Target Suitability

Within RAT, Cohen and Felson (2004) explain that target suitability is reflected through four main criteria: the value of the crime target (i.e. the desirability of a target for offenders), the inertia of a crime target (its ability to resist or inhibit victimization), visibility of a crime target, and the accessibility of a crime target (VIVA).

In conjunction with RCT, the value of the target is ultimately what an offender believes is of benefit to him/her. Value may not necessarily include monetary assets; rather, information in general can be more valuable to a hacker/cracker (which is not to imply that their ultimate goal is not pursuing and securing monetary gains). Something as

7 Trojan horses are impostors—files that claim to be something desirable but, in fact, are malicious. A very important distinction between Trojan horse programs and true viruses is that they do not replicate themselves. Trojan horses contain malicious code that when triggered cause loss, or even theft, of data (Symantec Corporation, 2006).

8 A keylogger is an application that monitors a victim's keystrokes and then sends this information back to the malicious user (Shetty, 2005).

relatively trivial as a victim's Internet Protocol[9] (IP) address can be of value to a hacker/cracker.

In our findings, the value of crime targets varied widely depending on circumstances surrounding each hacking/cracking incident. Value included such things as:

Participant 1: "...5,000+ AOL usernames and passwords…credit card information [which] was turned over by users via instant message in response to [a] phishing attempt."

Participant 3: "...the accounts [and] passwords of users of...Battle.net"

Participant 4: "...information from people's computers...cd-keys [for Battle.net games] and proxies...Diablo II user's information...school teacher's password"

Participant 5: "I was looking for cd-keys [for Battle.net games] and whatever I could find really."

Regarding the inertia of targets in cyber space, Yar (2005) explains that if computer criminals have sufficiently capable resources and computer systems, a crime target's inertia is almost non-resistant to victimization. This, however, is not without exception as will be discussed further.

Moreover, the crime target's visibility and accessibility in cyberspace is very apparent when observing the data. One participant was able to crawl through public AOL chat rooms to send phishing attacks to over 5,000 visible targets.

9 A numerical label assigned to devices operating over a computer network.

> **Participant 1**: "One trojan [I wrote] ended up in the Symantec[10] database for having more than 1,000 known infections. At that time, it was not uncommon for me to have lists of 5,000+ AOL usernames and passwords."

Other participants also victimized large numbers of targets. Participant 4 admitted to stealing approximately $6,000 worth of cd-keys from popular Blizzard Entertainment[11] games via keyloggers, phishing, and trojans.

> **Researcher**: "In total, how much money do you think you've taken as a result of hacking/cracking?
> **Participant 4**: In money? Counting the costs of the games' cd-keys?
> **Researcher**: Sure.
> **Participant 4**: Probably like $6,000.

Additionally, Participant 2 also admitted to mass targeting:

---

10 "Symantec was founded in 1982 by visionary computer scientists. The company has evolved to become one of the world's largest software companies with more than 17,500 employees in more than 40 countries. [They] provide security, storage and systems management solutions to help [their] customers – from consumers and small businesses to the largest global organizations – secure and manage their information-driven world against more risks at more points, more completely and efficiently than any other company" (Symantec Corporation, 2010).

11 "Blizzard Entertainment® is a premier developer and publisher of entertainment software. After establishing the Blizzard Entertainment label in 1994, the company quickly became one of the most popular and well-respected makers of computer games. By focusing on creating well-designed, highly enjoyable entertainment experiences, Blizzard Entertainment has maintained an unparalleled reputation for quality since its inception" (Blizzard Entertainment, 2010).

Participant 2: "I infected a few hundred people with a keylogger and waited for them to log in [to Diablo II on Battle.net] and then stole all their items."

Capable Guardianship

As Cohen and Felson (2004) explain, the third tenet to RAT – guardianship – is implicit in everyday life but often overlooked because of an individual's absence of violations. They explain that two types of capable guardianship are important: formal capable guardianship (i.e. law enforcement) and informal capable guardianship (i.e. family, friends, co-workers, etc.) (Cohen & Felson, 2004). Additionally, Cohen and Felson (2004) argue that informal capable guardianship "may be one of the most neglected elements in sociological research on crime..." (p. 434). While their premise was based on the real world, the same ideals can be applied to cyberspace – if not even more than in the real world. In cyberspace, informal capable guardianship is arguably scarcer because of the lack of oversight on Internet activity within the confines of an individual's home.

Choi (2008) argues that the final elemental factor in RAT, the level of capable guardianship, is the "most viable tenet that can control the level of computer-crime victimization" (p. 312). By utilizing the target-hardening strategy via increased computer security, it will make it more difficult for computer criminals to commit computer crimes in cyber space (Choi, 2008). And those results can be correlated with the results of this study. While traditional forms of capable guardianship included both formal and informal, Choi's (2008) study utilizes "digital-capable guardianship" (anti-virus, anti-spyware, and firewall software) as tenets to reducing computer crime victimization. After looking at the responses of participants, each type of capable guardianship is analyzed and discussed below.

While all participants were not questioned on whether policing in cyberspace has or would reduce computer criminal behaviors, one participant did give some insight into his opinion on the issue:

Participant 1: "I was almost caught once, and haven't carded anything since."

Researcher: "Do you think police presence in cyber space is enough to deter people from committing hacking offenses?
Participant 1: "No... not everyone...myself personally, yes."

However, each participant *was* directly asked his current perception about the level of policing (formal capable guardianship) in cyber space. Here were their responses:

Participant 1: "If the government thinks it's worthy to go after you, they will."

Participant 2: "I don't think they put a lot of effort into it unless you break into a government network."
Participant 2: "I mean if I hacked a computer right now owned by some random person, nobody would come after me because now the government has to spend money and time to track down a person infecting a single person's computer."
Researcher: "So would you say little to no visible police presence? Or do you think it's there and they just don't pay attention to the small incidents?
Participant 2: "Yeah, they don't care about the small things."

Participant 3: "There is not enough of it, we need more. I personally think that each firm that operates online should have a department that is able to monitor their immediate cyberspace."

Participant 4: "Null...in my country, the government is busier catching drug dealers, robbers, [and] violators than hackers/crackers. "

In addition, each participant was questioned about their level of understanding regarding current cybercrime law and sanctions in their respective countries of residence. Results revealed that all five of the participants who were interviewed had very little to no knowledge of this information.

Participant 1: "Not really, I may have looked them up years ago, but I spend too much time programming, cracking, reversing to learn about law too...They would probably make me pay fines...[and] prison time depending on the crime."

Participant 2: "I've heard a lot of people going to prison for it...but I read an article about a 16 year old who hacked into government servers but didn't do anything bad while on the server and they just told him not to ever do it again and took his computer."

Participant 3: "Cybercrimes usually are tacked with high fines, I'm not 100% sure what the laws are for committing a cyber act in my state."

Participant 4: "Lol...fail, I don't know any [cyber laws]."

Participant 5: "I have no clue, maybe fines or something."

In regards to informal capable guardianship, several accounts showed that a poor level of its presence is partially (or perhaps fully) responsible for some computer criminal behavior. In this conversation, Participant 1 admits to the researcher that his mother was aware of his criminal activity in cyber space, but she did not attempt to correct or discourage his behavior:

Participant 1: "During these days you could order anything [with other individual's credit cards], and have it sent anywhere."
Participant 1: "I was almost caught once, and haven't carded anything since."
Participant 1: "I sent my mom flowers on Mother's Day."
Participant 1: "I received a call from the credit card company a few weeks later. She denied ever receiving the flowers and there was nothing ever said about it."
Researcher: "Did she actually get the flowers?"
Participant 1: "Yes."
Researcher: "So she knew what you did?"
Participant 1: "Yes."

Additionally, in two other cases participants admit to committing hacking/cracking offenses because of friends who encouraged their illegal behavior:

Participant 2: "...I had a friend come to me once and request that I break into some guy's computer who was messing with him, and I did."

Participant 3: "Well, I once had a friend ask me to hack her girlfriend...and her girlfriend noticed what I had done...

In at least one case in this project, increased informal capable guardianship did yield positive results in reducing an offender's interest or pursuit of engaging in some types of hacking/cracking:

Researcher: "Why did you eventually stop [hacking/cracking]?"
Participant 1: "Honestly, I pretty much stopped any widespread illegal activities since my oldest daughter was born in 2001."
Participant 1: "She is worth more than a jail sentence."

When asking all five participants their recommendation on how to reduce hacking/cracking in cyber space, none of the participants openly suggested using anti-virus programs. However, when explicitly asked whether they believed anti-virus, anti-spyware, and firewalls (digital-capable guardians) deterred or reduced hacking/cracking offenses, all five participants agreed that in some capacity victimization is reduced:

Participant 1: "Firewalls definitely, hardware firewalls...I believe the software firewalls are very fallible...anti-virus and spyware, maybe. They are only as good as what they are able to detect."

Participant 2: "To be honest, I think anti-spyware programs are useless...firewalls have some chance of stopping [hackers] unless they disable it...anti-virus programs...are the only thing you can hope to keep you reasonably safe."

Participant 3: "They could help prevent some types of hacking/cracking but deter? No, I don't think it could."

Participant 4: "Yes, it will prevent some attacks, but if someone really wants to hack/crack [they] will probably succeed even if you have those programs installed."

Participant 5: "Yes, those programs will help in stopping most attackers, especially scripters [cyberpunks]"

As is evident through this research, RAT should be warranted further exploration in future assessments of an individual's computer criminal behavior. Each tenet of RAT was evident throughout our findings, and in some cases manipulation of those tenets led to a decrease in computer criminality among participants. It was clear through our interactions with participants that monetary gain was a major motivating factor among offenders, which is something that should be addressed in future policies and continually tested in the future. Additional testing of RAT in regards to hackers/crackers should be conducted to further assess the manipulation of each of the three tenets of Cohen and Felson's theoretical perspective. Additionally, further research in this field could be developed to seek out the potential causation factors relative to Akers and Burgess' Social Learning Theory as well as Sampson and Laub's Life-Course Theory which are discussed in further detail later.

METHODOLOGICAL CONSIDERATION

Qualitative Approach

The approach taken during this research was from a qualitative perspective seeking to find common causation factors among hackers/crackers. Our research was designed to recruit and communicate with participants entirely in cyber space through instant messaging and e-mail. Thus, this posed a problem in gaining a participant's trust and willingness to participate in our study. Several steps were taken to increase the probability of participation; however, exact numbers on individuals who refused to participate due to mistrust was unknown.

Throughout the research process, we would always contact participants (potential or otherwise) through an official college-issued "*.edu*" e-mail address and our names were disclosed to participants both by e-mail and in the informed consent documentation.

Participant Selection

In order to be considered for participation, an individual must be actively or previously involved in committing some type of hacking/cracking related offense. Participants were selected using two methods: through social networking websites, and through the use of snowball sampling. In the first method, several websites were used to locate and recruit potential hackers – two of which were related to hacking/cracking the popular gaming service Battle.net and one, which was focused on hacking/cracking cellular phone software/firmware. These two websites were selected because of their vast amount of users (upwards of 50,000 and 290,000 respectively) as well as the enriched hacking and reverse-engineering content they provided. The former became the most useful in recruiting participants likely because the PI had knowledge and common interest in the services offered on Battle.net. One important detail to note was that inadvertent relationships with potential interviewees had been established prior to their questioning to participate, which probably greatly increased their likelihood of participation (Spradley, 1979).

Additionally, because this research attempted to locate active and/or inactive hackers/crackers on the Internet, the snowball method proved to be a valuable sampling method. As mentioned earlier, Maxfield and Babbie (2008) explain that snowball sampling can be defined in simple terms as "identifying a single subject or small number of subjects and then ask[ing] the subject(s) to identify others like him or her who might be willing to participate in a study" (p. 238). After each successful interview, participants were asked to contact or identify other potential participants on our behalf. This became very helpful in establishing credibility and trust as academic researchers studying computer criminal behavior because those participants who completed their interview process could vouch for our credibility and neutrality.

Further, each participant was e-mailed a copy of the informed consent document prior to their involvement in any research questioning or interviews. The consent document clearly articulated the nature, purpose, and research process to potential participants, as well as their right and guarantee of confidentiality. After reading through and acknowledging their participation in the interview process, participants were required to digitally sign their name as well as consent to whether their chat logs could be published in any analysis or findings as a result of their responses and information obtained during the interview process.

Once a participant gave his/her consent, and digitally signed their name, they were asked to fill out a pre-interview questionnaire consisting of 12 questions. The questionnaire's goal/purpose was two-fold: to collect general demographic information from participants, and to use information obtained from the questionnaire to further provide the participant with more specific information relevant to their computer criminality. For example, one question asked participants their country of residence, which later became useful in providing participants with information regarding computer crime sanctions in their respective areas.

Additionally, the pre-interview questionnaire clearly defined vocabulary terms that were utilized in both the questionnaire and the interview. This critical piece helped elaborate and eliminate any confusion about specific terminology used by the PI throughout their interaction with participants.

Interview

The most informative, helpful, and rewarding part of the research project was revealed during the one-on-one interview with participants. The second data collecting method, interviewing, was used to understand the participant's involvement in hacking/cracking through their recollection and experiences. The interview process itself was conducted with participants one-on-one in cyberspace via AOL Instant Messenger[12] (AIM). The specific reasoning behind using AIM as opposed to other instant-messaging services was the simple fact that all of our participants were comfortable with and preferred its service over other providers. Had the participant used another service, the PI was

---

12 AOL Instant Messenger is an instant messaging service/program, which allows users to communicate textually over the Internet in real-time.

more than willing to install and utilize different instant-messaging software (within reasonable limitations).

Prior to beginning an interview, each participant was reminded of his confidentiality agreement. The tone and formality of each interviewee was taken into account when interviewing participants. The PI's use of proper punctuation and capitalization was utilized at their own discretion. Depending on the participant's attitude and perceived comfort level, improper punctuation may have been used to make participants feel more comfortable and related to the PI.

When conducting the interview, a series of formal open-ended questions were asked to participants. They were broken down into the tenets of Routine Activity Theory – motivated offenders, suitable targets, and absence of capable guardianship. Each participant was asked the same questions (in no particular sequence), and depending on responses, additional follow-up questions (not found on the formal interview) were asked at the PI's discretion.

In an attempt to let interviewees provide the PI with the most amount of information, any interruption was avoided until interviewees had stopped typing. AIM proved useful in this regard because it will notify each end of a conversation whether the other is currently typing in their AIM window. As soon as interviewees were done typing, interest was expressed by the PI, or follow-up questions were pursued by the PI with the intent of obtaining more in-depth responses and information.

The interviewees in this research were categorized into three different groups: hackers, crackers, and cyberpunks. Each participant was required to self-identify themselves as one of these three in the pre-interview questionnaire, and then these responses were cross-referenced with information obtained in interviews as well as the formal definitions discussed earlier. This was done to see whether or not participants responded truthfully in their self-identification.

METHODOLOGICAL CHALLENGES

In order to conduct a research project involving human subjects at a state university in New England, we were required to submit our research documentation to the institutional review board of the university prior to the beginning of the study. This approval process is required for all research studies involving the use of human subjects to prevent any potential psychological or physical harm to participants.

When dealing with privacy and issues of confidentiality, participants were ensured that their identity would not be revealed, because doing so could possibly lead to criminal charges or civil liabilities on the interviewee's behalf. Reasonable safeguards were utilized during this process to prevent the identification of subjects. One such measure was to redact any personal identifying information from chat logs such as an interviewee's AIM account, as well as any sufficiently narrow identification details from their interview responses.

Regardless of these procedures, there were still a few problems that were encountered during the research process including trust difficulties, falsified data, and controlling for validity issues.

Trust Difficulties

Perhaps one of the major issues encountered in this research project was the inability to gain a hacker/cracker's trust so that the PI can research and collect valuable information from participants. It was probably more difficult for an individual to believe the PI's identity in cyberspace because of their fear that we are law enforcement officers posing as researchers conducting a study. The anonymity of the Internet is what makes hackers/crackers flourish and taking away that barrier by identifying themselves to an unknown person may seem very risky to them. For this reason, there were people who declined to participate in this research for fear that he/she was being deceived by researchers, much in the way potential sex predators are deceived by law enforcement pretending to be young children.

In one particular case, a participant was very troubled by the idea of his own security, and believed that law enforcement would be able to intercept data transmissions from his computer. As a result, his consent document and attached pre-interview questionnaire were sent to the researcher with digital signatures and encryption. Further, he provided the PI with false identity information to which he confessed, and additionally requested that the interview take place in an encrypted chat environment. While we were willing to meet the requests of the participant, his eventual participation as an interviewee was dropped when he failed to show up at the agreed meeting time and became unreachable. Follow-up instant messages by the PI to this individual did not receive a response by the participant, so he was removed from the research.

Falsified Data

Another issue that we experienced during our research was participant's dishonesty toward researchers, particularly on the pre-interview questionnaire. In two cases, participants revealed to researchers that they were going to lie about their own identity, and digitally signed their names as "Jane Doe." Additionally, one of these individual's thought it would be humorous to mark down female as his gender (even though he was male), and for his occupation wrote "Entrepreneurial Street Salesman" (which he later confessed was a glorified term for drug dealer). Needless to say, this issue was not taken lightly, and the unverifiable nature of his statements led us to drop his involvement in the study because his dishonesty clearly threatened the validity of this research.

Moreover, three participants in the research incorrectly/falsely identified themselves as white hat hackers, when in fact, throughout the course of the interview actually admitted to many cyberpunk and black hat-related activities with no mention of white hat-related hacking. In one particular incident, our falsely identified "Jane Doe" confessed to us that he was not going to identify himself as a cyberpunk and announced to the PI: "i ain't no script [kiddie] bitch."

Validity Issues

Because participants were actively involved in engaging in illegal behaviors on the Internet, it is unknown whether or not their stories and experiences were truthful. We took several necessary steps to reduce the likelihood of the issue such as recruiting individuals on a completely voluntary basis, as well as reinforced (at least 3 times each) that their responses and information would remain confidential. It was our assumption that these steps would eliminate the need for participants to deceive researchers; however, that was not the case in a few known instances.

Another issue we faced during this research challenges our sample size. Because of the small sample size that was collected, it threatens the integrity of our study as being representative of the computer crime population. Because of the nature of our recruitment method, some individuals probably did not believe that we were researchers because we had never met any individual in the real world, only in cyber space. It was probably hard for participants to judge our attitudes and honesty through textual communication, rather than face-to-face interactions. Because of this, it may have dissuaded individuals from participating in our research.

Discussion and Future Research

Throughout the research process, our study has successfully gathered essential classification data to help identify and distinguish hackers/crackers. Validity issues were encountered during this process as some participants falsely identified their personal information as well as their hacking abilities. Additionally, the three main tenets of Routine Activity Theory – suitable targets, motivated offenders, and capable guardianship – were cross-referenced against data gathered in the interview to exemplify its importance in potentially reducing or preventing future cybercrimes. Although the information obtained during these processes was helpful and valuable, there were several considerations we recommend for future endeavors in this type of methodological approach to researching hackers/crackers.

Due to constraints with the sampling size, we acknowledge that the data collected is likely not applicable as a representative sample. However, the information collected is still valuable qualitative data, which could be explored further through additional research studies. The mere lack of availability or inability to recruit participants through cyberspace has demonstrated that trust issues or unknown factors threatened our sampling method, and better strategies may be utilized to overcome this issue.

One method, which was not explored in this research, was monetary incentives. For future research, we would recommend attempting to provide participants who complete the interview process with some form of monetary compensation. This could perhaps increase the number of participants in our study and therefore yield more significantly valid findings.

It was apparent through interactions with participants that their trustful attitude towards us was genuine (or so we thought). We did encounter a few potential participants who had issues believing our confidentiality agreement; he/she would agree to provide an interview, but would refuse to sign their real name on the informed consent. This issue could be refined in the future by having the participant acknowledge what he/she has read and mark a check-box consenting to their confidentiality agreement.

Other participants would willingly admit their falsified responses to researchers, which threatened our belief in the participants' responses. Some of the falsified information would include items such as a participant's occupation and gender – two things that led us to believe the individuals were not taking our research seriously. When dealing with this population, which is known for its vandalism and shenanigans, it should be expected that a few participants would try to deliberately deceive researchers for fun or otherwise.

Also, three out of the five participants falsely identified their hacking classification (black hat or white hat). It is believed that the participants' false classification was done purposely, to project themselves as being honest and upstanding users – not harmful Internet criminals. The definitions were re-analyzed after finding these false identifications to ensure there was no confusion among the terminology or wording, and our assessment upheld their validity.

There were a few interesting circumstances in our interviews with hackers/crackers which should warrant further exploration by utilizing other theoretical perspectives. In one instance, a participant explained a situation in which his mother was aware of his illegal activities on the computer, and even purchased items for her using illegal funding obtained through phishing. In two other instances, participants were also encouraged by their peers/friends to engage in deviant online behaviors. Both instances relate to Burgess and Akers (1966) Social Learning Theory, which is an expansion of Sutherland's differential association perspective. Burgess and Akers assert that

> "'operant' behavior (the voluntary actions of an individual) is conditioned or shaped by rewards or punishments...[and the same is applicable to] classical or 'respondent' conditioning (the conditioning of involuntary reflex behavior); discriminative stimuli (the environmental and internal stimuli that provide cues or signals for behavior); schedules of reinforcement (the rate and ratio in which rewards and punishments follow behavioral responses); and other principles of behavior modification" (Akers & Sellers, 2004, p. 84).

In those instances described above, it is possible that individuals engaging in computer crime activities were acting out of positive reinforcement from family and peers, something that should be explored further in future assessments of computer crime motivations.

Additionally, another conversational topic involving life-course changes sparked interest in pursuing future theoretical perspective. One participant explained that a majority of his hacking/cracking-related activity ceased after his daughter was born. Sampson and Laub (1993) explain that abrupt "turning points" and changes in life such as getting married, finding employment, or having children, increase social bonds to society. This life-course perspective explains why most individuals who are deviant at a younger age stop their deviant behaviors later in life, while other individuals at the same time do not. Future assessments of the life-course perspective in regards to computer crime could be beneficial in determining events, which lead to a discontinuation of an individual's computer criminal behaviors and as a result could be used advantageously as a crime prevention strategy.

Conclusion

Laws related to computer crime are constantly changing and being proposed. One notable finding in this research found that most participants were unaware or ignorant of the specific computer crime laws applicable to their state or country of residence. This is partially due to a weak emphasis on computer crime in the criminal justice system and also due to the lack of programs to educate citizens about the consequences and laws in regards to computer crime.

It was evident from this research that computer criminals are at least somewhat motivated by monetary incentives as a reason for engaging in illegal behaviors. Future sanctions regarding hacking/cracking should include monetary fines to offenders and perhaps community service as an alternative for those individuals who cannot afford payments. Ultimately, this might help reduce recidivism among computer criminals.

Additionally, the unique qualitative approach taken in this research should be given consideration in future recruitment of computer crime offenders. Although our sample size was considerably small, given more time and resources dedicated to locating and bonding with offenders, we might increase the sample size exponentially.

This research was only the first step in constructing a model in reducing computer criminal behavior in cyber space. Specific factors that lead to an individual's computer criminality were identified in this study. Additionally, this research demonstrated the usefulness and important underpinning of Routine Activity Theory in examining and researching motivational factors surrounding hackers/crackers in cyber space. The qualitative data collected in the project, while not empirically generalizable for the entire hacking community, demonstrated clear classification and theoretical foundations for future assessments of computer criminals and their online deviant behaviors.

Discussion 1: Search a recent cybercrime case, and explain how the suspect can be classified based on 12 Cyber Criminal Profiles.

Discussion 2: Which type of Electronic Vandalism would be your major concern and why?

Chapter 4 - Identity Theft, Phishing, and Online Fraud

In April 2011, one hacker claimed to have broken into the Sony PlayStation Network (PSN) and in the process discovered that sensitive customers' information (users' full names, home addresses, email addresses, and passwords, dates of birth, credit card numbers, expiration dates, and CCV security codes) was being saved and forwarded to Sony. On May 1, 2011, after many denials of the incident, Sony company finally admitted that the details of over 77 million customers' private information and around 12 million credit/debit card numbers and expiration dates were possibly stolen.

This case may be one of the biggest identity theft cases against world gaming customers. The stolen personal information can be sold on illegal online websites through simple registration and password set-up processes that are similar to purchasing items from common online shopping websites. These illegal websites encourage online users to engage in illegal online activities displaying banner ads that contain various advertisements for hacking and phishing tutorials. The variety of price ranges is determined by types of credit cards and level of credit limits. For example, platinum cards are $35 and corporate cards $45. Utilizing the hardware of credit card makers, which encodes the credit card information onto the magnetic strip, those purchased credit card numbers become physically cloned to use for shopping in both the physical and cyberworld.

In 2009 the Internet Crime Complaint Center (IC3) referred 336,655 complaints to enforcement agencies on behalf of individuals. These complaints included many different fraud types such as auction fraud, non-delivery, and credit/debit card fraud, as well as non-fraudulent complaints, such as computer intrusions, spam/unsolicited email, and child pornography. This is a 22.3 percent increase from 2008 when 275,284 complaints were referred. The total dollar loss from all referred cases of fraud was $559.7 million with a median dollar loss of $575 per complaint.

A 2009 survey by the Computer Security Institute (CSI) shows that 443 of respondents, consisting of computer security practitioners in U.S. corporations, government agencies, financial institutions, medical institutions and universities, reported significant jumps in incidence of financial fraud (19.5 percent, over 12 percent last year); malware infection (64.3 percent as compared to 50 percent last year); denials of service (29.2 percent, as compared to 21 percent last year), password sniffing (17.3 percent, as compared to 9 percent last year); and website defacement (13.5 percent as compared to 6 percent last year).

In 2009, there has been an increase in almost every kind of security threat that affects computers. One hundred thousand barriers were broken by known viruses, and the number of new viruses increased and phishing attempts, in which con-artists try to trick people into handing over confidential data, are becoming increasingly sophisticated. Also on the increase is the number of networks of remotely controlled computers, called "Bot-nets," used by malicious hackers and con-men to carry out many different cybercrimes.

Consumer Reports conducted a survey of online consumers in 2011. Using a nationally representative sample of 2,089 online households with Internet access at home, they found that: 1) about 30 percent of the respondents reported that a virus or spyware caused serious problems, leading to replacement of 1.3 million PCs, as well as financial losses of $2.3 billion last year; 2) Almost 30 percent of individuals' bank information, medical records, and other personal information stored on their smart phones could be fully exposed to identity theft due to their negligence of securing information in their phones. 3) Active Facebook users engage in risky online behaviors such as posting their full birth date (34 percent) and posting their current location, children's names, and photos (21 percent) that can lead to burglaries, identity theft, and stalking.

The concept of Internet fraud covers a wide range of fraudulent schemes. This chapter focuses on major types of fraud victimization of international concern: identity theft, phishing, auction fraud and Nigerian fraud.

VICTIMIZATION STATISTICS

As previously discussed in chapter 1, cyberspace, with its unique spatial and temporal structure, creates new opportunities for criminals to interact with victims. The increasing number of victims of cybercrimes who suffer financial loss, or who are threatened, merits investigation. Although research on cybercrime from the offender's perspective is growing, there is little, if any, research concerning the victims of cybercrimes.

Although it is almost impossible to capture true figures of world cybercrime victimization, examining statistics from major cybercrime victimization reports of world nations is essential to estimate the level of prevalence of crime victimization resulting in financial and time loss in both private and businesses of the world community.

World Financial Loss

According to the 2013 BJS (Bureau of Justice Statistics) report, approximately 16.6 million American people (4 percent of the adult population) experienced identity theft and monetary loss, which totaled over US$24 billion in 2012. The average financial loss per victim was around $1,500.

Similarly, the United Kingdom is also experiencing significant problems with identity fraud that cost an estimated £3.3 billion involving an estimated number of over 80,000 victims in 2012. Approximately, 27% of the UK adult population surveyed had been a victim of identity fraud (Annual Fraud Indicator, 2013).

According to the Australian Attorney General's Office (2014), identity crime is still one of the most common crime types in Australia. Between 750,000 to 900,000 people experience identity crimes each year in Australia, with an approximated annual cost of at least $1.6 billion.

In Canada, a national survey conducted for the Chartered Professional Accountants of Canada (CPA Canada) found that 29 percent of the respondents had been victims of financial fraud. Also, credit and debit card fraud (71 percent and 28 percent respectively) were identified as the most common types of fraud reported by victims (2014, CPA Canada). The Canadian Anti-fraud Centre (2014) estimated that total losses due to identity theft were approximated to be over Can$74 million in 2014.

McAfee, Cybersecurity Company, claims that more than 800 million individuals were victims of cybercrime throughout the world in 2013, and the estimated cost could be $160 billion per year. In addition, as cybercriminals switch their focus to attacking mobile platforms, low-income countries, which have relatively smaller losses, will be at greater risk of financial loss from identity fraud, phishing, and financial fraud (2014).

Time Loss and Psychological Harm

Victims of identity theft not only bear individual financial loss, they also need to restore their good names and credit ratings. A 2008 McMaster survey reported that Canadian victims of identity fraud personally spent more than CA $150 million and 20 million hours to resolve the fraud issues.

According to the Identity Theft Resource Center's (ITRC) 2003 survey, American victims spent an average of $739 dollars in out-of-pocket expense based on damages done to existing accounts and $951 from new accounts. Pontell et al. (2008) reported that the median amount of monetary loss from missing work to clear up victimization was $4,000. CALPIRG reported that the average amount of time victims spent to restore their financial status was 175 hours. Resolving existing credit card fraud problems appears to be easier and require less time as compared to victims of other identity theft related frauds. According to the FTC survey, victims with new account fraud took an average of 60 hours to resolve the problems associated with the crime, but victims of existing credit card fraud spent an average of 15 hours to resolve the crime problem (Synovate, 2003).

In addition to financial and time loss that occur when resolving the problems due to identity theft victimization, many victims tend to experience a great deal of emotional stress, including feelings of anger, helplessness and mistrust, disturbed sleeping patterns, and a feeling of a lack of security (Davis & Stevenson, 2004). The ITRC (2009) survey indicates that short-term feelings of being ruined, betrayed, and powerless are common symptoms among victims. Moreover, 30 percent of victims experienced distrusting people and 4 percent claimed to have experienced suicidal ideations.

TRENDS AND ISSUES: MAJOR TYPES OF INTERNET FRAUD CASES

Our society is changing significantly through the Internet in ways such as how we purchase things, how we communicate, and where we get entertainment. At the same time, cybercriminals are using the enormous benefits of the Internet to defraud people who are innocently utilizing the Internet as a communication method and a commerce tool.

Today's criminals have integrated highly technical methods with traditional crimes and have developed and created new types of crimes. Even though it is difficult for law enforcement to apprehend and prosecute this new type of criminal, I personally believe that there is no significant difference between street criminals and cybercriminals with the exception that cybercriminals utilize a new weapon of choice.

Identity Theft

Identity theft is a specific form of Identity Fraud that involves the illegal use of someone's personal data such as name, social security number, or driver's license to obtain money, merchandise, or services by deception, and requires illegal use of the stolen identification that belongs to another person (CRS Report, 2010 p3). Identity theft includes fraudulently obtaining credit, stealing money from the victim's bank accounts, using the victim's credit card number, establishing accounts with utility companies, renting an apartment, or even filing bankruptcy using the victim's name.

Although there is a considerable argument for whether the relationship between identity theft and data breach is empirically valid, the plausible correlation can be explained. The Identity Theft Resource Center (ITRC) reported that there was a 47 percent increase in data breaches between 2007 and 2008. In 2008, the business industry experienced the greatest number of data breaches (36.6 percent), followed by education (20 percent) and government/military (16.8 percent). In addition, identity theft complaints also escalated during the same time period. Moreover, media coverage of identity theft cases also clearly supports the argument. For example:

> In June, 2011, Daniel Spitler pleaded guilty to illegally accessing personal information on 114,000 iPad 3G owners from AT&T's servers. The stolen e-mail addresses included ones from the U.S.

government officials, NASA, and the Department of Homeland Security.

Over a two-year period and in March 2008, TJ Maxx lost details of approximately 90 million customers, while in 2008, federal prosecutors announced indictments against 11 people alleged of stealing more than 40 million credit and debit card account numbers from national wide retailers in the U.S.

Identity theft is often interrelated with various other criminal activities such as credit card fraud, Internet fraud, document fraud, immigration fraud, employment fraud, etc. Although a precise typology of identity theft is not clearly presented in the literature, three primary types of identity theft are commonly identified:

1. true name fraud
2. account takeover, and
3. criminal identity theft.

- True name fraud occurs when someone uses a consumer's personal information to open new accounts in his/her name.
- Account takeover occurs when criminals gain access to a person's existing account(s) and make fraudulent charges.
- Criminal identity theft is when a criminal provides a victim's personal information to law enforcement when the criminal gets arrested. Victims can have a criminal record or outstanding warrants attached to their name and personal information without even realizing it.

The suggested three forms of identity theft above may offer current trends and issues in identity theft victimization. According to FTC (2008), the most prevalent form of identity theft was credit card fraud, which is 20 percent of the reported 313,982 identity theft complaints, and about 12 percent of the identity theft complaints were rated as more than one form of identity theft. After the victim's identity is stolen, their information is frequently misused in the form of credit card fraud when perpetrators begin making purchases. They will often change addresses to avoid alerting the victim to fraudulent charges. In this case, a victim is unaware of the charges and does not pay them, possibly causing a negative impact on the victim's credit. In addition to abusing existing credit card accounts, opening new accounts in the victim's name generates more charges on the victim's line of credit. These criminal activities affect the victim's current financial stability and their future credit as well. Examples of true name fraud and account takeover are presented below:

> In 2009, a cybercriminal used the name and rank of an officer in the Canadian Snowbirds 431 Squadron demonstration team in conducting an online scheme wherein the criminal pretended to be selling a car from the United Kingdom.
>
> In 2010, three Bulgarian criminals, two residing in Toronto, were indicted in U.S. federal court on charges of using counterfeit ATM cards, bank fraud, and aggravated identity theft in connection with a skimming scheme in which they are alleged to have compromised numerous ATMs throughout eastern Massachusetts and stolen more than $120,000.

Victims' personal identifiable information can be also misused to create counterfeit documents or obtain benefits in a victim's name. These actions may facilitate international terrorism, using fake passports to illegally enter any nation. Identity theft can facilitate employment fraud using the victim's personal information, and this could adversely impact the victim's credit, public record, ability to file taxes, and ability to obtain future employment.

> In 2002, a woman in Florida was falsely accused and arrested for motor vehicle theft when another woman had stolen her identity, stolen a car, and continued using the victim's name and information during her sentencing and probation. The victim was released when it was discovered that her impersonator, maintaining the false identity, was serving eight years in prison for various felonies.

To victims of identity theft, the task of correcting incorrect information about their financial or personal status and trying to restore their names and reputations can be a terrible trial. At the same time, it seems to be almost impossible to bring back the original identities of the victims once they are victimized by cybercriminals.

Phishing, Nigerian Scam, and Internet Auction Fraud: Techniques of Social Engineering

The use of social engineering is not new to crime victimization research. Social engineering in Internet fraud cases is generally manifested as a process of personal persuasions or deceptions undertaken to illegally gain private information or organizational data using individuals' emotional weaknesses within the cyber-environment.

These social engineering tactics are designed to build a trust relationship between victims and the social engineers, who are seeking illegally-obtained information not only from cyberspace (i.e. chat-rooms, e-mail, message boards, or websites) but also from the physical world. Information found in the victim's home or workplace, on their cellphone, or even in their garbage can be a powerful tool for psychological attack. These con artists strike when cognitive biases (errors in mental processes) become prevalent in individuals. For example, an online user visits an unknown website and sees a famous company logo that enforces reliability of the site and influences personal decision-making processes.

Thus, the social engineer works to take advantage of human nature by forcing victims to follow societal orders or enforce potential victims' decisions to follow their ideal values. Any type of fraud scheme blends these types of social engineering techniques and additional components of the Internet to present fraudulent solicitations to potential victims, to conduct fraudulent transactions, or to transmit the proceeds of fraud to financial institutions or to others connected with the scheme. The advent of the Internet has allowed different types of fraud to occur faster than ever before. As the United States Department of Justice claims, "the same types of fraud schemes that have victimized consumers and investors for many years before the creation of the Internet are now appearing online (sometimes with particular refinements that are unique to Internet technology)." Phishing, the Nigerian scam, and auction fraud would be the best reflection of the social engineer at work.

Phishing

The term "phishing" is a play on the word "fishing," switching the "ph" in honor of the hacker/phreaker practice of telecommunication services. As recently as a decade ago these attacks were used to gain access to Internet service provider accounts, with American Online a popular target, and the term was coined in 1996 by hackers who were stealing America Online (AOL) accounts by scamming passwords from unsuspecting AOL users (Moore, 2011).

The first use on the internet of the word phishing occurred in the alt.2600 hacker newsgroup in January 1996. However, the term may have been used even earlier in the popular hacker newsletter 2600. By 1996, hacked accounts were called "phish." By 1997, phish were actively being traded between hackers as a form of electronic currency.

There are instances whereby phishers would routinely trade 10 working AOL phish for a piece of hacking software or "warez". For reference, warez refer to stolen copyrighted applications and games. Overtime, the definition of what constitutes a phishing attack has blurred and expanded. The term phishing covers not only obtaining user account details, but now includes access to all personal and financial data.

What originally was entailed in the meaning of phishing was tricking users into replying to emails or message with passwords and credit card details. But now, the term phishing is expanded to include using fake websites, installing Trojan horses, using key-loggers, screen loggers, and man-in-the-middle data proxies which are delivered through any electronic communication channel.

Phishing is currently one of the most rapidly proliferating and successful methods of obtaining personal data in fraudulent scams. Phishing e-mails involve our major communication tools coupled with social engineering design that targets unsuspecting online users in order to obtain personal information in response to an unsolicited message. The obtained information can be used for online sales or in the commission of identity fraud.

On June 1, 2011, Google disclosed that hundreds of Gmail passwords that belong to prominent people including major bank officers and senior government officials in the U.S. were disrupted by phishing attempts. Google stated that the attacks appeared to originate from China, targeting government officials of other Asian countries.

Phishing entails sending highly targeted emails that are disguised with authentic features appearing to be delivered from a trusted source with plausible messages that are difficult for recipients to detect. According to Symantec, the computer security company, the most common targets of phishing attacks are government agencies and high ranking officers in major corporations. Those who primarily attack corporations tend to seek new product designs and target engineers at national defense contractors, aiming at national security data to sell on the black market. Common forms of phishing techniques include sending an e-mail to the head of a company using the Internal Revenue Service email account, or using the company's human resources department email account asking for personal information to make a payment.

Using phishing techniques can also contribute to a massive number of individual victimizations. The victims who clicked on e-mail messages were sent to the fake bank websites disguised to look identical to authentic banking sites, where they were asked to provide personal information (bank account numbers, passwords, Social Security numbers, and drivers' license numbers).

In October 2009, the F.B.I. began arresting 53 people on charges of conducting a vast financial fraud-based phishing scheme associated with Bank of America and Wells Fargo's account holders. This case had the largest number of defendants charged in a cybercrime case and caused at least a $2 million financial loss. According to the indictment, the co-conspirators, Kenneth Joseph Lucas, John Clarke, and Nichole Merzi, retrieved account information and transferred funds into their own accounts, and then transferred some funds back to their accomplices in Egypt (New York Times, 2009).

Dhamija et al.'s study using 22 university-based participants examined 20 sites to determine their authenticity and found that 90 percent of participants were deceived by good quality phishing sites, 23 percent relied only on content to determine authenticity, and 68 percent ignored pop-up warnings as to content risk. In other words, people are highly exposed to phishing risks regardless of their level of education, age, sex, previous experience, and hours of computer use.

The 2010 Global Phishing Survey conducted by the Anti-Phishing Working Group (APWG) reported that at least 67,677 unique phishing attacks are currently in existence worldwide and cybercriminals aggressively target world e-commerce sites (Top-Level Domain (TLD):

.com, .net, and .org) and banks. Principally, all phishing attacks in the second half of 2010 (from July 1 to December 31, 2010) substantially increased from previous periods and were higher than any time period in the three years since APWG began to engage in research.

Since major business owners are proactively scanning Internet zones, many cybercriminals tend to place brand names in sub-domains rather than placing brand names in the domain name.. This technique makes it difficult for Internet users to cover the "base" or true domain name being used in a URL.

APWG also found cybercriminals using Internationalized Domain Names (IDNs), which deceive Internet users to impossibly distinguish from true domain names. On January 16, 2009, APWG discovered that the domain name "xn—hotmal-t9a.net," appeared as "hotmail.net" on IDN-enabled browsers. On July 12, 2010, the domain name "http://xn--fcebook-hwa.com" appeared as "http://fácebook.com" when rendered in IDN-enabled browsers. This attack is called the "The IDN homograph attack," and using characters in different language scripts makes online users nearly indistinguishable from well-known domain names.

Another important cybercrime trend has been an increase in anti-malware programs that can contribute to phishing activities, fraudulent scams, or the sales of worthless computer security products. APWG (2009) reported that detected anti-malware program cases significantly increased 225 percent from 2,850 in July 2008 to 9,287 in December 2008. The case listed below illustrates the fraudulent scheme that combines phishing and other frauds.

On June 23, 2011, two members of a major Latvian crime ring, Peteris Sahurovs and Marina Maslobojeva, who placed malware in online ads were arrested by Federal authority. The particular type of malware involved is also known as "scareware." Online users unknowingly download the program through online ads, then their computer screens are taken over by messages warning of a variety of virus infections. To restore the computer to its normal state, the user is forced to buy their fraudulent security software. Notably, however, this purchase is made knowingly and eagerly by the victim, because the cybercriminals have erroneously frightened them into thinking their machine is infected by a horde of viruses – hence "scareware." According to the Justice department, $72 million worth of scareware was sold by one group for over three years; another group caused at least $2 million in financial damages. Unintentional clicks on ads for phony virus scans on web-pages infected hundreds of thousands of computers, and the victims provided their credit card information to purchase software for up to $129.

Additionally, the criminal group bought online ads in the *Minneapolis Star Tribune's* website to distribute their malware. In order to make their fraudulent activities appear legitimate to the newspaper, they claimed to be representatives of the Best Western Motel Chain by creating a false advertising agency. Once the newspaper ran the ads, the scareware embedded in the ads infected the computers of users visiting the website.

The Nigerian Scam

There is another form of social engineering techniques in Internet fraud that is referred to as 419 fraud, the section of the Nigerian penal code that addresses fraud schemes. The Nigerian scam was initially conducted beginning in the early 1980s. As technology developed, their techniques evolved as well (Rosoff et. al, 2010).

The traditional form of the Nigerian e-mail scam is known as the "pigeon drop," which convinces a potential victim that unclear ownership of a sum of money can be shared, but requires the victim to pay "advance fees" of around $5,000 or more in order to cover legal charges or bribes of officials (Rosoff et. al, 2010).

Nigeria continues to develop and deliver innovative Internet scams that primarily target Americans, who they view as rich and easy to deceive (Rosoff et. al, 2010). The current scammers prefer to embellish their stories with details that can be retrieved from local newspapers. After obtaining a victim's information, such as email and personal relationships through social networking sites, the scammer breaks into a victim's e-mail account. As a next step, the scammer impersonates the victim and sends an email that appeals for emergency assistance to everyone in the account's e-mail list, asking them to wire-transfer money to Nigeria. The storyline in the email includes requesting money for immediate medical attention or losing a wallet during a trip to Nigeria. An example of the full text of the email sent from a victim's account, posted in the *New York Times* is listed below:

From: Drew Biondo (…@yahoo.com)
Subject:EMERGENCY!!!

HELLO
HOW ARE YOU DOING? I WANT YOU TO KEEP THIS CONFIDENTIAL BETWEEN BOTH OF US, I KNOW THAT I CAN PUT MY TRUST IN YOU ON THIS. PLEASE DO NOT LET ME DOWN. RIGHT NOW I AM IN AFRICA, NIGERIA. I CAME HERE ON A TRIP TO SEE A FRIEND AND WHEN I GOT HERE I LOST MY WALLET CONTAINING THE ADDRESS OF MY FRIEND AND HIS CONTACT PHONE NUMBER, ALONG WITH MY ATM CARD AND OTHER VALUABLES.
SO RIGHT NOW I DO NOT EVEN HAVE ANY MONEY ON ME. I AM STAYING IN A HOTEL NOW, AND THE MANAGER IS ALREADY RANTING OVER HIS MONEY AND AS TIME GOES BY THE BILLS ARE INCREASING.
I WOULD WANT YOU TO LOAN ME $2000. I PROMISE TO PAY YOU BACK AS SOON AS I GET BACK… I WOULD WANT YOU TO HELP SEND THE MONEY VIA WESTERN UNION. GET BACK AT ME ASAP.
HOPE TO READ FROM YOU…
DREW BIONDO

Internet Auction Fraud

Fraudulent schemes appearing on online auctions have been the most frequently reported by victims, with a high of 71.2 percent of all reported complaints in 2004. However, in 2010, 10.1 percent of referrals were rated in the auction fraud category and the total number of complaints and referrals of auction fraud has steadily declined over the last several years. Although the main reason for this reduction is unknown, current diversification in cybercrime types may provide cybercriminals more options to commit different types of cyber-schemes that allow searching for more targets that are suitable in cyberspace and minimize attention from law enforcement agencies.

These auction fraud schemes, and similar schemes for online retail goods, typically purport to offer high-value items, ranging from laptop computers to collectibles such as rare stamps or coins that are likely to attract many consumers. These schemes induce their victims to send money for the promised items, but then deliver nothing or only an item far less valuable than what was promised, including counterfeit or altered goods.

The problem associated with this type of fraud is that, as Chua et. al.'s study indicates, victims have little information about the sellers and rely heavily on the con-artist's reputation score posted on the auction site, which can be easily manipulated. They also argue that the con-artist exploits buyers' unfamiliarity with how the online auction market works. Non-delivery fraud is common in the laptop market, and the creation or alteration of an existing stamp is the most successful technique in the philatelic market because most buyers acknowledge constant traders in the market. In other words, selling non-existent products in the philatelic market would not be successful, and sending a phonebook or defected laptop in the laptop market would have a higher chance of defrauding buyers. A sample of an auction fraud case is presented below:

> …who ordered the laptop computer from an eBay.com seller about six weeks ago. Days later, he received a laptop-sized FedEx package – but inside was a Montreal phonebook.

Some Internet fraud schemes, which appear to be variations of online auction schemes, involve the use of unlawfully obtained credit card numbers to order goods or services online. One widely reported and intricate scheme involves offering consumers high value consumer items at very attractive prices on legitimate e-commerce websites. When a potential buyer contacts the "seller," the seller promises to ship the consumer the item before the consumer has to pay anything. If the consumer agrees, this impostor seller uses that consumer's real name, along with an unlawfully obtained credit card number belonging to another person, to buy the item at a legitimate website.

Once the website ships the item to the buyer, the buyer, believing that the transaction is legitimate, authorizes his credit card to be billed in favor of the impostor seller or sends payment directly. As a result, there are two victims of the scheme: the original e-commerce merchant who shipped the item based on the unlawfully used credit card and the consumer who sent his money after receiving the item that the impostor seller fraudulently ordered from the merchant. In the meantime, the impostor seller may have transferred his fraudulent proceeds to bank accounts beyond the effective reach of either the merchant or the consumer.

Discussion 1:
After examining the latest cybercrime reports, please answer the following questions:
Why is the number of cyber-victims growing? Why is cybercrime severely underreported? Which of the findings makes you seriously concerned and why?

Discussion 2:
What do you think society's perception of cybercriminals is? Without revealing specific details of any particular incident, do you think you are a cybercriminal? Why or why not?

PART III

Causations of Cybercrime: Criminological Explanations

The scientific process of criminology is similar to that of other disciplines. Empirical validity is approximated to the truth. In order to convey empirical validity, one must examine certain phenomena derived from cause and effect and then form a hypothesis, which is a tentative prediction. A careful research design that considers the conceptualization and operationalization process needs to be constructed. Once data collection is completed, analysis is undertaken. Finally, an inference is made from the findings, which becomes a theory.

There are many criminological theories that apply to traditional crimes. A criminal investigator, or any type of law-enforcement personnel, is concerned with understanding patterns of crimes with respect to what happened and when, where, and how it happened. Once this baseline information is obtained, the goal is to investigate additional facts and circumstances as quickly and as thoroughly as possible in order to determine who committed the offense.

On a more fundamental level, it is important for the protection of society to understand why social deviance, abuse, and crime occur because in so doing we are potentially better able to prevent crime. Understanding theoretical explanations of crime can also enable professionals to better gather and analyze crime and intelligence information, investigate and prosecute offenders, and design enforcement programs that target particular offending by individuals or groups. Unfortunately, criminologists have paid less attention to theoretical explanations of high-tech crime or to the role of technology in the criminology literature.

Our goal in this chapter then is to understand theoretical explanations for why some people commit crime using a computer whereas others do not. We will explore various theoretical perspectives to understand the mind of a cybercriminal and the motivations that contribute to their engagement in illegal activities.

Criminological theory and criminal justice policy have an indispensable relationship. According to Sutherland (1947), criminology is the body of knowledge that regards crime as a social phenomenon. It includes the process of "making laws, breaking laws, and enforcing law." Criminal justice policy and practices are strongly related to this process, especially the process of making law and enforcing law, because the direction of criminological theory guides empirical research. If the research supports the theory based on empirical validity, the theory often turns into criminal justice policy. In other words, if a theory is empirically valid, it can be used as the basis for criminal justice policy.

Throughout Part III, we will discuss various cybercrime issues via the application of several prominent crime theories. Classical Theories, Trait Theories, Social Process Theories, and Social Structure Theories will be discussed. After reviewing the general explanations of theoretical perspectives, it is crucial to apply them to issues associated with cybercrimes. Consider the questions that are intended to stimulate thought regarding the nature of cybercrime and cybercrime prevention strategies on micro and macro scales.

Chapter 5 - Traditional Criminological Theories

Classical Theories

One of the primary goals in criminal justice policy is crime deterrence. Initial deterrence perspectives in criminology begin with the classical school. Classical criminology developed from a reaction to the unjust laws and punishment systems that were in existence before 1789 (Vold, Bernard, and Snipes, 2002). The classical school was not interested in studying criminal behavior, but rather lawmaking and the legal process. The Declaration of Independence and the United States Constitution reflect the Classical movement; thus the law of today is classical in nature (Aker, 1997).

Beccaria and Bentham are two famous classical theorists, and both led the movement for human rights and free will. The basic premise of classical theory is that actions and decisions are made by persons in the exercise of free will. The classical theorists posited that people choose to obey or violate the law by rationally calculating the risk of pain versus the potential pleasure of reward. In regards to deterrence, Beccaria (1764) believed that criminals would be deterred from committing crimes when the costs outweighed the benefits. Beccaria thought punishment should be proportionate to the crime committed, and criminal behavior would be deterred by certainty, swiftness, and severity of punishment. Bentham (1843) was a proponent of utilitarianism, which assumed the greatest happiness for the greatest number. Bentham also believed that the cost of committing a crime should outweigh the benefits because people acted as human calculators, and that punishment should be proportionate to the crime committed. Based on Beccaria's and Bentham's ideas, criminologists could simply hypothesize how to deter criminal behavior and reduce crime, and the theories developed by classical criminologists eventually became the basis for all modern criminal justice systems (Vold, Bernard, and Snipes, 2002).

The most apparent link between deterrence theory and our criminal justice policies and practices involves the concept of severity of punishment. The classical school saw two forms of deterrence: specific and general deterrence. Specific deterrence means that punishing a criminal will deter the criminal from committing a crime. General deterrence means that punishing a criminal will deter others from committing crime.

Gibbs (1968) was the first to test the deterrence hypothesis by defining certainty and severity of punishment. Gibbs (1968) found that greater certainty and severity of imprisonment was associated with fewer homicides in the fifty states for the year 1960. Tittle (1969) also found that more certainty was associated with less crime for all the seven index offenses in the FBI Uniform Crime Reports. Paternoster (1987) found negative correlations between perceptual and objective deterrence and crime, but the correlations were very low. Paternoster (1989) also found, in a study of school children, that certainty of punishment had more impact than severity. In sum, certainty has a deterrent effect on crime, but the deterrent effect of severity is only present when certainty is high (Vold, Bernard, and Snipes, 2002).

Deterrence theory has been utilized in current criminal justice policies such as "three strikes," "truth-in-sentencing," and "mandatory minimums" that are mainly focused on one aspect of the theory: severity. The results of deterrence—the "Get Tough" movement and the "War on Drugs"—have generated a substantial impact on the rising prison population as a significant side effect in the criminal justice system. Our current criminal justice policies still tend to focus more on severity and less on another component of deterrence theory: certainty. As stated previously, certainty has been associated with deterring criminal behavior. Thus, many criminologists emphasize that those who implement criminal justice policy should focus on the certainty of apprehension and conviction, rather than on the severity, when they use deterrence theory in policy implementation.

The U.S. became concerned about crime because of a considerable rise in crime during the 1980s, when deterrence theory was revised and reimagined as "rational choice". Rational choice theory was introduced by the economist Becker in 1968, and Cornish and Clarke developed the theory in 1986 (Williams III and McShane, 1999). Rational choice focuses on criminal decision making and motives. Rational choice makes no hard distinction between offenders and the law-abiding because the theory assumes that all of us will commit an offense when we think we can get away with it (i.e., everyone is born bad). Thus, rational choice theory mainly seeks to make criminal choices less attractive.

Rational choice perspective has influenced criminal justice policies and practices in several ways. Clarke (1997) identified four rational choice objectives to reduce criminal opportunities: first, increase the perceived effort required to commit a crime; second, increase the perceived risk; third, reduce the anticipated reward; fourth, remove excuses for crime. These objectives have resulted in many crime prevention successes.

Cohen and Felson (1979) proposed their Routine Activity Theory as another version of deterrence theory. The theory mainly focuses on opportunities for crime. Cohen and Felson (1979) suggested that there will always be a vast supply of crime motivation and that motivated offenders are a given. They strongly believed that crime is based on situational factors, which provide criminal opportunity. The researchers asserted that three crucial elements are necessary for a predatory criminal act: motivated offender, suitable target, and lack of a capable guardian. If one of the elements is absent, crime is not likely to occur. If all three elements are present, then the chances for crime increase.

The Routine Activity approach has led to the practical application of situational crime prevention measures by changing conditions and circumstances. One situational crime prevention strategy is target hardening. Target hardening makes it more difficult for offenders to commit crimes on specific targets. Increasing police patrol in "hot spot" areas, the use of locked doors, windows, alarm systems, and community crime watch programs are all examples of target hardening.

Policy Implications-Classical Theories

Classical school theories operate from a perspective of choice. The assumption is that individuals have the ability to make a rational choice to either follow the law or to violate it. In order to deter crime, punishments must sufficiently outweigh the pleasure received by committing a criminal act. If the deterrence theory is true, crime will be deterred by employing harsh punishment with great certainty.

Various programs have been tried around the country using deterrence and choice as primary elements. Programs such as Scared Straight have attempted to use fear and deterrence to prevent young offenders from committing additional crimes by exposing them to the realities of prison life. Boot camps have attempted to use fear, discipline, and brief incarceration to keep offenders from committing additional crimes. These types of programs are controversial and have yielded mixed results.

Consider Classical Theories:

Can you see how the concept of weighing potential benefits against potential costs is fundamental to making choices? And how rational choice theory can also be applied to changing circumstances in people's lives? A key to using the classical theories to understand criminal behavior is realizing that what seems irrational to you may be very rationale or even necessary to the offender.

CONTROL THEORIES

Control theories are logically consistent with their propositions. Their explanation of delinquency is based not on the question of "Why did he do it?" but, instead, on "Why did he not do it?" Control theorists assume that delinquency will naturally occur in the absence of controls against it. Control theories mainly focus on social control, social bonds, and attachments (Hirschi, 1969).

Sykes and Matza (1957) developed a different perspective on social control to explain why some delinquents drift in and out of delinquency. According to Sykes and Matza, delinquents hold values, beliefs, and attitudes very similar to law-abiding citizens, so the delinquents develop a special set of justifications before the delinquent acts. They learn techniques that allow them to neutralize such values and attitudes temporarily and thus, drift back and forth between legitimate and illegitimate behaviors. These techniques act as defense mechanisms that release the delinquent from the constraints bonded with moral order.

Sykes and Matza proposed the five techniques of Neutralization. They are presented below, along with sample responses provided by a hacker:

Denial of responsibility: Delinquents will propose that they are the victims and they are pushed or pulled into situations beyond their control	"My friends encouraged me to send the virus."
Denial of injury: Delinquents suppose that his acts really do not cause any harm or that the victim can afford the loss	"Why is everyone making a big deal about it? No one got physically injured."
Denial of the victim: Delinquents view the act as not being wrong and the victims deserve the injury, or there is no real victim	"Microsoft corp. needs to know how much their systems are vulnerable."
Condemnation of the condemners: Delinquents shift the blame to others	"Microsoft corp. does worse things to their consumers by charging extreme costs for their useless software."
Appeal to higher loyalties: It is equivalent of Robin-hood syndrome	"I hacked into their computer system to reveal the security loopholes."

Sykes and Matza claim that individuals who accept more techniques of neutralization are generally more likely to engage in crime, and neutralization is more likely to lead to crime among individuals who associate with delinquent peers. Sykes and Matza further argued that these neutralizations are available not just to delinquents, but they can be found throughout society. Unfortunately, Sykes and Matza's theory has not received much attention due to the lack of empirical validity regarding the specific content of rationalizations, neutralization, and attitudes. Hirschi asked an important question: Do delinquents neutralize law-violating behavior before or after they commit an act? Neutralization theory loses its credibility if juveniles use techniques of neutralization before the commission of a delinquent act. There are methodological problems, findings are not consistent, and the relationships are weak—but the theory of Sykes and Matza has received some support from empirical research.

Hirschi's social bond theory assumes that delinquent acts will result when one's bond to society is weak or broken. Individuals who are tightly bonded to the various agents of social control—such as family, school, or church—are less likely to engage in criminal behavior. Hirschi (1969) asserted that humans possess the natural inclination to commit delinquent acts, and delinquent acts are controlled through four main elements of the social bond: attachment, commitment, involvement, and belief. First, attachment refers to psychological and emotional connection to significant others such as family, friends, and community. Hirschi (1969) emphasizes that attachment to parents is extremely important. This element is the true heart of social bond theory. Second, commitment involves the time, energy, and effort expended in conventional lines of action. Prospects of employment and educational opportunities prevent a person from becoming deviant. Third, involvement refers to participation in conventional and legitimate activities, such as school activities, recreations and athletic events, which restrict a person from the opportunities of criminal behavior. Fourth, belief involves the acceptance of a conventional value system. The theory posits that if common moral beliefs are absent or weakened, individuals are more likely to participate in antisocial behaviors.

Hirschi (1969) argues that attachment and commitment are positively associated, regardless of social class position. In addition, attachment, commitment, involvement, and belief are also positively associated with one another. The theory assumes that attachments are the most powerful protection against delinquency (Shoemaker, 2000).

Self-control theory posits that the major element of social control is self-control. Gottfredson and Hirschi (1990) proposed that a person develops the personal attribute that controls an individual's propensity to commit crime, that this latent trait, "self-control," appears early in life (by age 8) and remains stable over time. People with low self-control tend to be impulsive, insensitive, physical, risk taking, short-sighted, and nonverbal. Low self-control is associated not only with crime but with "analogous behavior" such as drinking, smoking, and illicit sex (Akers, 2004). In addition, Gottfredson and Hirschi (1993) also indicate that low self-control is not the "motivating force" leading to criminal behavior, and "the link between self-control and crime is not deterministic, but probabilistic, affected by opportunities and other constraints."

According to Gottfredson and Hirschi (1990), ineffective parenting is the most important contributor to low self-control. Adequate parental management, which results in high self-control in the child, occurs when the child's behavior is monitored and any deviant behavior is immediately recognized and punished. Gottfredson and Hirschi (1990) pinpoint the role of parents as the most essential source of socialization for children.

Policy Implications-Control Theories

Hirschi's social bond theory (1992) argues that juveniles are less likely to engage in delinquent behavior when they are more attached to others and have stronger belief in the moral validity of law. The policy implications can be derived from the four elements of the social bond: attachment, commitment, involvement, and belief. Big brother and sister programs or curfew laws can increase social attachment and also provide supervision. After-school activities increase involvement in legitimate activity. Providing jobs for youth can be effective by increasing their commitment to the economic system. In addition, moral education programs can strengthen beliefs in the legitimacy of law by teaching that all people benefit from society when everyone obeys the rules.

Policy implications can be derived from self-control theory's key concept that effective parenting during childhood can create high self-control in the child that will inhibit deviant behavior. Thus, policies need to focus on early education and effective child-care programs. Requiring parenting classes in high school for potential parents would be a very effective way to reduce delinquency and crimes.

Consider Social Control Theories:

What is it about people who use computers responsibly rather than to cause harm? Were they raised by nurturing parents who encouraged responsible use of computers from a very young age? Were most law-abiding IT users influenced in positive ways while growing up in regard to their use of computers and other communications devices?

SOCIAL LEARNING THEORIES

As a general concept, social learning theory has been applied to the fields of sociology, psychology, criminal justice, and criminology to explain how criminal values, ideas, techniques, and expressions are transmitted from one individual to another.

Sutherland (1939) formally proposed a theory of differential association (7 propositions) in the third edition of his textbook, *Principles of Criminology*, to explain causes of criminal behaviors. His final version of the theory was revised in 1947 and expanded to 9 propositions. The theory presents a social learning process, which rejects claims of both the biological and pathological explanations toward deviance, and became one of the most recognized social learning theories.

Sutherland's theory is influenced by three major components used to present a better formulation. These three major components included the ecological theory, symbolic interactions, and culture conflict theory. The theory shows that Sutherland used the different crime rates from the culture-conflict approach, while the symbolic interactions approach was used to describe the process through which individuals turned into criminals. The objective of the theory was to explain individual criminal behavior, as well as the criminal behavior of various societal groups.

Sutherland says crime is caused by the social environment of individuals rather than the individual themselves. The main principles of the theory note that deviant behavior is learned behavior through interaction with significant others, such as family members or friends. In order to become a criminal, a person must not only have a propensity toward illegal activity, he/she must also learn how to commit criminal acts. The most important principle of differential association is the sixth, which states that individuals become criminals "because of an excess of definitions favorable to violation of the law over definitions unfavorable to violations of the law" (Sutherland, 1947). In other words, if individuals repeatedly see and feel that law violation brings various benefits (conditions favorable to deviance), the individuals are more likely to become criminals. In addition, the learning process depends on priority, intensity, and duration.

Differential association theory specifies the process by which an individual will learn specific techniques for criminal activities and the criminal mindset, such as values, motives, rationalizations, attitudes, and justifications to adopt criminal behavior.

Burgess and Akers (1966) expanded Sutherland's differential association theory by adding components of operant and respondent conditioning, and by adding components of rational choice theory. The basic premise of the social learning theory is that social behavior is determined neither by inner personality nor by outer sociological and environmental factors. It is a cognitive process in which personality and environment are a continuous process of reciprocal interaction (Akers, 2004). The main view of social learning theory is based on the forces from a group that lead to a positive view of crime (Agnew, 1992).

Akers' theory focuses on four major concepts: 1) differential association; 2) definitions; 3) differential reinforcement; and 4) imitation. Differential association refers to the process whereby one is exposed to normative definitions favorable or unfavorable to illegal or law-abiding behavior. Definitions refer to the personal attitudes that one attaches to a given behavior. Differential reinforcement refers to the balance of actual rewards and punishments based on consequences of behavior. Imitation refers to the engagement in behavior after the observation of similar behavior in others.

According to Akers (2001), the process will more likely produce deviant behaviors when individuals are differentially associated with deviant peers, when their own definitions favorably set them to commit deviant act, when the deviant behavior is differentially reinforced over conforming behavior, and when individuals are more exposed to deviant models than conforming models.

In addition, social behavior responds to rewards and punishments. Any given behavior is likely to continue or to increase if it is followed by more rewards than punishments. The theory proposes that criminal and delinquent behavior is acquired, repeated, and changed by the same process as conforming behavior.

Policy Implications-Social Learning Theories

Learning theorists believe that deviant behavior can be eliminated or modified by taking away the reward of the behavior, increasing the negative consequences of the behavior, or changing the balance of reward/punishment for the behavior. The solution to crime should be aimed at these perspectives. The strategies to deter crime need to focus on segregating offenders and keeping people away from bad influences. In addition, rehabilitation through reeducation and resocialization will be very effective to deter crime. In order to accomplish this, teaching the value of law through education and resocializing through parental skills and peer-evaluation training will help to reduce crime.

Sutherland truly believed that an individual's association is the most significant factor to explain a cause of criminal behavior because a person learns deviant behaviors though interaction with deviant others. The policy implication can be derived from the major concept of the theory: limit individual exposure to delinquent associates. This can be accomplished through appropriate parental management: by watching and supervising their children's choice of friends.

The policy implications that can be derived from each theory are different. The focus of the policy implications should be on the interactions and reinforcements individuals experience and receive. There are several existing examples of how social learning theory has already been used for policies.

Mentoring programs can be a policy to prevent some future criminal behavior in theory. The idea behind mentoring programs is that an adult is paired with a child who theoretically learns from the behavior of the adult. Furthermore, the child is positively reinforced, in most of these programs, by receiving something positive (Jones-Brown, 1997).

Treatment and prevention programs in peer, family, school, and institutional programs have relied on the application of social learning theory. For example, G.R.E.A.T. (Gang Resistance Education and Training) is a prevention program for middle school students with the goal of promoting anti-gang attitudes, reducing involvement in gangs, and increasing positive relationships with law enforcement (Akers, 2004).

Consider Social Learning Theories:

Young people enticed by computers will naturally look to technologically-adept peers to imitate, impress, and receive approval from—especially in the absence of parents or other respected adults who may be unable to teach them about IT, or unwilling to extend praise for computing accomplishments. When you think back to your early computing experiences, from whom did you learn the most? Can you see how learning to abuse computers and other electronic IT devices may result from falling in with the wrong crowd?

SOCIAL STRUCTURE THEORIES

Merton (1938) believes that crime occurs because of the discrepancy between the cultural structure and social structure of America (Vold, Bernard, and Snipes, 2002). Cultural structure means that the main goal of American society is to obtain monetary success, which leads to status and prestige. Social structure refers to the means available for an individual to attain the cultural goal of monetary success. Merton explains high crime rates in the lower classes by stating that all people strive for the same cultural goal of monetary success, but legitimate means are disproportionately available to the higher classes (Cullen and Agnew, 2003).

Merton's theory is at macro level, since he seeks to explain why certain groups of people, rather than certain individuals, are more likely to commit crime. Merton hypothesized that a high level of anomie in lower class causes crime and delinquency. Research provides some support for the hypothesis regarding class and race, but the relationships are usually weak.

Like Merton, Cohen (1955) also believed that people seek cultural goals. However, Cohen thought that youths were concerned with goals other than monetary success (Vold, Bernard, and Snipes, 2002). Cohen (1955) describes two types of status: achieved status and ascribed status. Achieved status refers to status that one has earned; ascribed status is the status that one was born into. Achieved status can be usually obtained through good education, however most among the lower class fail to gain the achieved status in school due a lack of ascribed status. This situation puts a serious strain on individuals in the lower class, and they set up their own value and status system by forming and joining gangs (Vold, Bernard, and Snipes, 2002).

Cloward and Ohlin (1960) developed another macro-level perspective of strain theory related to delinquent subculture in gangs. Cloward and Ohlin's (1960) differential opportunity theory describes three types of gangs. First, a "criminal gang" would be formed from the combination of no legitimate means and the presence of illegitimate means. They strive to gain monetary success through criminal behavior. Second, "violent gangs" or "conflict gangs" would be formed when neither legitimate nor illegitimate means are present. Third, "retreatist gangs" fail to achieve legitimate or illegitimate means, and they subsequently turn to "alcohol or drugs, and drop out" (Vold, Bernard, and Snipes, 2002). In general, Cloward and Ohlin offer a reasonably good explanation of the content of gang delinquency. However, the theory does not provide an adequate explanation of why the delinquency originally develops.

In terms of policy implications, Cloward and Ohlin developed a comprehensive policy program, known as Juvenile Delinquency Prevention and Control Act of 1961. The program includes improving education, creating work opportunities, organizing lower-class communities, and providing services to individuals, gangs, and families (Vold, Bernard, and Snipes, 2002).

Agnew's general strain theory (1992) is micro-level. Unlike social control and differential association theory, which focus on absence of positive relationship with others, general strain theory is the only major criminological theory that focuses on negative relationship with others (Agnew and White, 1992). In other words, the strain theory mainly focuses on the pressure that is placed on the individual to commit crime (Agnew, 1992).

Agnew (1992) identifies three major types of strain. The first is the failure to achieve positively valued goals, such as monetary success, respect, and autonomy. Agnew (1992) posits that strain is increased when a person’s actual achievements are less than his or her expectations. The second is the loss of positive stimuli, such as a death or a broken relationship with a family member or friend. The third is the presentation of negative stimuli, such as child abuse, neglect, and adverse relationships with parents and teachers.

From these negative relationships, negative emotions develop, which Agnew defines as strain (Akers, 2004; Vold, Bernard, and Snipes, 2002; Shoemaker, 2000). These negative feelings such as anger and frustration energize an individual for action, and also create a desire for revenge and lower inhibitions (Akers, 2004). According to Agnew (1992), crime is most likely to occur when the response to strain is anger.

However, crime is not the only way that people respond to strain. Through coping mechanisms, people can handle the strain in their life. Examples of coping mechanisms are the support of family and friends, self-efficacy, and personal intelligence. If positive coping mechanisms are not in place, the juveniles are likely to commit delinquent acts. In addition, if the juveniles are not able to remove themselves from the negative relationship that produced the strain, they are likely to become delinquent. In sum, the basic thought behind general strain theory is that when people get treated badly, they may get upset and engage in crime (Agnew, 1992).

Social disorganization theory explains why such patterns of criminal activity occur in specific geographic areas. The theory examines the movement of people and their concentration in specific locations. Initial social disorganization perspectives in criminology began at the Chicago School. The Chicago School theorists began to look at the consensus and coordination of activities within a society. They believed that rapid change due to immigration, urbanization, or industrialization puts stress on a society to progress or else a breakdown can occur. When a breakdown occurs people are left morally isolated, and disconnected from the social consensus. Deviance can follow because individuals become unaware of the consensus and the rules, or they find that the consensus no longer benefits them (Shoemaker, 2000).

Park and Burgess (1928) introduced an ecological analysis of crime causation. The theorists examined an area's characteristics instead of criminal behaviors to explain high crime. They developed the idea of natural urban areas, which consisted of concentric zones (from the downtown central business district to the commuter zone). Each zone had its own structure, characteristics and unique inhabitants.

Shaw and McKay (1942) were interested in Parks and Burgess's conception of the "natural urban area" of Chicago, and used this model to investigate the relationship between crime rates (mainly delinquency) and the various zones in Chicago. They found that the delinquency rates always remained high for a certain zone of the city (Zone 2) no matter what immigrant group lived there. The area was characterized by a high percentage of immigrants (non-whites and lower income families) and had an acceptance of non-conventional norms, which competed with the conventional. Crime was a function of the characteristics of certain types of neighborhoods. The researchers found that poverty, resident mobility, and racial heterogeneity indicated the presence of social disorganization, and social disorganization produced high rates of crime.

Social disorganization theory offers a different explanation to the problem of high crime rates among youth. It shifts the focus away from the youth, to their broader social situation. The theory explains that the youth's thinking process, which leads to the criminal behaviors, was affected by their social environment. The youth have fallen victim to their environment, causing them to become morally isolated and disconnected from the social consensus. This explanation involves soft determinism, where the youths are left to make their own choices, but they are not bound by society's common morals.

Policy Implications-Social Structure Theories

The policy implications that can be derived from each theory are different. Considering general strain theory focuses on negative relationships, negative emotions, and coping mechanisms, policies should focus on the key concepts. Agnew (1995) proposed several different programs to reduce delinquency. Family-based programs are designed to teach members how to solve problems in a constructive manner, and parents are taught how to effectively discipline their children (Agnew, 1995). This will reduce the amount of negative emotions that result from conflict in the family, and will decrease the amount of strain in the home. Family-based programs, school-based programs and peer-based programs also help to improve positive coping mechanisms, enabling juveniles to refrain from delinquent behavior.

The crime solution strategies associated with social disorganization theory mainly focus on acculturation and assimilation, along with community empowerment. The examples of acculturation and assimilation include helping immigrants embrace the culture of their new country, new neighborhoods in towns, and urban renewal. Community empowerment includes strengthening grassroots organizations and integrating networks with wider political, social, and economic resources.

The policy implications can be derived from social disorganization theory. The solution for ecology theorists would be aimed at the social environment, rather than at the individual youths. The ecology theorists would implement community development programs aimed at reducing the amount of time youths spent at the risk of their environment, such as community-based after-school programs and various educational programs. Most importantly, the youth will need to be re-connected to the social consensus, and overcome their moral isolation. This can be accomplished through the implementation of community-based educational programs where individuals introduce values of the community and teach others an appreciation for living responsibly in the community. These educational programs will allow for an integration of the youth back into society, and save them from further disconnection.

Consider Social Structure Theories:

You can imagine that many poor individuals are among the "computer have-nots," so presumably their ability to commit many types of cybercrimes is relatively limited. Do you agree with this premise? Can you think of exceptions? What about drug dealers who never use a desktop or laptop computer, but who do use cell phones or Tablets to organize contacts and sales data, and to send and receive messages to and from suppliers, customers, or confederates? Are the "computer haves," rather than the "have-nots," more likely to commit cybercrimes? With respect to cybercrimes and information security, who, in technological terms, comprises these supposedly different groups of individuals? Moreover, if a person's social class and quality of education allows considerable access to computers while growing up, how might the combination of these factors contribute to that person committing cybercrimes in his or her formative years or later in life? Do you think that coming from a relatively wealthy family and having routine access to computers and other types of electronic devices could actually contribute to one's ability and propensity to commit cybercrimes? Would this view help explain the classical stereotype of hackers being generally young, of middle to higher socioeconomic class standing, technically inclined, and without a criminal record? (McQuade, 2006).

Discussion 1:
Please discuss your own views about cybercrimes and punishment. Provide your own judgments about deterrent effects against committing cybercrimes such as sending out spam, launching denial-of-service

(DoS) attacks, distributing malware, or committing credit card fraud. Should society strive to increase perceptions of the possibility of being caught and more harshly punished? Please elaborate with classical theoretical perspectives.

Discussion 2:
Please consider gaming addiction issues. Utilize theoretical perspectives to explain these Internet addiction disorders and develop preventive measures.

Chapter 6 - Theoretical Application to Cybercrimes

Can the major criminological theories we previously discussed empirically explain deviant behaviors in cyberspace?

This chapter explores how major traditional theories can interact with cybercrime. Five major criminological theories, 1) Social Learning Theory, 2) Social Control Theory, 3) General Strain Theory, 4) Social Bond Theory, and 5) Deterrence Theory will be discussed, and the tenets of these theories will be applied to cybercrime issues.

Social Learning Theory

Skinner and Fream (1999) examined computer crimes and used social learning theory to explain computer crime behaviors. Utilizing two major components of social learning theory, differential association and definitions, they determined that these components do influence the reported computer crimes. Differential association, hanging out with friends who did commit computer crimes, was the strongest predictor of computer piracy and computer crime index. Imitation of other sources, family members or friends, also increased the likelihood that the individual will commit similar computer crimes. This further indicates that computer crime is a learned behavior. Higgins (2005) agrees with this finding as well. Higgins believes social learning theory rather than social control has a stronger effect on determining software piracy behavior.

SOCIAL CONTROL THEORY

Higgins (2007) in his work entitled, *Digital Piracy, Self-Control Theory, and Rational Choice: An Examination of the Role of Value*, tested low levels of self-control and digital piracy. Digital piracy, defined by Higgins' research, is "the illegal copying of digital goods, software, digital documents, digital audio (including music and voice), and digital video for any other reason other than to back up without explicit permission from and compensation to the copyright holder" (Gopal, Sanders, Bahattacharjee, Agrawal, & Wagner, 2004 in Higgins, 2007, p 33). The research looked at digital piracy and the role of value in regard to self-control and rational choice theory. The research concluded that there were indirect and direct effects in regard to digital piracy. The lower an individual's level of self-control, the more likely they are to conduct the deviant behavior of digital piracy. This is supported by LaGrange and Silverman (1999) who also found that levels of low self-control are significant predictors of increased offending. They are also unlikely to see the consequences of their deviant behavior if they have low self-control levels.

Higgins (2005) looked at cyber piracy as it is related to levels of self-control among college students, whom are the most likely to commit software piracy. The research examined college students based on measures of low self-control, software pirating peers, software pirating attitudes, and moral beliefs toward software piracy. The findings show that there is a relationship between the level of self-control and software piracy. Higgins' (2005) study agrees with Evans et. al's (1997) findings "that individuals with low self-control may not recognize or acknowledge the consequences of software piracy" (Higgins, 2005, p. 16). This is also supported in Higgins' 2007 research as well.

Holt, Bossler, and May (2011) examined low self-control and deviant peer associations in order to explain cyber deviant behaviors. These cyber deviant behaviors include media piracy, pornography, harassment, hacking, and software piracy. They studied middle school and high school students in Kentucky and collected and analyzed 435 cases. The sample they used represented 25% of the total high school population and 35% of the total middle school population.

Holt, Bossler, and May (2011) concluded that self-control did not predict any form of cyber deviance as they defined. This differs from

Nagin and Paternoster's (1993) and Waitrowski, Griswold, and Roberts' (1981) research. Nagin and Paternoster (1993) found that lack of self-control does play a significant role in influencing the likelihood of committing theft, drunk driving, or sexual assaults. Waitrowski et. al (1981) also stated that the social control variables they tested are significant predictors of delinquent behaviors.

Holt et. al (2011) found that peer offending has a stronger relationship than self-control in determining cyber deviant behaviors. This finding supports social learning theory elements. They also stated that a very important element in cyber deviance of juveniles is anonymity in cyberspace: "The anonymity afforded by the Internet and computer technology, coupled with the relative ease and innocuous appearance of most online activities in public settings, may make cyber deviance more attractive to some youths than real world offenses" (Holt et. al, 2011, p. 392). In regards to self-control theory, they did determine that deviant peers aggravate the effects of low self-control on cyber deviance.

STRAIN THEORY

Moon, Blurton, and McCluskey's (2008) research argues that Agnew's general strain theory has been applied to crimes before but has not adequately looked at particular strains. Agnew's theory argues that "strain, when perceived as unjust, high in magnitude (i.e., duration, redundancy, and centrality), associated with low social control, or creating incentives for criminal coping, is more likely to be related to delinquent behaviors" (Moon et al., 2008, p. 583). Moon et al.'s (2008) research takes into account seven main strains that are believed to cause juvenile delinquency: family conflict, parental punishment, teachers' punishment, financial strain, examination-related strain, bullying, and criminal victimization. The study used middle school students in South Korea and examined mainly the effect of anger between strains and delinquent behaviors of juveniles.

Hinduja and Patchin (2007) conducted a study on the effects of Agnew's General Strain Theory to see if there are possible offline consequences of online cyberbullying victimization. The research tried to determine if cyberbullying victimization is in fact a form of strain. Stated in this research is the idea that bullies are presenting "negative valued stimuli (whether it is physical or emotional abuse) to his or her victim" (p. 93-94). Hinduja and Patchin (2007) conducted an online survey of 1,388 Internet-using adolescents between December 22, 2004 and January 22, 2005. They found their sample by targeting websites whose visitors had similar demographic characteristics to the target population of the study.

The results of Hinduja and Patchin's (2007) study indicated that 32 percent of males and 36 percent of females were victims of cyberbullying. As for the theoretical element, there is a significant relationship between strain and offline behaviors of juveniles. The strain that was caused by the online cyberbullying has caused the juveniles to act in deviant ways offline. Hinduja and Patchin's (2007) study "has pointed to the emotional and psychological costs of cyberbullying victimization and empirically linked cyberbullying victimization with offline delinquent and deviant behavior" (p. 103).

Social Bond Theory

Stack, Wasserman, and Kern (2004) conducted research on adult social bonds and the use of Internet pornography. This research offers insight into the relationship between social bonds of individuals and cyber deviance. The research utilizes social bonds to predict the use of cyber-porn among adults. The adult bonds refer to marital bonds, religious bonds, bonds to conservative beliefs, and socioeconomic bonds.

Stack et al.'s (2004) data was collected from the 2000 General Social Survey on 531 Internet users. The research found that there is a statistical relationship between social bonds and cyber-porn use. The religious bond factor had stronger negative influences on predicting cyber-porn use than a happily married marital status. The study suggests that strengthening adult social bonds may reduce cyber-porn usage in general, but also the problem of child pornography as well.

Deterrence Theory

Higgins, Wilson, and Fell (2005) conducted research on the effect of deterrence theory on software piracy. The research was conducted on 382 undergraduate students examining the role of deterrence on reducing the frequency of software piracy incidents. The researchers reiterate the concepts of deterrence theory as they apply it to their research on software piracy. Higgins et al. (2005) utilized certainty and severity of punishment to predict the deterrence effect on software piracy of college undergraduate students. They utilized real-life scenarios in their survey, which added to the findings of their study.

Skinner and Fream's (1999) research took punishment into consideration as a factor influencing computer crime behaviors. They found that unlike traditional crimes, certainty of being apprehended was not negatively associated with computer piracy. Skinner and Fream (1999) also found that severity of punishment did not predict computer piracy behaviors. This finding differs from Higgins, Wilson and Fells' (2005) findings regarding deterrence theory. They found certainty of punishment to negatively correlate to software piracy. However, Skinner and Fream (1999) found no support for perceived punishment being an influential factor in determining computer crime behaviors. This differs from Jenson, Gibbs, and Erickson (1978) who found an inverse relationship between personal perceived risk of punishment and self-reported delinquency.

Discussion:
Review the cyber-piracy issue. How do you think college communities, including university officials, faculty, or IT administrators, could capitalize on control theoretical perspectives to encourage responsible use of computers by students?

PART IV

Cybercrime Victimization

We have partially discussed cybercrime victimization topics in previous chapters. Part IV focuses on cybercrime victimization based on individual and public awareness, profiles of victims, nature and extent of victimization, and responses from victims of cybercrime. In addition, chapter 7 is strongly associated with the target suitability factor in the Routine Activities Theory. Focus on my argument about why individual online lifestyle factors should be compatible with the target suitability factor in Cohen and Felson's Routine Activities Theory for properly examining cybercrime victimization. Chapter 8 introduces "Cyber-Routine Activities Theory (2008; 2010)," in which I proposed and empirically tested the patterns of computer crime victimization.

Chapter 7 - Types of Cybercrime Victimization

Cyberspace creates new opportunities for criminals to interact with victims. The increasing number of victims of cybercrimes who suffer financial loss, or who are threatened or stalked, merits investigation. Although research on cybercrime from offender perspectives is growing, there is little if any research concerning the victims of cybercrimes.

In the physical world, prostitution and illegal drug use are examples of victimless crimes. How about in cyberspace? Illegal online gambling and cyber-piracy are good examples, since they harm society and individuals who voluntarily participate in these crimes. It is also important to consider other examples of victimless crimes in cyberspace. We will discuss this issue more in a later chapter.

Cybercriminal Opportunity and Harmful Impact

Wall (2005) illustrates the impact of the Internet on criminal opportunity and criminal behavior as shown through the three levels on the Y-axis of the table below. The Internet has created more opportunities for traditional crime, such as phreaking, chipping, fraud, and stalking. These types of crime were already extant, but the Internet increases the rate and prevalence of these crimes by creating more opportunities for criminals.

Another level of the Internet's impact on criminal opportunity includes new opportunities for traditional crime, such as cracking/hacking, viruses, large-scale fraud, online gender trade (sex), and hate speech.

Level of Criminal Opportunity by type of Cybercrime

	Integrity-related (Harmful Trespass)	Computer-related (Acquisition theft/deception)	Content-related (Obscenity)	Content-related (Violence)
More opportunities for traditional crime	Phreaking Chipping	Frauds Pyramid schemes	Trading sexual materials	Stalking, Personal Harassment
New opportunities for traditional crime	Cracking/Hacking Viruses Hactivism	Online Frauds 419 Scams Trade secret theft ID Theft	Online Gender Trade/ Cam-girl sites	General hate speech/ Organized pedophile rings (Child abuse)
New opportunities for new types of crime	Spam/ Denial of Service/ Information warfare	Cyber-piracy/ Online Gaming/ Internet Auction Scams	Cyber-sex Cyber-pimping	Bomb talk/ Drug talk/ Hate speech

Source: Wall , David S. 2005. "The Internet as a Conduit for Criminal Activity." pp. 77-98 in Information Technology and the Criminal Justice System, edited by April Pattavina. Sage Publications.

The third level is new opportunities for new types of crime, such as spam, denial of service, intellectual property piracy, online gambling, e-auction scams, and cybersex.

As Wall argues, for each type of these crimes there are three levels of harm: least; middle; and most harmful. So, for example, in the integrity-related harmful type, phreaking and chipping are least harmful, whereas denial of service and information warfare is most harmful. How Wall has defined the level of harmful impact is unclear. In fact, harms can be categorized as financial loss, emotional, and psychological harm, and physical harm. Although his argument doesn't appear to be empirically validated, Wall's examples help guide us to examine different types of criminal opportunities.

How Cybercrime Happens?

As we discussed in the nature of cyberspace, the unique features of the Internet—such as anonymity and user-friendliness—provide new ways for criminals to commit their crimes. This chapter will illustrate the nature of cybercrime victimization via actual cases.

The Internet enables cybercriminals to communicate quickly, and efficiently transmit large quantities of information to many victims via chat rooms, email, message boards, or web sites. In most cases, cybercriminals need basic computer skills and a computer with an Internet connection.

"Consequently, a single computer provides a diverse medium for conducting an array of crimes. Criminals can use the computer to initiate and maintain contact with potential victims via the Internet, to conduct fraudulent financial transactions, to illegally replicate and/or distribute legitimate products or information, or to co-opt confidential, personal information. Computer crimes frequently overlap each other during their commission" (NW3C, 2002, p. 1).

Cybercrimes include fraudulent marketing schemes, on-line auctions, work-at-home schemes, gambling operations, and spam (NW3C, 2002 a). According to NW3C (2002), criminals in online banking schemes collect confidential personal information by "spoofing a valid web site, creating a deceptive web site, or even touting a legitimate-sounding scam in a chat room." When a criminal gets bank account information, illegal transfers of money, for example, can happen in one quick transaction (NW3C, 2002).

Personal information that is electronically stored on the Internet is subject to theft by criminals, and includes social security numbers, mother's maiden name, bank PIN numbers, or photographs, and has become a marketable commodity (NW3C, 2002 a). The NW3C report claims that criminals can commit identity theft when an Internet user "co-opts" his/her name or credit card number for their own use. How does it happen? The report shows that: "One method for acquiring personal information occurs when an employee in a position of trust steals confidential information from clients by accessing electronic files. Another means of attaining information is by illegally replicating credit card numbers with a computer during the course of a legitimate business transaction. Often victims of identity theft may never know the person who stole their information."

In Chapter 4, we discussed various examples of Internet fraud and ID theft cases. Internet fraud is defined by The United States Department of Justice as "...any type of fraud scheme that uses one or more components of the Internet—such as social networking services, chat rooms, email, message boards, or web sites—to present fraudulent solicitations to prospective victims, to conduct fraudulent transactions, or to transmit the proceeds of fraud to financial institutions or others connected with the scheme." The advent of the Internet has allowed different types of fraud to occur faster than ever before. As the United States Department of Justice claims, "The same types of fraud schemes that have victimized consumers and investors for many years before the creation of the Internet are now appearing online (sometimes with particular refinements that are unique to Internet technology)."

There are different types of Internet fraud that could qualify as 419 fraud (NW3C, 2002 b), but the major types reported by the United States Department of Justice are: auction and retail schemes online; business opportunity/work-at-home schemes online; identity theft and fraud; investment schemes online; market manipulation schemes; and credit-card schemes.

Auction fraud happens when an online user buys something from ebay, craiglist, etc., and he or she does not receive the item he or she purchased. The problem associated with this type of fraud is that, as NW3C (2002 b) indicates, victims have little information about the sellers. All they know is the email address of the sellers.

Identity theft is defined by NW3C (2002 b) as "the illegal use of someone's personal data such as name, social security number, or driver's license to obtain money, merchandise, or services by deception" (p. 2). Identity theft includes fraudulently obtaining credit, stealing money from the victim's bank accounts, using the victim's credit card number, establishing accounts with utility companies, renting an apartment, or even filing bankruptcy using the victim's name.

Stock market manipulation also happens when victims try to benefit from an online opportunity to make money. Criminals can use different methods through spam email or Internet message boards in order to increase prices in traded stocks. When the price doubles or triples, the criminals sell off their holdings for "significant profit margins." Victims, on the other hand, are left with less-valued stocks. The Internet can also be used to bring down stock with rumors or lies (NW3C, 2002 b).

Violent Crime Victimization in Cyberspace: Human-trafficking, sexual harassment, catfishing, stalking, and cyberbullying

Victimization has spread to become an issue in not only the physical world but also the online world. This leads to the bigger issue of how people can protect themselves from danger on the Internet. The issue becomes an even bigger problem when the time comes to prosecute the offenders because of jurisdictional and crime definition issues. As outlined above, issues such as stalking, human-trafficking, catfishing, sexual harassment, and cyberbullying are big problems that can directly impact people's lives. Problems such as these become further compounded by the popularity of social networking sites. Social networking sites open people up to a greater risk of victimization.

In a 2009 Pew Research Poll, over 80% of adolescents have accessed the Internet in their homes (Marcum , Ricketts, & Higgins, 2010). More recently social networking sites such as Facebook and Twitter have become popular. These sites are used as a way for people to communicate with family, friends, and others who share similar interests. Along with the rise in social networking sites has come the rise in the use of smartphones. Smartphones are phones that have abilities similar to computers, allowing users to access the Internet as well as download applications or programs onto their phone. In a study done by the Pew Research Center's Internet & American Life Project (2012), it was found that 56% of adults have a smartphone compared to

80% of young adults (ages 18-29). This increase in use of smartphones along with the prevalence of social networking sites in everyday life can open people up to the risk of sexual victimization. This risk of sexual victimization becomes even more prevalent when people engage in risky online behaviors.

Human-trafficking

Human-trafficking victimization has spread to become a transnational issue in not only the physical world but also the online world. This leads to the bigger issue of how people can protect themselves from danger on the Internet. The issue becomes an even bigger problem when the time comes to prosecute the offenders because of jurisdictional and crime definition issues.

NaJat Maalla M'jid (2014) argued that sexual exploitation could lead to child trafficking for sexual and economic purposes, child sex tourism and online child sexual exploitation (UN News, 2014 March). Also M'jid insisted that advanced technologies allowed criminals easy access to child trafficking and online child prostitution (UN News, 2014 March). According to the United Nations Convention on the Right of the Child (2002), children's rights must be protected from any crime and child trafficking, and it also states that prostitution is an anti-human behavior. In other words, online prostitution has made our children more at risk, has spoiled our society, and must be prevented by law enforcement systems.

In America, human-trafficking is defined as using a person under the age of 18 for a commercial sex act. In other words, pimp, who prostitutes minors, is also considered a human-trafficker in the U.S. Thus, human-trafficking is not just an international issue, but this issue is also a prevalent problem in the U.S. considering minor sexual exploitations.

As outlined above, facilitated human-trafficking can directly impact people's lives. Problems such as these become further compounded with the popularity of social networking sites and mobile applications. The available technology opens people up to a greater risk of human-trafficking victimization.

Unlike traditional human-traffickers, they approach potential victims and gain their trust through social networking sites. The offenders often promise to make the victim a star or offer a voucher for travel to a new location away from the victim's home. In addition, the offender may post a fraudulent online employment advertisement offering relocation and a very high salary. A joint investigation by Polish and Italian police also indicated that employment agency websites are the primary means of recruitment for human-trafficking victims. Once the victim has joined the offender, typically the victim is restricted from communicating with home and must travel under the offender's supervision. Typically, human-trafficked women are trapped in the sex-industry and the offender often controls the victims with threats, drugs, and physical violence.

Common online human-trafficking cases are highlighted below:

In a case in Ottawa, two teenage girls recently pleaded guilty to befriending other girls and forcing them to become "escorts" in their prostitution ring. The victims, ranging in age from thirteen to seventeen, reported being assaulted, robbed, beaten, and photographed. The teenagers' prostitution ring was broken up in June 2012 when the leaders were arrested (The Canadian Press, 2012). This instance in Ottawa, Canada is just one example of how social media can lead to people becoming the victims of sexual crimes. Instances such as the case in Ottawa show how social networking can have an effect on human-trafficking. Human-trafficking rings can now utilize social networking sites to both look for victims and conduct transactions with clients.

In Denmark, law enforcement agencies alerted the public of suspicious advertisements for nannies, waitresses, and dancers on websites in Latvia and Lithuania. The offenders used Internet sites to post advertisements for employments in Western Europe. According to the anti-trafficking group in Poland, 30 percent of its trafficked women were recruited through the Internet.

In Illinois, a 19-year-old female applied to an Internet advertisement of modeling opportunities. Instead of offering her modeling work, the trafficker lured the girl to wait in a hotel room where she was expected to have sex with an unknown person. The trafficker, who would become her pimp, intended to sell the young woman for sex at an hourly rate. In this case, the pimp's would-be client was an undercover police officer who brought the victim to safety.

Sexual Violence on Craigslist

Some of the more prominent cases involving sexual victimization transferring from online to the physical world involve the website craigslist. Dr. Jacqueline Lipton (2011) wrote a book about the issues involving the prosecution of crimes that occur in both cyberspace and the physical world. One of the issues that she discusses is the victim's inability to fight back when their online and offline worlds collide.

For example, a person was victimized in the real world due to a craigslist posting about a rape fantasy. The victim was actually raped in the real world by a third party who claimed he was acting on the victim's invitation because her personal information was posted on the site. It is hard for the victims to gain closure because of the difficulty of establishing who exactly posted the information online (Lipton, 2011).

Catfishing Scheme

Online sexual victimization starts with activities such as using social networks, online auction sites, and gaming sites. While many cyber sexual victimization cases spill over to the offline world, some do stay purely on the Internet. The most recent cases in the news are instances of "catfishing", also known as impersonating someone else online and interacting with others (Shaw, 2013). Typically, instances of catfishing involve two victims and the offender. The victims generally consist of the direct victim who is being manipulated by the offender, and the secondary victim whose likeness (often photos) is used to create the false profile (Viacom International Inc, 2014). Catfishing schemes have consequences for the person being deceived as well as for the person whose likeness is being used by the perpetrator.

The most well-known instance of catfishing involved NFL linebacker Manti Te'o in the months leading up to the 2013 NFL draft. While Te'o was at the University of Notre Dame he began a relationship with a women named Lennay Kekua. The relationship between the two was strictly online and over the phone. During the relationship Kekua was in a serious car accident and later diagnosed with leukemia. Te'o was later informed that she had died and used the death as motivation for his senior year play at Notre Dame. Before the college football BCS title game Te'o was informed that Kekua was not dead and in fact never existed. After investigation by the university, it was discovered that Te'o was the victim of an elaborate catfishing scheme concocted by a man named Ronaiah Tuiasosopo using photos of a women from his high school (Burke & Dickey, 2013). Tuiasosopo said that he created Kekua as an extension of himself and an escape from his real life where he was not comfortable with himself (Associated Press, 2013). Te'o ended up being drafted in the second round thirty-eighth overall by the San Diego Chargers, and had a very successful rookie season.

In another case from New York, a model is suing the dating website Match.com for allowing someone to steal her likeness via the web and use it to scam a man for money until he had none left to give and was driven to suicide (Fishbien, 2013). This is a common result of catfishing schemes where victims are sought to provide money in order to assist the catfisher. There are many cases of people falling in love with the person they met online. Then, a "problem" arises such as past due bills and, wanting to help, they send money. While catfishers are sometimes hard to catch, their presence is becoming more widely known.

Cyberstalking

Another type of cybercrime is cyberstalking. It is defined by NW3C (2003) as "one individual harassing another individual on the Internet using various modes of transmission such as electronic mail, chat rooms, newsgroups, mail exploders, and the World Wide Web."

Cyberstalkers can also obtain personal information about their victims (e.g., home address, phone number) from the Internet and utilize this information to meet their victims in person (1). Cyberstalking takes different forms, such as: email that contains a threatening message; spamming (in which a stalker sends a victim a multitude of junk email); live chat harassment (online verbal abuse); sending electronic viruses; and tracing another person's computer and Internet activity. Cyberstalking occurs through three ways: email, Internet, and computer (Ogilvie, 2000).

Cyberstalkers are usually male, and victims of cyberstalking are more likely to be women and children. Working to Halt Online Abuse (WHOA) reports that 1,221 cases were handled by the organization from 2000 to 2004. The demographic information of the victims, as reported by WHOA, is as follows:

> *Age*: forty-eight percent of the victims are in the age group of 18-30; twenty seven percent are in the age group 31-40; and twenty three percent are older than 40.
>
> *Race*: seventy-eight percent of the victims are Caucasian; 3.5 percent are Hispanic; 3 percent are African-American; and 3 percent are Asian.
>
> *Gender*: Sixty-nine percent of the victims of cyberstalking are female; and eighteen percent are male. 13 percent are unknown.

In Kings County, Washington, a man was arrested in a cyberstalking case. According to a KIRO(2010) news article, in less than four months the twenty-three year old suspect sent 269 emails and voicemails to a seventeen year old girl demanding that she send him nude photos or he would kill her and her family (KIRO News Seattle, 2010). According to the police, the suspect stalked the girl on MySpace where she had copious amounts of personal information. The stalking went on for several months prior to law enforcement involvement. Cyberstalking can easily happen due to the fact that people tend to expose personal information on social networking sites. Instances of cyberstalking can be very dangerous to the person being stalked which makes the presence of online security that much more important.

Cyber Sexual Harassment

Digital communication today is used almost universally by the younger generation and is, without dispute, one vehicle for harassment and threat. Similar to cyberstalking, sexual harassment is when someone is being sent messages, including photos and videos, which are unwanted and sometimes lewd in nature. These can be sent over cell phone, email, instant message, or through social networking services. While the users may know each other, sometimes these messages can come from strangers met on the Internet. Similar to other cybercrimes, online sexual harassment is harder to prosecute due to jurisdictional issues associated with the Internet and the underreported nature of these instances. However, the New Jersey Senate panel has recently approved a bill that would make cyberharassment illegal. The bill bans people from using electronic means as well as social media to threaten to injure, commit a crime against, or send obscene material to or about someone (Johnson & Friedman, 2013).

Cyberbullying

Being bullied in school is as old as time itself. People of many generations can tell stories of how they or someone they knew growing up were bullied in school. This kind of familiarity with the issue is what may cloud the ability to effectively handle the growing issue of cyberbullying. Many adults' response to cyberbullying is very nonchalant and unperturbed, as they feel bullying is a part of growing up. The problem with this approach is that bullying has changed significantly since the turn of the 21st century.

Many would argue that personal devices give us a greater rate of accessibility. The downside to this kind of accessibility is when it is used for the wrong reasons. Bullying in schools may not be a new concept, but the difference today is that children cannot escape their bullies. If a child is being bullied at school it is very likely that they will go home and the torment will continue through social media sites, emails and even text messages. This kind of relentless bullying is what has driven some children to take their own lives.

There were two significant cases of bullycide in Massachusetts that brought the seriousness of bullying in the state to the public's attention. The tragic bullycides of Carl Joseph Walker-Hoover in Springfield, Massachusetts and Phoebe Prince in South Hadley, Massachusetts showed just how severe the outcomes of bullying could be. Eleven-year-old Carl took his life on April 6, 2009 because he was being repeatedly called "gay" (Donaldson James, 2009). Fifteen-year-old Phoebe took her own life on January 14, 2010 as a result of relentless traditional and cyber-bullying (Huus, 2011). Anti-bullying legislation was passed in Massachusetts in May of 2010 as a result of the tragic bullycides of the young Massachusetts residents (Huus, 2011). The bill makes anti-bullying curriculum mandatory for all students, kindergarten to twelfth grade, in both private and public schools. The bill also requires that all adults in the school be trained on how to handle bullying (Huus, 2011).

The Carl Joseph Walker-Hoover and Phoebe Prince cases were nationally followed and significant. However, a recent case of cyber-bullying in California has proven to be significant as well. In 2012,

Audrie Pott, a fifteen-year-old girl, went to a party and passed out from consuming Gatorade mixed with alcohol. While she was passed out, she was sexually assaulted. Photos taken during the assault were circulated and within days after the incident, Audrie committed suicide/bullycide as a tragic result.

There was an unpleasant reaction from Audrie's parents and supporters after the conclusion of the trial of the perpetrators that ultimately caused Audrie's death. The three perpetrators were tried in private juvenile proceedings and were sentenced to a mere thirty to forty-five days in juvenile hall (Mendoza, 2014). Two of the offenders actually still attend Audrie's school, Saratoga High; the other individual transferred to a school about an hour away in Gilroy, California.

On March 7th, 2014, Audrie's Law was proposed (Mendoza, 2014). Within Audrie's Law, there is a cyber-bullying statute that makes it a felony to share obscene or sexual photos of young people or their body parts on social media or smartphones to harass or bully them. Attorney Sue Burrell of the San Francisco-based Youth Law Center has an issue with giving youth perpetrators harsher sentences because she fears that simply locking them up until they are well into adulthood is not the answer, and instead argues that officials should look for interventions to set youths on a better path (Mendoza, 2014).

While bullying has been around for generations, cyberbullying is a fairly new problem that has been developing more recently over the last few decades as technology has been increasing. "The claim is made that the term originated either with Canadian Bill Belsey or US lawyer Nancy Willard (2003). Whatever the date at which the term was first used to describe the behavior, online harassment, and the careful study of such behavior, date back at least to the 1980s" (2012, pp.118). Today the biggest problem with cyberbullying is not so much what to do about it as it is about how to clearly define it. Like with any crime, it needs to have a clear definition so there is no confusion when it comes time for punishment. This, however, has proven rather difficult. Hinduja and Patchin define cyberbullying as "willful and repeated harm inflicted through the use of computers, cell phones, and other electronic devices" (2010, pp. 208). The other problem that comes along with cyberbullying is where to draw the line. Many may argue that what someone writes on an online social media site falls under freedom of speech. "The judiciary has long struggled to balance freedom of speech against the darker side of digital communication" (Holladay, 2010). Unfortunately, usually it is not until something tragic happens as a result of those things posted online that we actually try and do something about it.

Other Online Victimization Issues

Online Gaming Addiction

Earlier we briefly discussed the concept of victimless crime in cyberspace. Gaming addiction can be categorized in this victimless-crime, or sometimes violent-crime, category. Though on the surface it might appear that simply playing games for hours at a time is not a criminal act, real and tangible harm can be done via online gaming addiction.

South Korea is one of the most wired societies in the world. More than half the population has access to the Internet, and there are more than 25,000 cyber cafes—known there as PC rooms—which are open 24 hours a day across the country. South Korea is a global leader when it comes to the number of people who can access broadband or high-speed Internet services, with the number of broadband subscribers exceeding 10 million. It is a paradise for online gamers, who come from all over the world to play in South Korea. In fact, the government has been behind efforts to promote South Korea as an IT and cyber leader, but the more negative impacts of over-reliance on the web have only been recently acknowledged and are starting to be seriously addressed due to the sad case detailed below:

> In September 2009, South Korea's gaming obsession threw shockwaves across the world. A couple was arrested for the death of their 3-month-old baby girl, Sarang, which means "love" in Korean. Sarang starved to death while her parents went on all-night gaming binges. The parents were actually caring for a virtual child in 6- to 12-hour online binges. The virtual baby was a cooing and cherubic mini-avatar called Anima, which players earned after reaching a certain level in the game Prius.

Online Pornography

On December 1st, 2014, the UK government introduced a range of new restrictions on the type of content allowed in online pornographic films made in the UK. According to the Department of Culture, Media and Sport (DCMS), the purpose of the changes is to attempt to crack down on material "harmful to minors." However, critics addressed the move as "arbitrary censorship" and also pointed out that online viewers would still be able to access content banned in the UK by watching videos filmed abroad (the Guardian, December 2nd, 2014).

McQuade makes an excellent point in regard to this issue:

> *Proponents argue that legal pornography provides a way for people not offended by such materials to explore human sexuality for personal, social, and even professional reasons having nothing to do with deviance, abuse, or crime. Nonetheless, pornography remains controversial, substantially because of the inherently private nature of sex, and because of obvious harm experienced by children groomed into sexual encounters for molestation by pedophiles or criminally forced into pornographic modeling or prostitution, as well as potential harm inflicted on children exposed to porn of any nature (p.243).*

Drug Abuse and Drug Trafficking via Online

One of the most available designer drugs in cyberspace is bath salts. Bath salts, or synthetic cathinone, and its derivatives such as methcathinone, mephedrone, methedron, methyleone and MDPV, are hallucinogenic central nervous system stimulants. These substances have a history of abuse in European countries, particularity in the UK, because their effects are similar to MDMA (Ecstasy) and cocaine (Spiller et al., 2011). Bath salts soon became an alternative to these two stimulants after their purity and availability decreased in the UK (Prosser et al., 2011). According to caller data at UK Poisons Information Service center, the number of telephone inquiries about synthetic cathinone was zero prior to 2009, but between 2009 and 2010 the number was equal to the number of calls regarding cocaine and MDMA (Prosser et al., 2011).

Although synthetic cathinone products have been successfully regulated in the UK by the Misuse of Drugs Act 1971, they are gaining popularity in the US among young adults, club goers, and other substance users despite the Federal Analogue Act of 1986. This federal law was designed to treat controlled substances that are intended for human consumption as schedule I (deadiversion.usdoj.gov). It was passed in an attempt to prevent the use of "designer drugs" that are manufactured with small chemical changes to subvert existing regulatory laws against the use of other illegal drugs. The Federal Analogue Act, however, does not criminalize possession or manufacture of the designer substances, unless intended for human consumption (Prosser et al., 2011). This allows other hallucinogenic substances to be legal whether or not they are actually intended for human consumption. In addition, bath salts are currently not regulated in many states, including California, Montana, Nevada, New Hampshire, Oregon, Vermont, and Washington as well as Puerto Rico (NCSL, 2012; Prosser et al., 2011).

Additionally, unlike other traditional psychoactive drugs such as ecstasy or cocaine, bath salts are available on the Internet where they can be easily purchased with a quick search. The potential users can easily obtain product information and reviews and anywhere in the world. The online sellers take PayPal, money orders and credit cards to make it easier for the potential drug users to order. This availability on the Internet can increase the drug abuse of young individuals who spend considerably more time using the Internet than previous generations. Also, even though the police detect bath salts trafficking through the Internet, it is almost impossible to punish the online dealers and buyers due to the jurisdiction issue in cyberspace.

The bath salts usage report that was conducted among students in Tayside, Scotland by the Tayside Police Force Information and Intelligence Analyst Unit was used to analyze and compare the bath salts abusers' age, purchase preference and usage frequency. In that study, 1,006 students at five Scottish secondary schools, three colleges, and two universities participated in a voluntary anonymous survey. 20.3% (205) of them reported they had used mephedrone on at least one occasion. Among mephedrone users, 48.8% of them purchased the drug from the local drug dealer, and 10.7% (among the student in the age group 13-15) of them bought mephodrone from the Internet. However, sourcing of mephedrone from the Internet increased to 30.8% as the age of the user increased (24 years old). Approximately 97.9% of the participants answered that the drug was very easy to obtain, and their reasons for using bath salts were their legal status and accessibility (Wood et al., 2011).

In October 2013, the Federal Bureau of Investigation (FBI) arrested 29-year-old Ross Ulbricht, who was selling narcotics, fake IDs and illegal weapons via the internet from his apartment in San Francisco, California (The Time Magazine, 2013). He earned $80 million from his trade, but it took years for the FBI to track his activity since he had been using various methods to dodge investigators. In the last five years, the "legal" drug market has been dramatically expanded, and it has never been easier and cheaper to buy drugs online (The Guardian, 2014). Since the Internet is available anywhere in the world, online drug trafficking is not a geographically limited problem. From the previous history of the bath salts' popularity and their trafficking routine in the UK, it is not too difficult to anticipate the "new bath salts" in the drug market. Therefore, it is important to have proper policies in place, including specific statutes against designer drugs as well as active media campaigns to educate citizens to avoid questionable substances both online and offline. There will be an in-depth discussion about this issue in Chapter 10.

Discussion:
Please review your state statues regarding cyberstalking, cyberharassment, or cyberbullying, and discuss its limitation for your criminal investigation.

Chapter 8 - Computer Crime Victimization: Empirical Explanation

Criminologists in the early 1970s began to realize the importance of victimization studies. Previously they had placed their focus on the criminal offender and ignored the victim (Karmen, 2006). Creation of "the self-report survey," and the emergence of national victimization studies in 1972, facilitated the development of victimization theories in this era (Karmen, 2006, p. 51).

Lifestyle-exposure theory and Routine Activity Theory were introduced based on the evidence of "the new victimization statistics" as a section of a rational theoretical perspective embedded in sociological orientation (Williams and McShane, 1999, p.235). The two theories appear to be ideally suited for understanding why individuals are predisposed to crime, and how an individual's activities, interactions, and social structure provide opportunities for offenders. This chapter presents 'Cyber Routine Activity Theory (2008),' an integrated theory combining the main concept of traditional lifestyle exposure theory and routine activity theory, and applying them to empirically access computer crime victimization.

Target Suitability Revisited: Lifestyle-Exposure Theory

Why Do Online Users Become Victims?

In 1978, Hindelang, Gottfredson, and Garofalo developed the lifestyle exposure model which focuses on the victims' daily social interactions, rather than concentrating on the characteristics of individual offenders or individual causal variables. Lifestyle-exposure theory holds that criminal victimization results from the daily living patterns of the victims (Goldstein, 1994; Kennedy & Ford, 1990). Hindelang et al. (1978) defined lifestyle as "routine daily activities" including "vocational activities (work, school, keeping house, etc.) and leisure activities" (p. 241). The current project interest in lifestyle-exposure theory is to assess online lifestyles by examining the individual's online vocational activities and leisure activities that may contribute to computer-crime victimization. This section briefly introduces the concepts of the original lifestyle-exposure theory. Then, the lifestyle-exposure theory is applied to online lifestyles, such as vocational activities and leisure activities in cyberspace, online risk-taking behavior, and properly maintaining installed computer security systems.

Hindelang et al. (1978) posited that the lifestyles of individuals are determined by "differences in role expectations, structural constraints, and individual and subcultural adaptations" (p. 245). In the first phase of the lifestyle exposure theoretical model, Hindelang et al. (1978) discussed how role expectations and social structure create constraints. They conceptualized "role expectation" as expected behaviors that correspond to cultural norms, which link with the individuals' "achieved and ascribed statuses" (Hindelang et al., p. 242). Hindelang et al. argued that an individual's age and gender are substantially associated with role expectations, because certain age and gender differences are expected to follow normative roles in American society. The researchers defined "structural constraints" as "limitations on behavioral options" which constantly create conflicts for individuals by corresponding with "the economic, familial, educational, and legal orders" (Hindelang, et al., p. 242).

Research by Kennedy and Forde (1990) found that personal variables associated with lifestyle, such as age, sex, marital status, family income, and race, significantly influence daily activities and the level of criminal victimization risk. The study also suggests that lifestyle factors significantly reflect the individuals' amount of exposure time in places associated with victimization risk (Kennedy & Forde, 1990).

An adaptation process occurs when individuals or groups initiate gaining knowledge of skills and attitudes in order to manage the constraints associated with role expectations and social structure. This process develops some individual traits, including the individual's attitudes and beliefs. In the course of continuing these processes, the individuals modify their attitudes and beliefs, and these learned traits naturally become a part of daily routine behavioral patterns (Hindelang et al., 1978). In the second phase of the model, differential lifestyle patterns are associated with "role expectations, structural constraints, and individual and subcultural adaptations (Hindelang et al.).

Hindelang et al. (1978) addressed the importance of the relationship between victimization and vocational and leisure activities. Vocational and leisure activities are the daily activities that are central to a person's life. These lifestyle activities are predictive of personal interactions with others as formal roles. Hindelang et al. asserted that lifestyle and exposure to the level of victimization risk are directly related in the model. Moreover, Hindelang et al. (1978) suggested that association, which refers to the level of personal relationships among individuals who share common interests, is another factor that indirectly links exposure to personal victimization. In other words, personal associations increase level of the exposure to individual victimization.

So, how can we define lifestyle activities in cyberspace? Like the physical world, in cyberspace online users have online daily activities, such as checking e-mail, seeking information, purchasing items, socializing with friends, and obtaining online entertainment, which are becoming a major portion of the users' lives. Through online activities in cyberspace, people can constantly interact with others via various online tools, such as e-mail and electronic messengers, and create their own online lifestyle by engaging in various online communities based on their particular interests, such as social networking sites, cyber-cafés, clubs, and bulletin boards.

However, online lifestyles can result in catastrophic events for online users. For instance, on May 3, 2000, many online users received and opened an e-mail from significant others, coworkers, or government officials with the subject line "ILOVEYOU" without sensing that the email was one of the most malicious viruses ever experienced by Internet users. Clicking on an icon contained in the email activated the virus, which quickly changed Window's registry settings and then e-mailed copies of itself to everyone in the original victim's Microsoft Outlook Express address book. (Winston Salem

Journal, 2000).

The worldwide monetary damage due to the ILOVEYOU virus infection was estimated at between $4 billion to $10 billion, all occurring during a mere couple of days (Winston Salem Journal, 2000). This disastrous case clearly indicates that the Internet has become one of the most significant communication tools by combining online vocational and leisure activities into one method of “mail, telephone, and mass media” in cyberspace (Britz, 2004). The case presented above also illuminates that as digital necessity, in the form of going online, is becoming an increasing part of more peoples’ lifestyles it is a crucial lifestyle activity that could also carry with it a very great threat to our personal lives.

Lifestyle-exposure theory attempts to estimate the “differences in the risks of violent victimization across social groups” (Meier et al., 1993, p. 466). It has been applied to various types of crime, and it has succeeded in various ways in explaining the causes of victimization (Meier et al., 1993). Gover (2004) tested victimization theories by utilizing a public high-school student population in South Carolina. This study suggested that the effects of social interaction indirectly influence violent victimization in dating relationships (Gover, 2004). Key factors were measured through risk-taking behaviors such as drug abuse, alcohol abuse, driving under the influence, and a promiscuous sexual lifestyle (Gover, 2004). The concept of risk taking factors can be applied to cyberspace.

In cyberspace, computer criminals attract online users through fraudulent schemes. In many hacking incidents, computer criminals typically attract a victim, and thus their computer systems, by offering free computer software, free MP3 music downloads, or free movie downloads. Various types of software—such as Trojan horses, logic bombs, and time bombs—are designed to threaten computer security, and many computer criminals use those viruses and worms by placing hidden virus codes in these free programs. Clicking on an icon without precaution in social networking sites can contribute to computer-crime victimization. According to the 2005 FBI Computer Crime Survey (2006), “the virus, worm, and Trojan category” was rated as the highest category of financial loss, which is a rate over three times higher than any other category (p. 10).

Like Routine Activities Theory, lifestyle-exposure theory asserts that differential lifestyle patterns involve the likelihood of being in certain locations at certain times and having contact with people with certain characteristics. Thus, the occurrence of criminal victimization relies on "high risk times, places, and people" (Hindelang et al, 1978, p. 245). As noted in the Routine Activities Theory section, temporality is not absolutely necessary in cyberspace because there is no time zone in cyberspace (Yar, 2005).

However, I strongly argue that visiting certain locations in cyberspace may have a correlation with computer-crime victimization. In other words, specific lifestyle patterns directly link with "differences in exposure to situations that have a high victimization risk" (Hindelang et al, 1978, p. 245). Miethe and Meier (1990) asserted that physical proximity to perpetrators and the level of exposure is statistically associated with risky environment based on burglary, personal theft, and assault victimization cases. Their research used data from the British Crime Survey (Miethe & Meier, 1990). Kennedy and Forde (1990) also indicated that criminal victimization is not a random occurrence, but is strongly associated with certain geographic locations.

Computer criminals search for suitable victims in cyberspace. Online users congregate based on their interests, and they socialize with others in cyberspace. Piazza (2006) stated that computer users' information can be easily sent to hackers by simply clicking a pop-up window in "social networking sites" such as free download places and online bulletin boards when a hacker plants a malicious JavaScript code on these Web sites (p. 54). High levels of network activity on a particular site and search engine tools can guide offenders to popular Web sites in cyberspace (Yar, 2005). These popular Web sites become a sort of shopping mall for offenders, as they cause a multitude of potential victims to congregate in one localized area, thus enabling the offenders to shop for their potential targets.

In addition, properly maintaining installed computer security is a crucial factor in terms of online vocational activities. If an online user connects to the Internet without properly updating computer security, and visits the delinquent Web sites planted with computer viruses, it maximizes the risk of computer-crime victimization. Thus, the project also hypothesizes that those online users who frequently visit the delinquent Web sites without precaution and neglect regularly updating installed computer security programs have a high likelihood of experiencing computer-crime victimization.

Visiting certain locations in cyberspace may have a correlation with computer-crime victimization. In other words, specific lifestyle patterns directly link with "differences in exposure to situations that have a high victimization risk" (Hindelang et al., 1978, p. 245). Miethe and Meier (1990) asserted that physical proximity to perpetrators and the level of exposure is statistically associated with a risky environment based on burglary, personal theft, and assault victimization cases. Their research used data from the British Crime Survey (Miethe and Meier). Kennedy and Forde (1990) also indicated that criminal victimization is not a random occurrence, but is strongly associated with certain geographic locations.

Computer criminals search for suitable victims in cyberspace, where online users congregate based on their interests and socialize with others. Piazza (2006) stated that computer users' information can be easily sent to hackers by simply clicking a pop-up window in "social networking sites," such as free download places and online bulletin boards, when a hacker plants a malicious JavaScript code on these web sites (p. 54). High levels of network activity on a Particular site and search engine tools can guide offenders to popular web sites in cyberspace (Yar, 2005). These popular web sites become a sort of shopping mall for offenders, as they cause a multitude of potential victims to congregate in one localized area, thus enabling the offenders to shop for their potential targets.

In addition, properly maintaining installed computer security is a crucial factor in terms of online vocational activities. If an online user connects to the Internet without properly updating computer security, and visits the delinquent web sites planted with computer viruses, it maximizes the risk of computer-crime victimization.

POTENTIAL THEORETICAL EXPANSION: CYBER-ROUTINE ACTIVITIES THEORY

Both Routine Activities Theory and lifestyle-exposure theory are widely applied to explain various criminal victimizations. In general, most studies found fairly strong support for both victimization theories with predatory and property crimes. Even though the two theories are empirically supported in criminological research, the major critique resides in the failure of these theories to specify testable propositions regarding certain offenders' and victims' conditions, as such specification would allow for more accurate predictions of crime

(Meier & Miethe, 1993). In addition, little research has been empirically tested on individual computer-crime victimization.

Moreover, it is proffered here that Routine Activities Theory is simply an expansion of the lifestyle-exposure theory espoused by Hindelang et al. in 1978. In other words, Routine Activities Theory is really a theoretical expansion of lifestyle-exposure theory, as it adopts the main tenet in lifestyle-exposure theory, the individual's vocational and leisure activities. It appears that Cohen and Felson (1979) absorbed this tenet into what they call their suitable target tenet and then added a motivated offender and a lack of capable guardianship. It is posited here that an individual's vocational and leisure activities are what makes him or her a suitable target. Even Cohen and Felson (1979) acknowledged this point. Cohen and Felson (1979) asserted that the individuals' lifestyles reflect the individuals' routine activities such as social interaction, social activities, "the timing of work, schooling, and leisure" (p. 591). These activities, in turn, create the level of target suitability that a motivated offender assigns to that particular target.

Thus, Routine Activities Theory shares more than an important common theme with the lifestyle variable from lifestyle-exposure theory; it has actually incorporated this tenet and added the additional tenets of capable guardianship and motivated offender. This is akin to what Akers (1985) acknowledged that he did with Sutherland's (1947) differential association theory when he developed his social learning theory. Akers (1985) noted that he simply incorporated that theory into his theory by expanding upon the already existent differential association theory tenets. Hence, it is suggested here that these two theories, Routine Activities Theory and lifestyle-exposure theory, are not two separate theories, but that Routine Activities Theory is simply an expansion of lifestyle-exposure theory. Therefore, this study will apply Routine Activities Theory while acknowledging that lifestyle-expansion theory provides a more complete explanation of the "suitable target" tenet found in Routine Activities Theory.

From the routine activities theoretical perspective, one of three tenets, capable guardian, contributes to the new computer-crime victimization model in this project. This project assumes that motivated offenders and suitable targets are given situational factors. In cyberspace, pools of motivated computer criminals can find suitable targets in the form of online users who connect to the Internet without precaution or without equipping adequate computer security. The routine activities approach would lead to the practical application of situational computer-crime prevention measures by changing the conditions and circumstances.

My research finds that the most feasible method of preventing computer-crime victimization that can be adapted from Routine Activities Theory is a target-hardening strategy. This is accomplished in the form of up-to-date, adequate computer security equipment. A target-hardening approach via computer security will make it more difficult for computer criminals to commit computer crimes in cyberspace. Since the operation of formal social control agents in cyberspace is very limited, establishing a viable target-hardening strategy can be made via equipping adequate computer security in the computer system. It is also of note that the individual can also increase the target-hardening strategy by updating and maintaining this computer security. However, updating and maintaining this computer security equates to the lifestyle choices made by the individual. Regardless of whether the person properly updates and maintains the computer security, the fact remains that equipping the computer with security is a crucial component in reducing computer criminal opportunities in the new theoretical model.

General research on the lifestyle-exposure theory is limited to explaining computer-crime victimization, but supportive of the new theoretical computer-crime victimization model. Although studies associated with lifestyle-exposure theory have not focused on computer-crime victimization, a victimology perspective based on a personal lifestyle measure under lifestyle-exposure theory is appropriate and useful for understanding computer-crime victimization. This is because the gist of lifestyle-exposure theory is that different lifestyles expose individuals to different levels of risk of victimization. Thus, one of the research interests is to estimate the level of target suitability by measuring risk-taking factors that potentially contribute to computer-crime victimization. The project assumes that online users, who are willing to visit unknown Web sites or download Web sites in order to gain free MP 3 files or free software programs, or who click on icons without precaution, are likely to be victimized by computer criminals. In other words, the levels of online vocational and leisure activities produce greater or lesser opportunities for computer-crime victimization. Numerous findings support that lifestyle factors play significant roles in individual crime victimization in the physical world.

This project hypothesizes that the level of online lifestyle activities would contribute to the potential for computer-crime victimization.

Hindelang et al. (1978) suggest that "vocational activities and leisure activities" are the most crucial components of a lifestyle, which have a direct impact on exposure to the level of victimization risk. Here, the specific tenets from lifestyle-exposure theory, as expanded upon by Routine Activities Theory, addressed herein as the online lifestyle activities measure, will be presented as an important theoretical component. In Routine Activities Theory, Felson (1998) stated that target suitability is likely to reflect four main criteria: the value of crime target, the inertia of crime target, the physical visibility of crime target, and the accessibility of crime target (VIVA). This statement is a crucial point, which is compatible with the main lifestyle exposure theoretical perspective that explains why online users become suitable targets for computer criminals. It is the vocational and leisure activities that translate into the level of target suitability ascribed to Felson's (1998) VIVA assessment.

Mustain and Tewksbury (1998) argued that people who engage in delinquent lifestyle activities are likely to become suitable targets "because of their anticipated lack of willingness to mobilize the legal system" (p. 836). More importantly, the victims tend to neglect their risk of victimization by failing to inspect themselves regarding "*where* you are, *what* your behaviors are, and what you are doing to protect yourself" (Mustain & Tewksbury, p. 852). This study is designed to follow Mustain and Tewksbury's statement above.

The model is tested using SEM and is followed by a presentation of the research methods used in this study. The model actually consists of what is commonly referred to as two distinct theories, Cohen and Felson's (1979) Routine Activities Theory and Hindelang et al.'s (1978) lifestyle-exposure theory. However, as shown above, Routine Activities Theory is an expansion of lifestyle-exposure theory. Thus, Routine Activities Theory's major concept, the target-hardening strategy, is represented by digital-capable guardianship. Hindelang et al.'s lifestyle-exposure theory's core concept, vocation and leisure activities, which is proffered here represents a more detailed explanation of the suitable target tenet in Routine Activities Theory, and is represented here by online lifestyle. This is done to estimate computer-crime victimization. The conceptual model posits that digital-capable guardianship and online lifestyle directly influence computer-crime victimization. This project also posits that convergence of the two variables has an interaction effect that contributes to a direct impact on computer-crime victimization.

Figure 8-1. The conceptual model for computer-crime victimization.

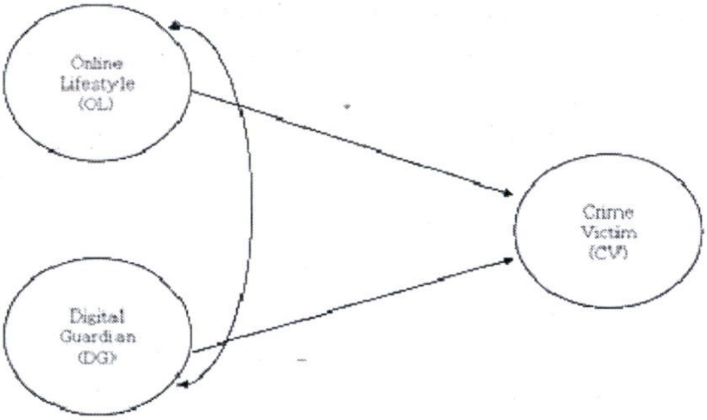

METHODOLOGY AND ANALYSIS

This study's methodology is divided into three phases: Phase 1 presents the sampling techniques and procedure of the sample; Phase 2 of the analysis examines psychometric properties of scales on two main factors, digital guardian and individuals' online lifestyle, and computer-crime victimization; Phase 3 of the analysis includes the measurement and structural models derived from the combination of two victimization theories were tested. Using structural equation modeling, the causal relationships among digital guardian, online lifestyle, and computer-crime victimization indexes are assessed, focusing on whether digital-capable guardianship and online lifestyle directly affect computer-crime victimization.

Phase 1: Sample and Procedure

In spring of 2007, students in nine liberal studies classes at a university in the Pennsylvania State System of Higher Education (PaSSHE) were given a self-report survey that was designed to measure the main constructs of Routine Activities Theory. The students were selected through a stratified-cluster, random-sample design. A list of all available liberal studies classes available in spring 2007 were entered into a computer, using the Statistical Package for the Social Sciences (SPSS). The lists were stratified by class level, and a proportionate subsample of classes was randomly selected using SPSS. The random number generator of SPSS randomly chose nine of these general studies classes, based on class level, for inclusion in the sample. A total of 345 respondents took part in the study. However, only 204 surveys were completed fully so those 204 surveys were analyzed for the purposes of this study.

The specific requirements for participating in the study included the following: (a) student must be enrolled in general studies class, (b) student must use his or her own personal computer or laptop.

Entering ten predictors (two observed variables from the digital-capable guardianship latent variable, three observed variables from online lifestyle latent variable, and three observed variables from online victimization latent variable, and two demographic variables) with a power of .95, and a medium effect size of f = .15, into the G*Power program computed the total sample (N = 172) at the .05 alpha level. Thus, threats to statistical conclusion validity were not an issue in this research. Surveying a minimum of 172 students allowed the researcher to have a large enough sample from which to assure that the sample size accurately represented the student population at the state university.

A self-report survey instrument was used to investigate the computer-crime victimization patterns among the university student population. Using university students in this study provided the researcher with several advantages: (a) university students are expected to be literate and experienced in completing self-administered, self-report instruments; (b) because the price of owning a computer has decreased and because most students are required to word process their assignments, students are constantly using a computer for their work and entertainment. Additionally young people are assumed to be more likely adopters of technology than older generations are (Internet Fraud Complaint Center 2003).

Phase 2: Properties of Measures

Digital Guardian

Each digital guardian has its own distinctive function to protect computer systems from computer criminals. There are three common digital-capable guardians available to online users: antivirus programs, antispyware programs, and firewall programs. Each of the digital guardians has its own distinctive function to protect computer system from computer criminals. Antivirus programs monitor whether computer viruses have gained an access through digital files, software, or hardware, and if the antivirus computer software finds a virus, the software attempts to delete or isolate it to prevent a threat to the computer system (Moore, 2005). Firewall programs are designed to prevent computer criminals from accessing the computer system over the online network; however, unlike the antivirus software, firewalls do not detect or eliminate viruses (Casey, 2000). Antispyware programs are mainly designed to prevent spyware from being installed in the computer system (Casey 2000). Spyware intercepts users' valuable digital information such as passwords or credit card numbers as a user enters them into a Web form or other applications and sends that information to the computer criminal. (Ramsastry 2004).

Before administering the self-report survey, all participants were supplied with a pre-survey guideline that provided definitions of the three digital guardian measures and asked the participants to examine their personal or laptop computer so that they could determine, prior to participation in the actual survey, whether they had any of the digital guardian measures already installed on their computers. The purpose of the pre-survey guideline was to ensure content validity in the portion of the actual survey focusing on digital guardian measure.

It was hypothesized that the level of capable digital guardianship, in the form of installed computer-security systems, will differentiate the level of computer-crime victimization. Hence, the number of installed software security programs was measured in order to determine the level of digital-capable guardianship.

The first observed variable consisted of three items that asked the respondents to state what types of computer security they had in their own computer prior to participation in the survey. The three items were based on dichotomous structure, which was identified 0 as *absence of security* and 1 as *presence of security*. The possible range for the number of installed computer-security programs was between 0 to 3. The value 0 refers to absence of computer security and 3 means that computer users installed antivirus, anti-spyware, and firewall software in their own computer. The mean of the number of computer-security score for this sample was 2.6, with a standard deviation of .73, a skewness of -1.96, and a kurtosis of 3.37.

The internal consistency coefficient of .62 indicates an undesirable range of Cronbach's alpha based on DeVellis's (2003) reliability standards. However, the item-total correlations (Item 1 = .40, Item 2 = .43, and Item 3 = .44) were respectable, with all three items above the acceptable levels of item total correlations of .30.

The second observed variable also consisted of three items with a series of three visual analogues by asking the participants to indicate on a 10-centimeter line their responses regarding each of the three main computer-security measures. Their level of agreement with each statement was identified by asking whether they had the specific computer-security program on their personal or lap top computers during the 10-month period. Each line had a range of 0 to 10, with the total possible range for this capable guardian scale between 0 and 30. The mean of the duration of having computer-security score for this sample was 22.3, with a standard deviation of 7.65, a skewness of -.99, and a kurtosis of .25.

The findings showed that this digital guardian scale had an adequate alpha coefficient of .70, which was sufficient for research purposes. All three scale items (Item 1 = .50, Item 2 = .52, and Item 3 = .55) performed well and sufficiently met the acceptable levels of item-total correlation, and the unidimensionality of the scales was confirmed by Cattell's *Scree test* with principal components factor analysis using a varimax rotation.

Online Lifestyle

The researcher hypothesized that users' online lifestyle is substantial factor in minimizing computer-crime victimization. Individual online lifestyle was measured by three distinct observed variables: (a) vocational (job) and leisure (home) activities on the Internet, (b) online risky leisure activities (c) online risky vocational activities. For the first measure of online lifestyle, eight survey items made up the vocational and leisure activities scale along with their item-total correlations. As with the vocational and leisure activities scale, respondents were asked to indicate on a 10-centimeter response line their level of agreement or disagreement with each statement. The items were anchored by *strongly agree* at the lower limit and *strongly disagree* at the upper limit. The scale's possible aggregate range is 0 to 80 with higher scores reflecting higher online vocational and leisure activities. The mean vocational and leisure activities score for this sample is 53.62, with a standard deviation of 11.22. The scale based on eight items had satisfactory skewness and kurtosis levels, and the assessment of principal factor analysis and a *Scree test* validated the scale items as a unitary construct.

For the measures of two categories of online risky lifestyle, each of four survey items was designed to rate the respondents' online leisure and vocational activities that are risky. Like other online lifestyle scale, respondents were asked to indicate on a 10-centimeter response line their level of agreement or disagreement with each statement. The terms *strongly agree* and *strongly disagree* anchor the response line.

In the category of online risky activities ("Risky Leisure Activities"), the scale's possible aggregate range is from 0 to 40. The mean of the first risky activities score for this sample is 16.02, with standard deviation of 8.93. The second category of online risky activities ("Risky Vocational Activities") consisted of four items, so the scale's possible aggregate range is also from 0 to 40. Both categories have met the appropriate levels of skewness and kurtosis for SEM analysis, and the results based on principal components factor analysis and a *Scree test* suggested that each of the scale items consists of unitary construct.

Computer-Crime Victimization

Three computer-crime victimization items were developed for this study. The current project has adapted the construct of corporate computer-crime victimization to delineate individual-crime victimization.

The computer-crime victimization scale consists of three distinct observed variables: (a) total frequency of victimization, (b) total number of hour loss, and (c) total monetary loss. In terms of data quality, the descriptive statistics imply conditions of severe non-normality of data that are one of the violations in SEM assumptions. Three computer-crime victimization scales contained extreme values of skewness and kurtosis, and the reliability coefficient indicated poor variability and low item scale correlations due to strong outliers. In order to adjust a highly skewed distribution to better approximate a normal distribution, the original items were transformed, ratio level, to a Likert-like scale format based on 4 possible responses (0 to 3), which was applied through a recoding process by minimizing the magnitude of outliers.

The existing scales from the 2004 Australian Computer Crime and Security Survey were adapted for use in this study. In the first item, "During the last 10 months, how many times did you have computer virus infection incidents?," the original responses were coded to 0 to 3 scales (0 = *0 time*, 1 = *1 – 5 times*, 2 = *6 – 10 times*, 3 = *over 10*) that are equivalent to the scales from 2004 Australian Computer Crime and Security Survey. In the second item, "During the last 10 months, approximately how much money did you spend fixing your computer due to computer virus infections?" the original responses were labeled to a scale from 0 to 3 (0 = *$0*, 1 = *$1-$50*, 2 = *$51-$100*, 3 = *over $100*). In fact, there were no specific guidelines of monetary loss in the survey, so this category of the scales was developed based on the distribution of responses from participants and the adaptation of the survey structure. In the third item, "During the last 10 months, approximately how many hours were spent fixing your computer due to the virus infections?," the original values were transformed to a scale from 0 to 3 (0 = *0 hour*, 1 = *1 -12 hours*, 2 = *13 – 84 hours*, 3 = *over 84 hours*). In the 2004 Australian Computer Crime and Security Survey (2005), the time it took to recover from the most serious incident based on day, week, and month period was estimated. The research adapted this time period by calculating 12 hours for one day for fixing a computer, so scale 1, 2, and 3 respectively represent an hourly basis for days, weeks, and months.

After the application of the transformation to Likert-like format, the values of skewness and kurtosis have significantly decreased. In addition, both Cronbach's alpha and item total correlation values have significantly improved. Even though the transformation to Likert-like format could not achieve appropriate normal distribution, it offered the minimal acceptance of skewness and kurtosis levels for SEM analysis.

The computer-crime victimization scales also met the basic measurement criteria for SEM after the application of transformation to Likert-like scale. The scales have acceptable reliability (Cronbach's Alpha = .66), acceptable item-total correlations, acceptable skewness and kurtosis levels, and the observed variables are unidimensional.

Phase 3-1: Measurement Model

Nine fit indices were examined in order to determine the fitness of the measurement model (see Table 1). Table 2 from Gibbs et al. (2003) indicated the fit indices, their justifications, and standards. Five indexes of absolute fit including chi-square, adjusted chi-square, root mean square residual (RMR), root mean square error of approximation (RMSEA), and global fit index (GFI) are reported. In addition, the Tucker-Lewis Index (TLI), the comparative fit index (CFI), the parsimonious goodness of fit (PGFI), and the expected cross-validation (ECVI) are presented in order to measure relative fitness by comparing the specified model with the measurement model.

Table 1. Selected Fit Indexes for the Measurement Model

	Model Fitness	Index	Value	Standard point
1.	Absolute fit	Chi-square	34.47 (df = 18) P. = .011	p. > .05
2.	Absolute fit	Normal Chi-square	1.915	< 3
3.	Absolute fit	Root mean square residual (RMR)	1.73	Close to 0
4.	Absolute fit	Root mean square error of approximation (RMSEA)	.07	< .10
5.	Absolute fit	Goodness of fit index (GFI)	.96	.90
6.	Incremental fit	Tucker-Lewis Index (TLI)	.95	Close to 1
7.	Incremental fit	Comparative fit index (CFI)	.97	Close to 1
8.	Parsimony	Parsimony goodness of fit index (PGFI)	.48	Larger value = Better fit
9.	Comparative fit	Expected cross-validation index (ECVI)	.35	Smaller value = Better fit

Three out of five measures of absolute fit (adjusted chi-square, RMSEA, and GFI) sufficiently met their standards. Since the probability value of the chi-square test was smaller than the .05 level, the test result indicates the rejection of the null hypothesis that the model fits the data. However, such a rejection based on the chi-square test result was relatively less substantial compared to other descriptive fit statistics because the chi-square test is very sensitive to sample size and non-normal distribution of the input variables (Hu & Bentler 1999; Kline 1998; Kaplan 2000). Thus, examining other descriptive fit statistics would be of substantive interest in this project.

Even though there was no absolute RMR standard, the obtained RMR value of 1.70 appeared to be high because an RMR of 0 indicates a perfect fit. The CFI and TLI, which compare the absolute fit of the specified model to the absolute fit of the measurement model, also sufficiently met the standard for appropriate model fit. Although the PGFI and ECVI do not have precise standards, the guideline of Gibbs et al. (2003) suggest that these obtained values are very close to good model fit. Despite the fact that it is very difficult to construct a model that fits well at first, the measurement model has acquired the overall good model fit. Therefore, the measurement model fits well, based on the suggested descriptive measures of fit.

Figure 8-2 indicates that the digital guardian latent variable has statistically significant unstandardized regression coefficients. The negative statistical relationship between the digital guardian and crime victimization is illustrated by the statistically significant unstandardized regression coefficient of -.75. The standardized coefficient of -.74 also reveals that the digital guardian is the most substantial factor on computer-crime victimization. Among digital guardian observed variables, standardized coefficients indicate that both the number of equipped computer-security software and the duration of the presence of computer-security software provide almost an evenly substantial impact on minimizing computer-crime victimization. These findings sufficiently support the routine activities theoretical component, capable guardianship, by emphasizing the importance of computer security that contributes to reducing computer-crime victimization.

The research findings showed a strong relationship between the online lifestyle factors and computer-crime victimization. The unstandarized path coefficient of .04 revealed that a substantial, statistically significant relationship exists between the online lifestyle factor and computer crime victimization. The unstandarized coefficients of online lifestyle confirmed that the online users who spend significant time engaged in risky online behaviors in cyberspace are likely to be victimized. In addition, the standardized coefficient of .67 indicates that risky online leisure activities (visiting unknown Web sites, downloading games, music, and movies) provide the most substantial contribution to computer-crime victimization among online lifestyle categories. It is a very important finding because previous research has failed to identify certain types of online risky behaviors that are more susceptible to other online behaviors.

It was hypothesized that there would be an interaction effect between two factors, digital-capable guardianship and online lifestyle, which would directly contribute to the level of computer-crime victimization. Surprisingly, the results indicated that there was little correlation between two latent variables. Although the covariance between digital guardian and online lifestyle indicator suggested positive covariance, the result was insignificant (p = .056). Thus, the findings showed that there was no interaction effect between personal online lifestyle and equipping computer-security features on personal desktop or laptop computers.

Figure 8-2. Measurement model.

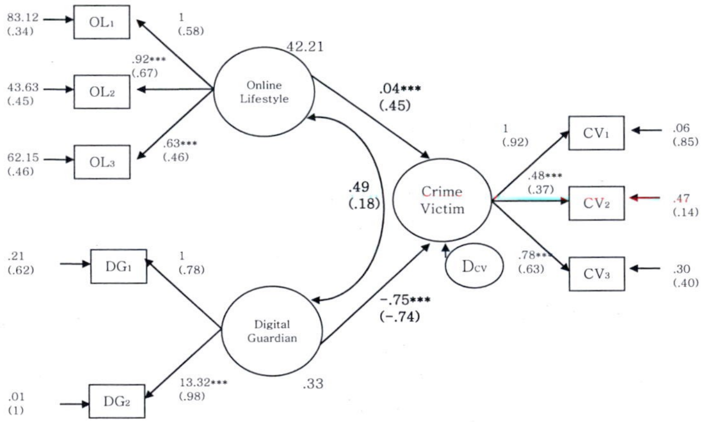

Phase 3-2: Structural Model

Similar to the measurement model, the probability value of the chi-square test (p. = .005) was less than the .05 level. As stated in the measurement model, such a rejection based on the chi-square test result appeared to be due to sample size. Three measures of absolute fit (adjusted chi-square, RMSEA, and GFI) met or exceeded their standards. The obtained RMR value of 3.03 was higher than the measurement model that indicated that the structural model did not offer a perfect fit. The CFI, TLI, PGFI, and ECVI values were similar to the measurement model, which sufficiently met the standard for appropriate model. Although the structural model was unable to convey an adequate fit for the model compared to the measurement model, the model had acquired the overall good model fit for the purposes of the research.

Table 2. Selected Fit Indexes for the Measurement Model

	Model Fitness	Index	Value	Standard Point
1.	Absolute fit	Chi-square	38.392 (df = 19) P. = .005	p. > .05
2.	Absolute fit	Normal Chi-square	2.02	< 3
3.	Absolute fit	Root mean square residual (RMR)	3.03	Close to 0
4.	Absolute fit	Root mean square error of approximation (RMSEA)	.07	< .10
5.	Absolute fit	Goodness of fit index (GFI)	.96	.90
6.	Incremental fit	Tucker-Lewis Index (TLI)	.94	Close to 1
7.	Incremental fit	Comparative fit index (CFI)	.96	Close to 1
8.	Parsimony	Parsimony goodness of fit index (PGFI)	.50	Larger value = Better fit
9.	Comparative fit	Expected cross-validation index (ECVI)	.36	Smaller value = Better fit

The structural model also provided empirical support for the components of Routine Activities Theory (See Figure 8-3). That is, individuals who have not installed computer-security programs or who use the Internet frequently and have risky online behaviors are more likely to be a victim of computer crime than those individuals who maintain and update regularly their computer security program and who use the Internet less and avoid risky online behavior.

Figure 8-3. Structural model.

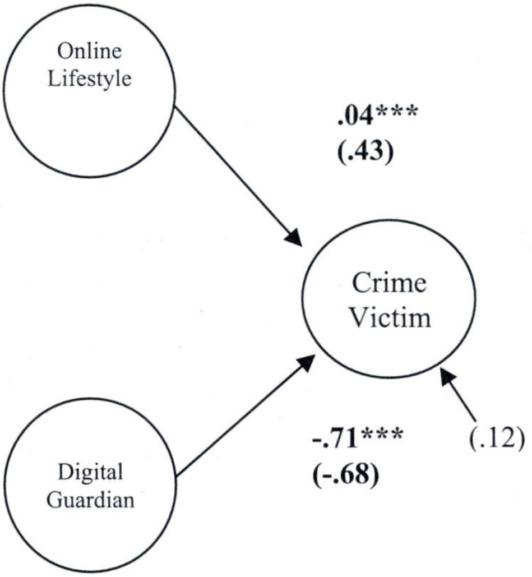

FINDINGS

This study investigated a new theoretical model that was derived from Hindelang et al.'s (1978) lifestyle-exposure theory and Cohen and Felson's (1979) Routine Activities Theory. The conceptual model advanced that digital-capable guardianship and online lifestyle both directly influence computer-crime victimization. The central measurement model in this study was shown to be superior as indicated by comparisons of structural coefficients and measures of fit.

Computer crimes are a significant threat to Internet users. Computer criminals cause significant monetary loss for their victims as well loss of productivity in the workplace. These losses occur when criminals are able to obtain personal information that gives them access to the victim's computer (Grabosky & Smith, 2001). The findings from this study are valuable for policy recommendations. First the findings show that college students who overlook their computer-oriented lifestyle in cyberspace or who fail to download the proper security software are more likely to become victims of cybercrime. Second, the findings showed that differential lifestyle patterns are linked directly with being victimized in cyberspace. The findings in this research show that the presence of computer security is the most important element in protecting an individual from cybercrime. The same finding has been suggested by MaQuade (2006), who suggested that "Routine Activities Theory has important implications for understanding crimes committed with or prevented with computers, other IT devices, or information systems" (p. 147).

The results of this study also show that establishing pro-social views of promoting adequate online lifestyle and downloading effective computer security will reduce the possibility of computer-crime victimization. These findings have been largely ignored by criminal justice crime prevention programs. And although the number of computer users increases daily, computer-crime prevention programs are not fully available to online users (Moitra, 2005). In fact, computer-crime prevention programs can be categorized as school-based crime prevention programs because some colleges and universities currently offer introductory and specialized courses in computer-crime and information security issues (McQuade, 2006).

Some researchers have suggested that the best way to minimize computer crime is through the incorporation of public awareness, formal education, and professional training (McQuade, 2006). Any program to prevent computer crime needs to provide online users with general knowledge of information security and valuable tips on how to avoid crime victimization. Programs should also emphasize laws and regulations that cover cybercrime in order to empower online users. Finally, programs should also alert students to the types of lifestyle behavior that predict victimization (Moitra, 2005).

Discussion

This study was the first attempt to create a computer-crime victimization model that is based on Routine Activities Theory. Routine Activities Theory was described in the main body of this study, using a combination of Hindelang et al.'s (1978) lifestyle-exposure theory and Cohen and Felson's (1979) Routine Activities Theory.

There has been much criticism of previous computer crime-related research, based on the issue of "generalizable data." Additionally, the small sample sizes used in qualitative studies have also been criticized for having potentially biased outcomes (Moitra 2005). The present research accomplished its main goals and contributes to the literature by using and integrating two criminological victimization theories with the empirical assessment of SEM in order to uncover computer crime victimization. Using the lifestyle-exposure theory, the daily living style, and the computer-oriented lifestyle in cyberspace, the present research developed one of the main tenets of the model. Routine Activities Theory helped reveal that a capable guardian reconstructed with a digital capable guardian provided computer security in this research. Thus, the findings of the study suggest that online lifestyle and digital guardianship are the essential aspects of a model that delineates patterns of computer crime victimization.

Limitations and Further Studies

There are a number of limitations to this study. Although the results accurately reflect a university's student population, it may be that the results cannot be generalized to the entire state university population, or the university population in the United States. For future research, the selection of potential universities for study should consider the level of computer technical support and the size of the student population at the university. It is important that any future research include diverse sites that represent the geographic locations and characteristics of the student population of the entire university population in the United States.

Another limitation of this study was that it is impossible to completely measure computer security. There might have been some error with the measurement of digital guardianship because some participants might not remember when they first downloaded security products on their computers. For future studies, it is important that the researcher be aware of this problem and attempt to identify specific dates of individual computer-security installations from the participants' computer systems. Doing such a check would increase the quality of computer-security measurement.

Because the study looked at content validity regarding computer security, it is possible that the study's participants did not understand the computer-security definitions or precise functions of the computer-security software. A lack of understanding could have led to under-reporting or over-reporting and thus would impact the content validity of the study. The researcher did attempt to increase the precision of measurement regarding these components by giving a pre-survey guideline, but that attempt was not infallible.

Criminology literature acknowledges that demographic factors are related to general crime victimization in the physical world. However, this relationship has not been completely revealed. There was no focus in this study on the relationship between cybercrime and demographic factors. Hence it is important that future research include an assessment of causal relationships between demographic variables (age, race, and gender) and cybercrime factors. Future research should also focus on how demographic variables are associated statistically with such variables as fear of cyber-crime, digital capable guardianship, online lifestyle activities, and computer crime victimization.

It should be noted that criminology literature has used other theories to explain risk-taking behavior. Early in the literature, some researchers believed that some personalities were more likely to exhibit risk-taking behaviors. Lyng (1990) delineated five terms for the two modal types (risk seeker vs. risk averter) from the early literature: (a) the "narcissistic" vs. the "anaclitic" (Freud 1925), (b) the "extrovert" vs. the "introvert" (Jung 1924), (c) the "Schizoid" vs. the "Cycloid" (Kretchmer 1936), (d) the "counterphobic" vs. "phobic" (Fenichel 1939), and (e) the "philobatic" vs. the "ocnophilic" (Balint 1959). Additionally, other terms such as "stress-seekers" (Klausner, 1968), "sensation-seekers" (Zucherman et al 1968), "eudaemonists" (Bernard 1968) were used to identify individuals who seek high-risk experiences (Lyng 1990, p. 853). These studies, however, were never able to convey adequate empirical validity because they were not able to explain casual factors in risking-taking behaviors (Lyng 1990).

Future studies also need to focus on why individuals continue to exhibit online risky behavior even when they are aware of potential dangers. Additionally future researchers need to develop more precise scales to measure computer security and online users' behaviors in order to investigate other theoretical perspectives for delineating a true crime victimization model.

Chapter 9 - Profiles of Computer Crime Victimization

In the previous chapter, I presented the computer crime victimization model derived from the combination of two victimization theories (Routine Activities and Lifestyle-exposure theory). Using structural equation modeling, the causal relationships among digital guardian, online lifestyle, and computer-crime victimization indexes were assessed in my research. The research revealed that digital-capable guardianship and online lifestyle directly influence computer-crime victimization. As a next step, I focus on how demographic factors influence computer crime victimization.

AN EMPIRICAL ASSESSMENT OF THE RELATIONSHIP BETWEEN DEMOGRAPHIC VARIABLES AND RISK FACTORS IN COMPUTER-CRIME

In criminology literature, it is commonly acknowledged that demographic factors such as race, age and gender are associated with general crime victimization in the physical world (Cohen et al., 1981; Gottfredson, 1984, 1986; Laub, 1990). However, the relationship between social context variables and factors associated with individual computer crime victimization has not been precisely revealed.

Similar to street crimes, the variations in age, income, and geographic location appear to be important variables that contribute to crime victimization. Anderson's (2006) analysis of the FTC's 2003 data indicates that online users between the ages of 25 and 54 with higher levels of income (greater than $75,000) who reside in the Pacific states are more likely to be exposed to the risk of identity theft victimization. In addition, the elderly (aged 75 and older), and persons who reside in the Mountain states, are rated as the lowest risk. Interestingly, educational level and marital status does not significantly contribute to the risk of victimization. Kresse, et al.'s study of identity thefts based on data from the Chicago Police Department from 2000 to 2006 also provided similar findings. Over 65 percent of the victims were aged between 20 and 44. Under age of 20 and over age of 65 were less likely to be exposed to the risk of victimization. NCVS reported that households headed by persons aged between 18 and 24 with the highest income category (over $75,000) are at the greatest risk of identity theft victimization.

The recent research suggests that risky online behaviors such as engaging in Internet purchases or using extensive hours of Internet increase the risk of suffering Internet Fraud victimization. Interestingly, Copes et al.'s (2010) study of profiles of victims of identity theft found that the typical victim of identity theft is white, female, between 35 and 54, earns between $50,000 and $75,000 per year, and has graduated from college. These victims typically report the crime, but not to crime control agencies. They rarely provide personal information or respond to unwanted solicitations. They did not appear to use the Internet more often than average Americans. Over 50 percent of victimization in the data was existing credit card fraud.

Computer criminals generate new viruses on a daily basis, so it is difficult to protect personal computer systems even with strong computer security software. Computer viruses can be easily spread through various online communication tools such as e-mail and online messengers by opening attachments or downloading computer applications. In addition, simply clicking pop-up messages, digital icons, or hyperlinks on Web sites or documents in cyberspace can swiftly launch malicious computer program applications and immediately implant them into online users' computer systems. Since a virus's activation depends on its design, many computer users are less likely to acknowledge their victimizations unless they experience failure gaining access to their operating system, data, or software. Furthermore, the infection is likely to spread rapidly to other computers if other online users share the same network.

The findings from lifestyle-exposure theory prove that online users must constantly be vigilant about any potential virus by abiding by adequate online lifestyle (Choi, 2008). In fact, many viruses are transmitted through various communication tools, so even if an attachment was sent from an acquaintance's email, online users must be cautious about executing or opening the attachment. Various free software and media files (MP3, MP4, MPEG, MOV, AVI, JPEG, WMA, ASF, etc) are widely available online, but they can be infectious. Since viruses are very easily implanted into any digital software or files, scanning software or files for potential virus infection has become a part of personal online lifestyle in cyberspace. Thus, online users should not overlook their online activities and must be aware of any potential victimization when downloading programs to see pictures, hear music, or obtain other features from unfamiliar web sites.

One of my main interests in this research was to examine how demographic variables interact with factors derived from Choi's (2008) computer crime victimization model. The assessment of social context factors in cyber spatial structures is crucial because the research assumes that social environments constantly interact with the traits of online spatiality. Two steps are used to assess the statistical relationships between demographic variables and factors based on computer crime victimization are as follows:

Step 1: Basic descriptive statistics, Chi-square test, and Cramer's' V were introduced to assess the statistical relationships between demographic factors (race, age, and gender) and fear of cybercrime.

Step 2: One-way analysis of variance (ANOVA), Fisher's LSD (Least Significant Difference) and OLS (Ordinary Least Squares) regression analysis were applied to estimate whether demographic variables (race and age) have a significant impact on main causal factors of computer crime (digital guardianship and online lifestyles), and computer crime victimization. In addition, the statistical relationship between gender and main causal factors was assessed via t-test to determine if there was a statistical difference between the means of male and female groups in this study.

DEMOGRAPHIC VARIABLES VS. FEAR OF CYBERCRIME

The respondents were asked to identify the most fearful cybercrime in the survey. Six different categories of cybercrime were offered as well as an "Other" category. While 1% (n=1) of respondents reported cyber-harassment as the least fearful crime, over 60% (n=130) of the survey participants chose identify theft as the most fearful cyber-crime (see Table 1). As expected, hacking was also fairly high on the list of cybercrime categories with 28% (n=57). Interestingly, only 2.5% (n=5) reported Internet fraud and 3.4% (n=7) reported online stalking as the most fearful crime within the category.

Table 1. Descriptive of Fear of Cybercrime (N=204)

Cybercrime Categories	Frequency (f)	Percentage (%)
Internet fraud	5	2.5
Identity theft	130	63.7
Hacking	57	27.9
Online stalking	7	3.4
Cyber-harassment	2	1.0
Other	3	1.5
Total (N)	204	100.0

Figure 9-1. Bar Chart of Fear of Cybercrime

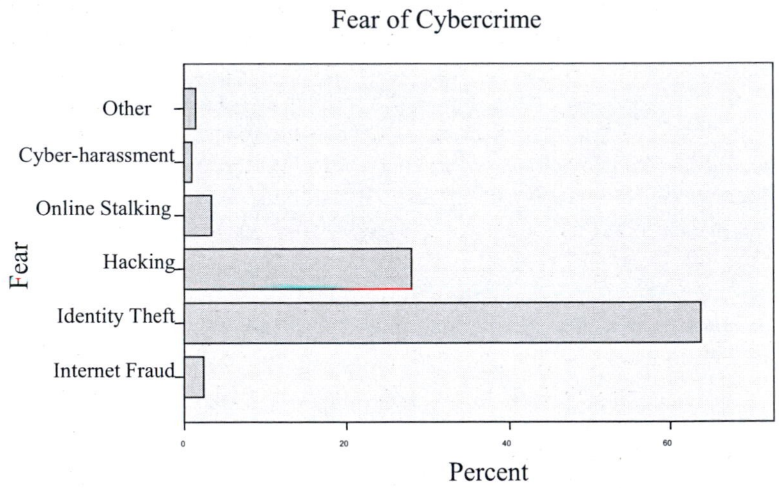

In the physical world, the assessment of demographic variables revealed that gender, age, and race variables play a substantial role in determining the level of fear. This research applied various statistical methods to estimate causal relationship between three demographic variables and fear of cybercrime; however, the research findings indicated that gender was found only to be a significant predictor of fear of cybercrime.

The chi-square test is a method to determine if two variables are independent of one another in nominal bivariate analyses. Since two variables, gender and the cybercrime categories, are nominal levels, the chi-square test was used to determine whether gender difference is statistically significant in identifying the most fearful cyber-crime among the six different crime categories.

In terms of percent within gender, females have a greater fear of identity theft (66.1%, n=74) and online stalking (6.3%, n=7), compared to 61% (n=56) and 0% (n=0) of males, respectively (See Table 2). While 33% (n=30) of males had identified hacking, 24% (n=27) of female respondents indicated it as the most fearful crime (see Table 2). The results of the Chi-square test verified the significant relationship between genders and identified the most fearful cybercrime from online users' perspectives (χ^2 = 11.937, df = 5, $p < .05$). Since the chi-square test suggests a statistical significant relationship between two variables, applying Cramer's V was necessary to determine the magnitude of nominal association. Cramer's V is a chi-square based on measure of association for tables larger than 2 × 2 (Bachman & Paternoster, 2004). In the findings, the magnitude of the Cramer's V of .242 indicated that about 24.2% of the variation in identifying the most fearful cybercrime is accounted for by gender difference (see Table 3).

Table 2. Pearson's Chi-Square Test for the Gender and the Types of Fear of Cybercrime (N=204)

		Gender		
		Male	Female	Total
	Internet frauds	4	1	5
	Identity theft	56	74	130
	Hacking	30	27	57
Fear	Online stalking	0	7	7
	Cyber-harassment	0	2	2
	Other	2	1	3
	Total	92	112	204

Note: Figure in parentheses indicates cell frequency.
* $p < .05$ (2-tailed test)

Table 3. Symmetric Measures for the Gender and the Types of Fear of Cybercrime

		Value	Approx. sig.
Nominal by nominal	Cramer's V	.242	.036
N of valid cases		204	

In sum, these findings suggest that identity theft was ranked as the most fearful cybercrime category and gender difference only differentially contributes to perceived risk of cybercrime among other demographic variables.

DEMOGRAPHIC VARIABLES VS. MAIN FACTORS IN COMPUTER CRIME VICTIMIZATION

This section presents how demographic variables (race, age, and gender) relate to main factors in computer crime victimization (capable guardianship, online lifestyle, and computer crime victimization), which are the major constructs in this research. In order to delineate significant relationships between demographic variables and the suggested main factors, different statistical analyses were applied by taking into consideration the scales of the variables.

First, the research examined the statistical relationship between race and the suggested three factors. Anderson (1972) asserts the advantage of utilizing Fisher's LSD (Least Significant Difference) is that "it can be easily applied to any fixed effects linear model, be it analysis of variance, regression, or analysis of covariance" (p. 30). Prior to utilizing LSD test, one-way ANOVA (analysis of variance) was used to test for determining the population means based on race are not equal as a first step. It was hypothesized that there is variability in the population based on race, which contributes to the level of digital guardianship, online lifestyle, and computer crime victimization. The F statistic offers the researcher the chance to estimate the existence of group variability among the three variables. If the F-test rejects the null hypothesis of equal means, then Fisher's LSD (Least Significant Difference) can be used to compare group means. An ANOVA analysis showed that race has a significant difference in the monetary loss category, which is one of three computer crime victimization variables at the .05 level (see Table 5).

Table 4. Descriptive: Race vs. Computer Crime Victimization (N=204)

		N	Mean	SD	Std. error
Frequency	African American	15	.73	.46	.12
	Asian	4	.50	.58	.29
	Caucasian	172	.65	.65	.05
	Hispanic	4	.75	.50	.25
	Other	9	.44	.73	.24
	Total	204	.65	.63	.04
Monetary loss	African American	15	.20	.78	.20
	Asian	4	1.50	1.73	.87
	Caucasian	172	.22	.68	.05
	Hispanic	4	.00	.00	.00
	Other	9	.33	1.00	.33
	Total	204	.25	.74	.05
Hour loss	African American	15	.73	.88	.23
	Asian	4	.75	.96	.48
	Caucasian	172	.52	.71	.05
	Hispanic	4	.25	.50	.25
	Other	9	.22	.44	.15
	Total	204	.53	.71	.05

Table 5. F-Test (ANOVA): Race vs. Computer Crime Victimization (N=204)

ANOVA

		Sum of squares	Df	Mean square	F	Sig.
Frequency of crime victimization	Between groups	.613	4	.153	.381	.822
	Within groups	79.975	199	.402		
	Total	80.588	203			
Monetary loss	Between Groups	6.740	4	1.685	3.194	.014*
	Within groups	105.005	199	.528		
	Total	111.745	203			
Hour loss	Between groups	1.982	4	.495	.977	.421
	Within groups	100.896	199	.507		
	Total	102.877	203			

*Significance at a .05 level

Table 6. Multiple Comparisons: LSD test

Multiple Comparisons: LSD

Dependent variable	(I) Race	(J) Race	Mean difference (I-J)	Std. Error	Sig.
Monetary loss	Asian	African American	1.30000(*)	.40877	.002
		Caucasian	1.27907(*)	.36740	.001
		Hispanic	1.50000(*)	.51364	.004
		Other	1.16667(*)	.43651	.008

* The mean difference is significant at the .05 level.

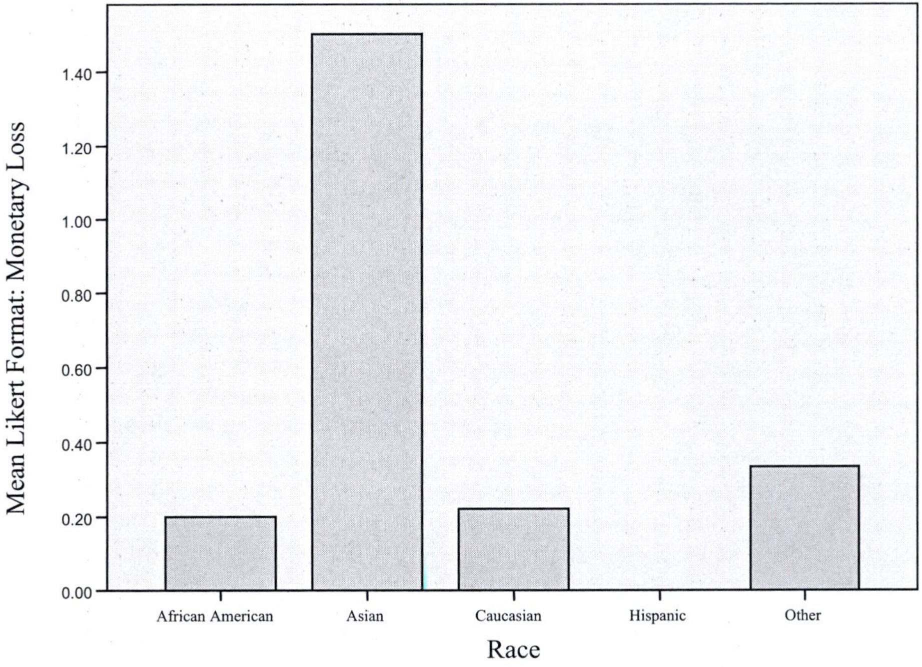
Mean Likert Format: Monetary Loss
1.40
1.20
1.00
0.80
0.60
0.40
0.20
0.00
African American
Asian
Caucasian
Hispanic
Other
Race

The results at the .05 significance level using Fisher's LSD test suggested that Asian students tend to experience higher monetary loss compared to other racial groups (see Table 6). Fisher's LSD method, which was based on the previous rejection of the null hypothesis with F test, indicated that racial difference significantly contributes to the level of monetary loss.

Second, the research also examined the statistical association between age difference and the computer crime victimization variables. In order to examine whether age has a substantial impact on the level of individual online lifestyle, capable guardianship, and crime victimization, Ordinary Least Squares (OLS) regression analysis was applied. The research naturally assumed that the regression assumptions were not being violated. Three specific hypotheses were tested in order to measure how age difference has substantial influences on the level of digital capable guardianship, individual online lifestyle, and computer crime victimization (see Table 7).

In the first hypothesis, the unstandarized coefficients of -.044 and -.470 indicated that age has negative and substantial impacts on the level of digital capable guardianship ($p < .05$). This result suggests that older individuals are less likely to install three major computer security software and unlikely to keep the computer security software active (Model 1). However, based on the R-Square, only 3% of the variation in the dependent variable can be explained by age difference. There is a weak, negative significant relationship between age and the level of digital capable guardianship. In other words, as age increases, the level of capable guardianship decreases, but the magnitude of this association is weak.

In the second hypothesis, online lifestyle was assessed by taking age difference into account via OLS analysis. Among four variables, the results found that age difference significantly contributes to two online lifestyle variables; the level of online vocational and leisure activities and risky vocational activities ($p <.05$). The unstandarized coefficients of -.926 and -.505 indicate that age has a negative influence on individual vocational and leisure activities and risky vocational activities (Model 2). R-square of .072 and .022 indicate that there are weak magnitude of associations between age and two online lifestyle variables.

Hence, older online users were less likely to spend extensive time on vocational and leisure activities, and they were also less likely to

Table 7. OLS Regression Unstandardized Coefficients for Model Predicting the Digital Capable Guardianship, Online Lifestyle, and Computer Crime Victimization by Age (N=204)

	Model 1		Model 2		Model 3
	Digital Capable Guardianship		Online Lifestyle		Computer Crime Victimization
	Number of Security	Duration of Having Security	Vocational & Leisure Activities	Risky Vocational Activities	Monetary Loss
Intercept	3.510	31.881	53.012	23.523	-.557
b	-.044	-.470	-.926	-.505	.039
p.	.000*	.021*	.000*	.032*	.046*
R^2	.026	.026	.072	.022	.019

Note: *b*= unstandardized regression coefficient
* $p < .05$

engage in risky vocational activities. However, the magnitude of association was fairly weak.

In the third hypothesis, age difference significantly contributes to the level of monetary loss for fixing a computer due to virus infections (Model 3). The unstandardized coefficient of .039 indicates that online users with older age are likely to spend more money to fix their computer due to virus infections compared to younger online users ($p <$ .05). The R-square of .019 suggests that approximately 98% of the variation in dependent variable cannot be explained by age difference. In other words, age difference has a significant impact on monetary loss, but the magnitude of association is very weak.

Third, the research inspected the statistical relationship between gender and the computer crime victimization variables. The t-test was utilized to determine if there was a statistical difference between the means of male and female groups in this study. The results from the independent samples t-test indicate that gender difference contributes to the level of risky leisure activities, risky vocational activities, and security management. Since the significance of the F test (Sig. >.05) in the online activities complies the variances for male and female groups are equal, examining the "Equal Variances are assumed" row should be used to interpret the significance of the t-value.

In risky leisure activities, the t value of 4.05 and the Sig. (2-tailed) column in the p-value (p = .000) is less than .05, suggesting that the average risky leisure activities score of males (M = 18.72, SD = 9.41) is significantly different from that of females (M = 13.81, SD = 7.89). In other words, males are more likely to engage in online risky leisure activities such as visiting unknown Web sites, downloading free games, free music, and free movies than females.

On the other hand, the t value of -2.5 and the Sig. (2-tailed) column in the p-value (p = .013) is less than .05 suggest that the average risky vocational activities score of male (M = 11.51, SD = 8.26) is significantly less that of female (M = 14.60, SD = 9.17). This finding suggests that compared to males, females tend to open any attachment in the e-mail, click on any web-links in the e-mails, open any file though the instant messenger, and click on a pop-up message that interested them.

Security management items were reversely coded for gaining the same directions with other online lifestyle variables. Thus, higher values represent higher negligence of security management. In recoded security management, the results indicate that there is a statistically significant difference in the level of security management between males and females, *t* (202) = -2.82, *p* = .005. That is, the average recoded security management score of males (*M* = 29.36, *SD* = 10.56) is significantly less than that of females (*M* = 33.79, *SD* = 11.61). In other words, males are more likely to update computer security, change the passwords for e-mail accounts, search for more effective computer security software, check the operation of computer security online, and use different passwords and user IDs for their Internet accounts than females.

Table 8. Group Statistics (N=204)

	Gender	N	M	SD	SE mean
Risky leisure activities	Male	92	18.72	9.41	.98
	Female	112	13.81	7.89	.75
Risky vocational activities	Male	92	11.51	8.28	.86
	Female	112	24.60	9.17	.97
Recoded security management	Male	92	29.36	10.56	1.10
	Female	112	33.49	11.61	1.10

Table 9. Independent Samples t-Test

	t	DF	Sig.
Risky leisure activities	4.05	202	.000*
Risky vocational activities	-2.50	202	.013*
Recoded security management	-2.822	202	.005*

* $p < .05$ (2-tailed test)

In summary, findings based on Step 1 suggest that identity theft was identified as the most feared cybercrime category and gender was not a significant variable to determine the perceived risk of cybercrime among demographic variables. Three specific findings based on Step 2 were revealed via the application of various statistical analyses. First,

ANOVA and Fisher's LSD test confirmed that racial difference has a substantial impact on monetary loss in computer crime victimization. Second, OLS regression indicated that age difference has a substantial influence on the level of digital capable guardianship and online lifestyle. Third, the independent samples t-test uncovered that gender difference differentially contributes to degree of engagement of online risky leisure and vocational activities, and the level of computer security management, which was one of the original online lifestyle variables.

FINDINGS AND DISCUSSION

The study assessed the relationship between demographic variables and computer crime victimization factors. Descriptive statistics suggested that identity theft was identified as the most fearful cybercrime category and gender was not a significant variable to determine the perceived risk of cybercrime among demographic variables. In addition, ANOVA and Fisher's LSD (Least Significant Difference) test confirmed that racial difference has a substantial impact on monetary loss in computer crime victimization. Results from OLS (Ordinary Least Squares) regression suggested that age difference has a significant influence on the level of digital capable guardianship and online lifestyle. Furthermore, the Independent samples t-test indicated that gender difference substantially contributes to the degree of engagement of risky leisure activities and risky vocational activities in cyberspace, and the level of computer security management.

This research is an initial step toward understanding how individual demographic variables interact with computer-crime victimization model based on Routine Activities Theory. As discussed, Routine Activities Theory is presented in detail in the main body of this study, via the combination of Hindelang et al.'s (1978) lifestyle-exposure theory and Cohen and Felson's (1979) Routine Activities Theory.

In fact, many criticisms on computer crime related quantitative and qualitative research are driven from lack of "generalizable data" based on computer-crime incidents against private victims in quantitative research, and small sample sizes in qualitative research that may draw biased outcomes (Moitra, 2005). The research has accomplished most of its main objectives. The main contribution of this research is that it constitutes an inventive attempt to uncover relationship between computer-crime victimization model and demographic variables. From lifestyle-exposure theory, the research transformed from its crucial theoretical component, individual's daily living patterns, to individual's computer oriented lifestyle in cyberspace as one of main tenet in the model. From the perspective of Routine Activities Theory, the crucial key element of a capable guardian was logically reconstructed with digital capable guardian, which represents computer security in this research. The relationships between demographic variables and the factors from victimization models are empirically explained in this study.

Discussion 1:
Write a short essay about a cybercrime incident you know about. Explain what happened and the types of primary, secondary, or tertiary harm experienced by the victim(s). Comment on whether you think the victim was well served by criminal justice officials or information security professionals with whom they interacted during or after the incident.

Discussion 2:
Suppose you met someone online and then eventually wanted to meet him or her in person. In what ways would you be concerned for your safety? What precautions would you take to protect yourself, your data, your money, and others in your life from harm?

Discussion 3:
Go online and either Google your name or find an example of what you consider to be a violation of privacy involving someone's personal information. Explain how you feel about your findings and the basis for your reviews. Then, explain steps that could have been taken to prevent any privacy violations from occurring.

PART V

Jurisdiction in Cyberspace and Managing Cybercrime

As previously addressed, cyberspace is different from the physical world because of its distinct temporal and spatial characteristics. Difficulties in prosecuting computer-related criminal activities arise because much of the property involved is intangible and does not mesh well with traditional theft or larceny statutes. In addition, jurisdiction has been traditionally based on geographic boundaries; however, the Internet generated a global jurisdiction due to its anti-spatiality. Because of this anti-spatiality, the law must determine whether an action that takes place on the Internet is controlled by the law of the country in which the site is located, where the Internet provider is situated, where the user is resident, or whether an entirely new jurisdictional base should be generated exclusively for cyberspace.

This chapter will examine the traditional concepts of legal jurisdiction and how these doctrines have been applied to cyberspace, both domestically and internationally, based on cases originating in the United States.

Due to the rapid growth of technology and the Internet, reexamining and reevaluating traditional legal principles have become significant tasks for legal professionals because they constantly encounter jurisdictional problems associated with cyberspace.

Chapter 10 - Jurisdiction in Cyberspace

JURISDICTION

Jurisdiction pertains to the general authority of a specific court to accept and resolve a dispute. Traditionally, a court's jurisdiction is based on geographic factors such as the location of a defendant's residence or place of business, where a crime or civil wrongdoing allegedly took place, the placement of disputed property, and so forth. A particular court may only consider a legal problem if the court has the authority to adjudicate that type of matter. This authority is referred to as jurisdiction.

The concept of jurisdiction includes two separate legal questions:

1. Does the court have the ability to hear the type of problem brought before it? (Subject Matter Jurisdiction).
2. Does the court have the ability to enforce its decision over the parties to the lawsuit? (Personal Jurisdiction).

Subject Matter Jurisdiction

Subject matter jurisdiction describes the court's ability to grant the type of relief sought by the allegedly injured party. Pursuant to American law, questions relating to the subject matter jurisdiction of a Particular court may be raised at any time during the judicial process, even for the first time at the appellate level.

- Bankruptcy cases are heard in bankruptcy courts.

- Disputes regarding the validity of a will are litigated in probate courts.

Intellectual property cases are heard in federal claims courts, which have jurisdiction over patent, copyright, trademark, and trade secret cases.

Subject Matter Jurisdiction: Example

The Constitution of the United States grants exclusive jurisdiction to the federal courts to determine matters regarding patents. A lawsuit based on a patent infringement was filed in a state court and the plaintiff prevailed. On appeal, for the first time, the defendant questioned the state court's ability to hear the matter. The appellate court agreed that the state court lacked subject matter jurisdiction to determine patent disputes, and the case was dismissed (Helewitz, 2005, p. 27).

Personal Jurisdiction

Personal jurisdiction refers to a court's ability to have its judgment enforced against the parties to the lawsuit. This type of jurisdiction is usually only applied to the defendant in the lawsuit, the person or institution that has been alleged to have committed a wrongdoing. Because the plaintiff (the person who institutes the lawsuit) has voluntarily requested the court to intervene, it is presumed that the plaintiff has accepted the court's jurisdiction over it. Unlike subject matter jurisdiction, which can never be waived, the personal jurisdiction may always be waived by the parties.

In order to acquire jurisdiction over the Parties, three separate bases may be applied by the court:

> Personal jurisdiction is the ability of a court to make decisions regarding defendants who reside or conduct business within specified geographical boundaries. Generally, most courts are empowered to exercise personal jurisdiction if the defendant meets any of the following criteria:

- The defendant is physically present in the geographic boundaries of the court's jurisdiction.

- If the defendant is domiciled, meaning that he or she is a permanent resident in the state, that court automatically has jurisdiction.
- If the defendant is doing business in the area of the court's jurisdiction on a regular and continual basis, the court may be able to exercise jurisdiction over it.
- Most courts have what is referred to as long-arm jurisdiction over a defendant if the defendant transacts any business within the court's geographical area of authority, or commits any tortuous act that has an effect in such area.

The third criterion is very important. This method of acquiring personal jurisdiction raises a host of questions with respect to Internet uses. Internet use is global, meaning that a website owner may be considered to be "doing business" everywhere in which the site may be accessed. It is the method of obtaining personal jurisdiction over a defendant that has caused the greatest concern with respect to applying traditional principles to cyber-law (Helewitz, 2005).

Long-Arm Jurisdiction

Long-arm jurisdiction refers to the authority of a court in one state to have jurisdiction over an out-of-state (non-resident) defendant when that defendant has sufficient minimum contacts with that geographical area. Understanding long-arm jurisdiction is important. Courts have also held that an out-of-state corporation doing business in another state is under the jurisdiction of the courts in the state where it primarily does business.

However, individuals committing a crime, causing an accident, or breaching contract in a state other than the one they live in will find themselves subject to the jurisdiction of the state in which the harm was done—regardless of where they primarily live, or conduct most of their travels or business.

Rem Jurisdiction

Rem jurisdiction has to do with a court's authority over property located within its geographical boundary. For example, an Ohio-based firm with a computer system located in Pennsylvania would be subject to Pennsylvania courts on the basis of rem jurisdiction. Although the basis of acquiring this jurisdiction is usually limited to physical property, it may be possible to assert that cyberspace is physically present within such boundaries, especially if the issue is coupled with some property located within the state.

Rem Jurisdiction: Example

Two people are disputing the ownership of a domain name. Because the title to the domain name is in question, and the name may appear in cyberspace within a given jurisdiction, it is conceivable that it might be able to be litigated in any state.

Quasi-in-rem Jurisdiction

Quasi-in-rem jurisdiction grants a court authority to hear a dispute if the defendant has property in the state, even if that property is not the subject of the lawsuit, which may be used to satisfy the plaintiff's claim. Quasi-in-rem jurisdiction is rarely asserted.

Quasi-in-rem Jurisdiction: Example

A U.S. retailer has purchased computers from a German manufacturer, and the contract has been breached. The German manufacturer maintains a bank account in Chicago. The retailer may be able to sue the German manufacturer in Chicago based on the bank account which can be used to satisfy the claim.

Helewitz (2005), a cyber-law expert, emphasizes the importance of understanding the service of process in cyber jurisdiction issues. Once it is determined that the court has jurisdiction, the person must be served with the initial pleading to commence the lawsuit. This notification to a person that he or she is being sued is referred to as service of process. Each jurisdiction, as well as the federal courts, has its own rules with respect to the appropriate method of serving a party to a lawsuit. In order to meet these requirements, the person who initiates the lawsuit must follow the statutory requirements of the court where the matter will be heard. This is true even if the subject matter of the litigation involves a question of cyber-law. Therefore, the rules followed by the Particular court must be analyzed to determine the correct method of service (p. 30).

Original Jurisdiction

Original jurisdiction refers to the jurisdictional requirements of a court when a dispute first enters the judicial system.

Appellate Jurisdiction

Appellate jurisdiction defines the types of cases accepted by the intermediate and final, or supreme, levels of appellate courts.

Concurrent Jurisdiction

Concurrent jurisdiction exists when both federal and state courts have the legal authority to hear the same case. Federal courts also have jurisdiction when a case involves litigants with different state citizenship. To qualify the diversity of citizenship under federal court rules, litigants must be residents of different states and the dispute must involve a controversy involving $75,000 or more.

Exclusive Jurisdiction

Exclusive jurisdiction exists when a case can only be tried in state court, or only be tried in federal court. Federal courts have exclusive jurisdiction over federal crimes, intellectual property, and certain other types of cases involving interstate rights or claims of wrongdoing. State courts have exclusive jurisdiction over disputes regarding traffic violations, divorce, adoption, state crimes, and interpretation of a state constitution.

Within the U.S., the general rule is that a person may be charged with a cybercrime by every state alleging a violation of its law:

- In criminal matters, the state in which the crime was committed, or from which it was launched will normally claim original jurisdiction.
- In civil matters, original jurisdiction is normally determined on grounds of where harm occurred.

Typically, a person or entity will answer to charges made against them and stand trial initially in the state that first files formal charges, or in the state in which the defendant was apprehended and is being held in custody. After the first state has finished its legal business with the accused, a convicted defendant may then be extradited to stand trial in a second state.

However, if the defendant was found innocent in the first trial, he or she may be subpoenaed to appear or be rearrested and transported to a different state to stand trial on new charges. In international criminal and civil cases, legal jurisdiction also depends on the laws of affected nations, as well as on international agreements between nations, such as extradition agreements specifying the conditions under which an accused person may be forcefully transported from one country to another in order to stand trial for a crime. People are not extradited in civil cases, however defendants may be tried in absentia in either criminal or civil cases, depending on existing laws and legal precedents.

VENUE

Whereas jurisdiction has to do with whether a court has authority over a Particular case, venue is the legal concept that defines the most appropriate forum for a trial. Very often two or more courts will have proper jurisdiction, but it would be more appropriate to hear the case in a Particular forum.

Two Massachusetts companies are involved in a breach of contract dispute, and Company B sues Company A. The e-commerce transaction involved ordering that took place over a website with a server in Massachusetts, and the order was shipped from A's warehouse in Florida to B's branch office, also in Florida. A number of courts may have jurisdiction over the case, given the contracts. However, a court may decide that Florida is the best venue for the dispute to be litigated because it is where the principal offices of both Parties are located. Presumably, it is the most convenient forum for both Parties.

"The Zippo Standard: A leading case that attempts to build a framework for minimum contacts is Zippo Manufacturing v. Zippo Dot Com, Inc., 952 F. Supp. 1119 (W.D. Pa. 1997). The Zippo standard was adopted by the Fifth Circuit Court of Appeals and is likely to be adopted by other appellate courts. The case centers on trademark infringement. Zippo (ZMC) is a famous lighter manufacturing company, and Zippo Dot Com (Z.com) is an Internet news subscription service. When ZMC sued Z.com, Z.com filed a motion to dismiss the case, claiming the court did not have jurisdiction over the parities because Z.com had such limited contact with Pennsylvania.

"The court articulated a sliding-scale test in which a court's determination of jurisdiction is based on the amount of business that an individual or firm transacts over the Internet. The court pointed to three examples along the scale: (1) an information-only website that could be accessed by any user, (2) the middle ground, where the service provides interactive websites on which a user can exchange information, and (3) the far end of the scale, where the party is an Internet vendor who regularly transacts business (through shipping of products, etc.) with residents of that state. The court ruled that Z.com occupied the middle ground and that the analysis should be determined by examining the level of interactivity and commercial nature of the exchange of information that occurs on the website. Ultimately, the court ruled that since Z.com contracted with 3,000 residents and seven Internet access providers, all located in Pennsylvania, the court did have personal jurisdiction over the case" (Melvin, 2005, p. 165).

INTERNATIONAL AGREEMENT

The cyber-attacks against U.S. and South Korean government websites on Saturday, July 4, 2009, would be a good example of an international agreement. Cyber criminals launched sophisticated and powerful attacks against major U.S. federal web sites, knocking them offline throughout the weekend. On Tuesday, the same types of attacks were made upon South Korean government and major commercial websites. Even though both U.S. and South Korean government officials presume that these attacks are linked to North Korea, the true identity of these attacks has not yet been revealed.

What nations would have jurisdiction over the perpetrators? Could the defendants, if identified, be tried in the nation from which the malware was originally distributed, or in one or more nations to which the malware was bounced and subsequently redistributed? Would prosecution depend on the number of victims involved, and amount of harm caused within one nation as opposed to others? What if the transgressors resided in a country that did not have computer-crime laws? Could they be charged under the laws of nations or states that do?

McQuade (2006) provides the short answer to all of these questions:

> "It depends on several factors, because cyber society lacks all of the requisite attributes of a state as outlined in the 1933 Montevideo Convention on the Rights and Duties of States, which specifies that a bona fide country must have a permanent population, a defined territory, a government, and the capacity to enter into relations with other states (p. 282)."

International agreement is a generic term widely used to label agreement between nations and, as such, means the same thing as articles of agreement, charter, concordant, convention, declaration, pact, protocol, and treaty. Many nations have entered into specific treaties to determine jurisdiction and applications of legal doctrines. The most recent of these treaties, the Convent on Cybercrime, was enacted on November 23, 2001. These treaties attempt to create a consensus among the signatory nations to provide a unified doctrine regarding cyber jurisdiction.

According to Helewitz (2005), American courts, when attempting to exert jurisdiction over foreign nationals who don't have a specific treaty on point, use a three-pronged test to ascertain whether jurisdiction may be asserted:

1. Whether the foreign national knowingly and purposefully directed its activities to an American market, or availed itself of the protection of American law. If so, the first test has been met.
2. Whether the foreign national actually has a presence in the forum country. This can be met if the defendant was soliciting business in the forum state.
3. Whether the assertion of jurisdiction meets the constitutional standards of fair play and substantial justice. To answer this question, several factors must be analyzed:

a) The extent of the defendant's activity in the forum state
b) The cost to the defendant to defend the action
c) The conflict that may exist with the law of the defendants' own country
d) The forum's interest in deciding the merits
e) The most practical manner to settle the dispute
f) The availability of an alternative forum

The question of a particular court's jurisdiction is far more problematic in the international area than it is locally. Because the Internet has global application, a plaintiff may forum shop to locate a court whose law would provide the relief sought, so as to adjudicate a problem that might not be able to be asserted in either party's home country. Because of this potentially conflicting application of legal principles, the most reasonable approach might be to create an international tribunal for the adjudication of Internet problems.

Chapter 11 - Use of Synthetic Cathinones: Legal Issues and Availability of Darknet

Kyung-Shick Choi Ph.D, Kevin J. Earl , Arang Park , Jo-Ann Della Giustina Ph.D & J.D.

With the growth of e-business, "Darknet" marketplaces where online users can purchase illegal drugs over the Internet are also rapidly growing. Bath salts, or synthetic cathinone products, are one of the most popular drugs that are available among darknets and gradually spreading in the U.S. Even though the Federal Analogue Act of 1986 is intended to prevent the distribution of designer drugs, its vague language makes it difficult to enforce the regulation of bath salts. An online voluntary survey was conducted among students at a University located in Massachusetts to see the possibility of switching purchasing methods from traditional to online. A total of 413 students participated in this study and all the responses were analyzed via Paired t test, ANOVA, and Vignettes. The study findings suggest that there are high chances of replacing the purchase method from direct contact with a drug dealer to purchasing drugs online. This study discusses the implications of such results, as well as the efforts being undertaken to curtail the proliferation of drugs through the darker regions of cyberspace. Policy implications, calls for future research, and the importance of international cooperation are discussed.

KEYWORDS: Bath Salts, Synthetic Cathinone, Drug Abuse, Drug Federal Regulation, Drugs Online, and Illegal Drug Purchase Online

INTRODUCTION

There is an overwhelming abundance of drugs that are available for purchase online. "Darknet" marketplaces provide an anonymous place that allows users of the site to purchase illegal drugs, including bath salts, or synthetic cathinone, which is a hallucinogenic central nervous system stimulant. Many illegal drugs have been bought and sold through these types of underground Internet forums. This is an issue because the anonymity that the Internet and darknets provide its users makes it difficult to crack down on bath salt sales taking place worldwide. These issues have been brought to light by the case against Ross Ulbricht, the man accused of running the darknet marketplace called Silk Road.

On the first of October in 2013, the FBI arrested 29-year-old Ross Ulbricht on charges of running the underground website Silk Road, a "darknet" marketplace that provided an online haven for anonymous drug trafficking to about a million registrants worldwide, with about 30% of them being in the United States (Hume, 2013). Silk Road's worldwide customer base supports the United Nations Office on Drugs and Crime's (UNODC) claim that international cooperation is a key element in bringing down organized crime (UNODC, 2014). It took the FBI years to track his activity since he had been using various methods to dodge investigators. Ulbricht was accused of arranging 1 billion dollars in transactions of illegal drugs, fake IDs and illegal weapons via the Internet from his apartment in San Francisco under the pseudonym "Dread Pirate Roberts" (Mosk, 2014; *Time Magazine*, 2013). Silk Road was subsequently shut down by a federal judge. However, the Digital Citizens Alliance found that the website is back up and running under new management, and is more lively than it was before. This is despite the arrests of prominent figures of the reborn Silk Road, now known as Silk Road 2.0 (Mosk, 2014).

The Digital Citizens Alliance reported that before Ulbricht was arrested there were 13,000 drug listings available on Silk Road. After his arrest, there were about 13,648 listings and the darknet economy as a whole had 75 percent more listings (Mosk, 2014). These findings show that the anonymous online drug market is resilient. Moreover, what the Digital Citizens Alliance continue to uncover in their research is that the darknet drug marketplace is not only resilient in that it was able to bounce back to its original strength, but that it has continued to grow more powerful. In April of 2014, there were 10 darknet drug markets with 32,000 listed drugs available; in August of 2014, there were 18 darknet drug markets with 47,000 listings (Ingraham, 2014). These findings show the increasing online availability of illegal drugs.

The darknet drug marketplace provides an underground, anonymous place in which individuals can buy and sell drugs. The Ross Ulbricht case provides an opportunity to realize just how immense the issue of drug sales through the Internet, which ultimately leads to drug use, is. Bath salts, along with many other drugs, were available on Silk Road, providing an open opportunity for any individual considering using the drug. Silk Road's shutdown and subsequent revival show just how immense an issue darknets are in providing drugs like bath salts to people all around the world.

THE HISTORY OF BATH SALTS

Darknets sell various illegal drugs including bath salts. Bath salts, or synthetic cathinone, and its derivatives such as methcathinone, mephedrone, methedron, methyleone and MDPV are known as being hallucinogenic central nervous system stimulants. These substances have a history of abuse in European countries, particularity in the UK, because their effects are similar to MDMA[13] (Ecstasy) and cocaine (Spiller et al., 2011). After the purity and availability of these two stimulants decreased in the UK, bath salts soon became an alternative to them (Prosser et al., 2011). According to caller data at UK Poisons Information Service center, the number of telephone inquiries about synthetic cathinone was zero prior to 2009, but between 2009 and 2010 the number was equal to the number of calls regarding cocaine and MDMA (Prosser et al., 2011).

Although synthetic cathinone products have been successfully regulated in the UK by the Misuse of Drugs Act of 1971, synthetic cathinones are gaining popularity in the US among young adults, club goers, and other substance users despite the Federal Analogue Act of

---

13 MDMA is one of the most popular recreational psychoactives, most commonly sold in the form of "ecstasy" tablets. It is known for its empathogenic, euphoric, and stimulant effects, and has also been used in psychotherapy (ereowid.org)

1986. This federal law was designed to treat controlled substances that are intended for human consumption as a controlled substance in schedule I (deadiversion.usdoj.gov). It was passed in an attempt to prevent the use of "designer drugs" that are manufactured with small chemical changes in order to subvert existing regulatory laws against the use of other illegal drugs. The Federal Analogue Act, however, does not criminalize possession or manufacture of the designer substances, unless intended for human consumption (Prosser et al., 2011). This allows other hallucinogenic substances to be legal, regardless of whether they are actually intended for human consumption or not. In addition, bath salts are currently not regulated in many states, including California, Montana, Nevada, New Hampshire, Oregon, Vermont, and Washington, as well as Puerto Rico (NCSL, 2012; Prosser et al., 2011).

As mentioned earlier, bath salts are fully available on the Internet where they can be easily purchased with a quick search. Potential users can easily obtain product information and product reviews, and can purchase and have them delivered anywhere in the world. The online sellers accept PayPal, money orders and credit cards to make it easier for the potential drug users to order. This availability on the Internet can increase the drug abuse potential of young individuals, who spend comparably more time using the internet than previous generations. Also, even though law enforcement can detect bath salts trafficking through the Internet, it is practically impossible to punish the online dealers and buyers due to issues of cyber-jurisdiction[14].

Bath salts and other synthetic drugs are highly potent with high potential for abuse that should be regulated in all states in the U.S. The purpose of this study is to assess the potential risk of bath salts abuse via online drug marketplaces and the perception about bath salts among U.S. college students. This study suggests that increased federal regulation of the substances should prevent further abuse and online distribution of the substances. This study also aims to provide a better understanding of the substance to the drug users, educators, policy makers and health care professionals. The significance of this research is that little existing research has empirically assessed this new phenomenon.

---

14 General authority of a specific court to accept and resolve a dispute in cyberspace. (Choi, 2010)

THEORETICAL PERSPECTIVE

Routine Activities Theory (RAT) can be helpful in understanding the phenomenon of purchasing bath salts and other drugs online. RAT was developed by Cohen and Felson in 1979 and their work was concerned with three main tenets: motivated offenders, suitable targets, and the absence of capable guardians against a violation (Choi, 2010; Cohen and Felson, 1979; Cohen, Felson, and Land, 1980; Felson, 1986, 1988, Kennedy and Forde, 1990; Massey, Krohn, and Bonati, 1989; Miethe, Stafford, and Long, 1987; Roneck and Maier, 1991; Sherman, Gartin, and Buerger, 1989). The lack of any of the major tenets would likely prevent a crime occurrence (Choi, 2010; Cohen and Felson, 1979). Even though RAT was initially developed to explain crimes in the physical world, it can easily be applied to crimes in cyberspace, including the phenomenon being examined by the present study. An interesting concept is that physical space and cyberspace differ in that cyberspace is not limited to physical separation, distance, and proximity as it is in physical space (Choi, 2010; Yar, 2005). Castells (2002) provides an argument that may help to better understand the link between RAT, a physical world crime theory, and a crime theory that can be applied to cyberspace. The argument presented by Castells is that cyberspace is "real space" that is closely related to the real world. Internet users are able to view different websites everyday as a part of their routine activities (Choi, 2010). It is possible that Silk Road 2.0 subscribers visit the site and possibly other darknets that sell drugs on a daily basis as a part of their routine activities.

It was found that "unstructured peer interaction in the absence of authority figures" is positively related to deviance (Bernburg and Thorlindsson, 2001, pp. 546-547; Choi, 2010). Silk Road and other darknets would be good examples of places in cyberspace that would allow for unstructured peer interaction in the absence of authority figures where deviance could, and does, take place. Darknets enable unstructured interaction between tech-savvy individuals that could have deviant intentions.

The temporal structure of cyberspace is unique, as users are from around the world and the World Wide Web is not limited by time zones; thus, it is available anytime and to anyone (Choi, 2010; Yar, 2005). This is why it is nearly impossible to know the number of cyber criminals that are committing criminal acts at any time. RAT assumes that there will always be a likely or motivated offender looking for the opportunity to commit a crime (Choi, 2010). The fact that Ross Ulbricht's Silk Road had about a million registrants from all over the world, and that the Digital Citizens Alliance reportedly found that the number of drug listings actually increased on Silk Road after Ulbricht's arrest, support this assumption that there are always likely offenders waiting for the opportunity to commit crime (Hume, 2013; Mosk, 2014).

The World Wide Web provides users who want to commit cybercrimes with the advantage of a great amount of accessibility to targets or, in this case, commodities like bath salts for sale on darknets. The measurement of accessibility is the "ability of an offender to get to the target and then get away from the scene of the crime" (Choi, 2010; Felson, 1998, pp. 58). The sophistication of computer criminal techniques and anonymity in cyberspace improves the amount of accessibility, which increases the criminal's ability to get away in cyberspace (Choi, 2010). The IC3 2004 Internet Crime Report (2005) suggests that one of the largest issues in investigating and prosecuting cybercrime is that the victim and offender may physically be anywhere in the world (Choi, 2010).

There are three types of categories of guardianship: formal social control, informal social control, and target-hardening activities (Choi, 2010; Cohen, Kluegel, and Land, 1981). Formal social controls are that of the criminal justice system (Choi, 2010). The criminal justice system has stressed the need for innovative crime prevention strategies to combat new and existing cybercrimes. Despite the efforts of federal agencies in guiding law enforcement initiatives against cybercrimes, most state and local law enforcement officers are not adequately knowledgeable in the processing of digital data and other related evidence (Choi, 2010; Taylor, et al., 2006). The lack of resources, new technology and training within state and local agencies inhibit their ability to fight new types of cybercrimes (Choi, 2010; Hinduja, 2009). Although there are specialized forces charged with the duty to patrol cyberspace, these forces are limited and they have a difficult time building a strong formal guardianship online (Choi, 2010; Grabosky, 2000; Grabosky & Smith, 2001).

Technology is continuously developing, and with these developments come the opportunity for cybercriminals to conceal their identities by using different computer programs. This makes it hard to successfully identify suspects (Choi, 2010; Grabosky, 2000). Examples of this have been seen in the way users of darknets protect themselves when purchasing drugs. They will use anonymizing programs like Tor and virtual currencies like Bitcoin in an attempt to hide their identities. However, for some, this is not enough. They seek out the utilization of desk-top Bitcoin services and Bitcoin laundry services, and Ross Ulbricht admitted using Tumblers and Mixers to hide the identities of Silk Road users (Greenberg, 2013).

In the physical world, informal social guardians can come in the forms of friends, teachers, parents, and security personnel (Choi, 2010; Eck, 1995; Felson, 1986). However, informal social controls in cyberspace can be anyone from "private network administrators and systems security staff" to "ordinary online citizens" (Choi, 2010; Yar, 2005, pp. 423). As an administrator, Ulbricht had the capacity to be an informal guardian on Silk Road if he had wanted it to be a completely legitimate site, as it did offer some listings for legal goods, but did not exercise this capacity.

Legal Issues and Online Purchase

Synthesized cathinones have been around since the late 1920s and their abuse, particularly of mephedrone, has increased sharply in the UK since 2009 (Prosser et al., 2011). Since 2010, these synthetic drugs have spread quickly in the US (Spiller et al., 2011).

Even though the Federal Analogue Act of 1986 is intended to prevent the distribution of designer drugs, its vague language makes it difficult to enforce the regulation of bath salts. The law designates only substances designed for human consumption, while bath salts are marketed as "not intended for human consumption." As a result, manufacturers can produce such designer drugs legally. There needs to be strong federal regulation that clearly prohibits designer drugs such as bath salts. Without such regulation, enforcement is hampered. In addition, every state should pass legislation that prohibits the use, sale and distribution of these drugs since most drug enforcement occurs at the local and state levels. Without comprehensive state legislation pertaining to bath salts, illegal use of these drugs will potentially increase.

More importantly, there is a strong possibility of substantial growth in online recruitment for illegal drug abuse. According to the

2014 Global Drug Survey, which was based on 79,630 drug users from 43 countries, purchasing illegal drugs via the Internet is a growing phenomenon. The survey clearly confirmed that the percentage of people purchasing illegal drugs over the Internet is increasing in the U.K. and that many users purchase illegal drugs over the Internet due to its convenience, reasonable price, and a better product range. The survey also uncovered that around a third of drug users aged 18 to 25 admitted taking a "mysterious white powder," which appears to be synthetic drugs (The Guardian News, Sunday 13 April 2014).

A survey that asked the participants if they had ever bought drugs on the Internet was distributed to seventeen different countries, including the United Kingdom and the United States. The survey results have been broken down into two sample size categories, the first with 600-1,500 respondents and the second with over 1,500 respondents. Both the United Kingdom and the United States were in the second category. All of the countries that were included in the survey had an 11% "yes" response rate, which means that of everyone surveyed, 11% of them had purchased drugs on the Internet (Winstock, 2014). Of the seventeen countries included, the United Kingdom had the highest percentage of participants that had bought drugs on the Internet, with 22.1% of respondents having done so (Winstock, 2014). The results from the United States' responses were above the average of the whole sample, with 14.3% of participants from the United States having purchased drugs on the Internet (Winstock, 2014).

The same study was also concerned with the top 20 drugs used within the 12-month period before the survey was distributed. While the results do not reflect bath salts specifically, bath salts can be included under the drug category "MDMA" because Winstock (2014) uses MDMA to serve as a broad drug category that denotes all types and preparations of it. As discussed previously, bath salts are similar to MDMA. 23.4% of all respondents had used MDMA in the last 12 months; this was the fifth-most used drug in all, behind alcohol, tobacco, cannabis and caffeinated energy drinks (Winstock, 2014). This finding shows that MDMA is prevalent across the world.

In order to confirm the feasibility of the threat discussed above, we searched and examined randomly selected 100 existing websites that supply illicit drugs online. The following table presents the media content analysis about the availability of illegal drugs online and available purchasing methods.

Table 1 indicates that 36% (63 out of 174) of websites accept credit cards for payment. Interestingly, 10% (17 out of 174) of websites allow drug users to use the virtual currency Bitcoin to make transactions. Bank transfers (13%) and Western Union (11%) also allow drug users to wire money internationally for expanding their purchase. The websites can be easily accessed via any web browser, and their advertisements introduce their products as herbal incense spice or a herbal blend and assert that they are legal products.

Table 1: Purchasing Illegal Drugs via Websites

	Major Type of Drugs Available Online			
Purchase Methods*	Bath Salts (18 Websites)	Ecstasy (4 Websites)	Research Chemical (61 Websites)	Legal High (17 Websites)
Credit Card	15	3	35	10
Western Union	7	0	12	0
Money Gram	7	0	12	0
PayPal	1	0	7	1
Bitcoin	1	2	14	0
Money Order	1	0	1	7
Bank Transfer	1	0	13	9
Inquiry Only	1	1	11	2
Total	34	6	105	29

*Note that multiple payment methods were applied per website.

From the website content analysis, it is also reasonable to assume that new and more clandestine forms of illegal online drug industries will continue to emerge, and drug users are likely to switch their main purchasing methods from street dealers to online purchase in the near future. When a drug user is free to access and use the substance with impunity, there will be a high level of abuse. When the drug produces effects comparable to other illegal substances, a potential abuser will tend to favor the drug without any legal repercussions. It is a logical employment of these theories that informs us regarding how bath salts will be used and abused.

We now turn our attention to the U.S. college population. The current study is particularly interested in learning how U.S. college students perceive the use of synthetic drugs, bath salts, and their willingness to switch purchasing methods from the traditional way to online purchase, which will be analyzed using a self-reported survey.

METHODOLOGY

To study how the negative associations with bath salts, legal status, and availability impact the current and possible future usage of the drug, an anonymous and entirely voluntary online survey was conducted among the students, faculty members, and staff at a state university located in Massachusetts, USA. After the International Review Board's approval, the survey invitation was sent to school email accounts, and each recipient was allowed to decide whether or not to participate in the online survey at any time during the survey period from December 6th, 2012 to January 22nd, 2013. The informed consent form was on the first page of the survey so that only the individuals who consented were able to proceed with the survey. The participants who declined to consent were withdrawn automatically before the survey began. The participants were permitted to withdraw from the survey at any time.

The survey asked a series of questions regarding demographic factors, previous/current experience with substances such as tobacco cigarettes, marijuana, ecstasy and bath salts, and their preferred purchase method. For the clarity of the study, the term ecstasy includes all street drugs named as ecstasy regardless of its chemical compounds, since the chemical composition of ecstasy in the drug market varies greatly. Bath salts are limited to the products that are sold as "bath salts" with the label "not intended for human consumption".

Only responses from the students (both undergraduate and graduate students) were analyzed using paired t tests, for comparison to another research study that was conducted in the UK. All the responses from the faculty members and staff were discarded to match the UK samples.

BATH SALTS USAGE IN TAYSIDE AREA OF SCOTLAND

The bath salts usage report that was conducted among the students in Tayside, Scotland by the Tayside Police Force Information and Intelligence Analyst Unit was used to analyze and compare the bath salts abusers' age, purchase preference and usage frequency. In that study, 1,006 students at five Scottish secondary schools, three colleges, and two universities participated in a voluntary anonymous survey. 20.3% (205) of them reported they had used mephedrone on at least one occasion. Among mephedrone users, 48.8% of them purchased the drug from the local drug dealer, and 10.7% (among the student in the age group 13-15) of them bought mephodrone from the Internet. However, sourcing of mephedrone from the Internet increased to 30.8% as the age of the user increased (24 years old). Approximately 97.9% of the participants answered that the drug was very easy to obtain, and their reasons for using bath salts were their legal status and accessibility (Wood et al., 2011).

THE STUDY RESULTS

This study measured how the negativity of bath salts, legal status, and availability has an impact on current and possible future usage of the drug. A total of 413 people participated in this study. The sample was composed of 64.4% undergraduate students (n=266), 12.6% graduate students (n=52), 12.6% faculty members (n=52), 9% staff (37) and 1.5% others. The responses from the students, both undergraduate and graduate students (n=318), were used to compare to the Tayside study.

Among 318 students at a state university in MA, 56.92% (n=181) have had experience with marijuana, and 12.89% (n=41) of them have used ecstasy, and only 0.31% (n=1) of students have tried bath salts at least once for a recreational purpose (Figure 11-1).

The most preferred purchase method among marijuana, ecstasy and bath salt users was via a local drug dealer. The percentage of the students who obtained the drug via the Internet was the lowest, after gas stations and adult shops (Figure 11-2).

The preferred purchase method among US and UK students was via the local drug dealer. While 30.8% of students in the UK had bought bath salts online, none of the US students had purchased the drug online (Figure 11-3).

Figure 11-1. The percentages of students that had experience with each of the three substances.

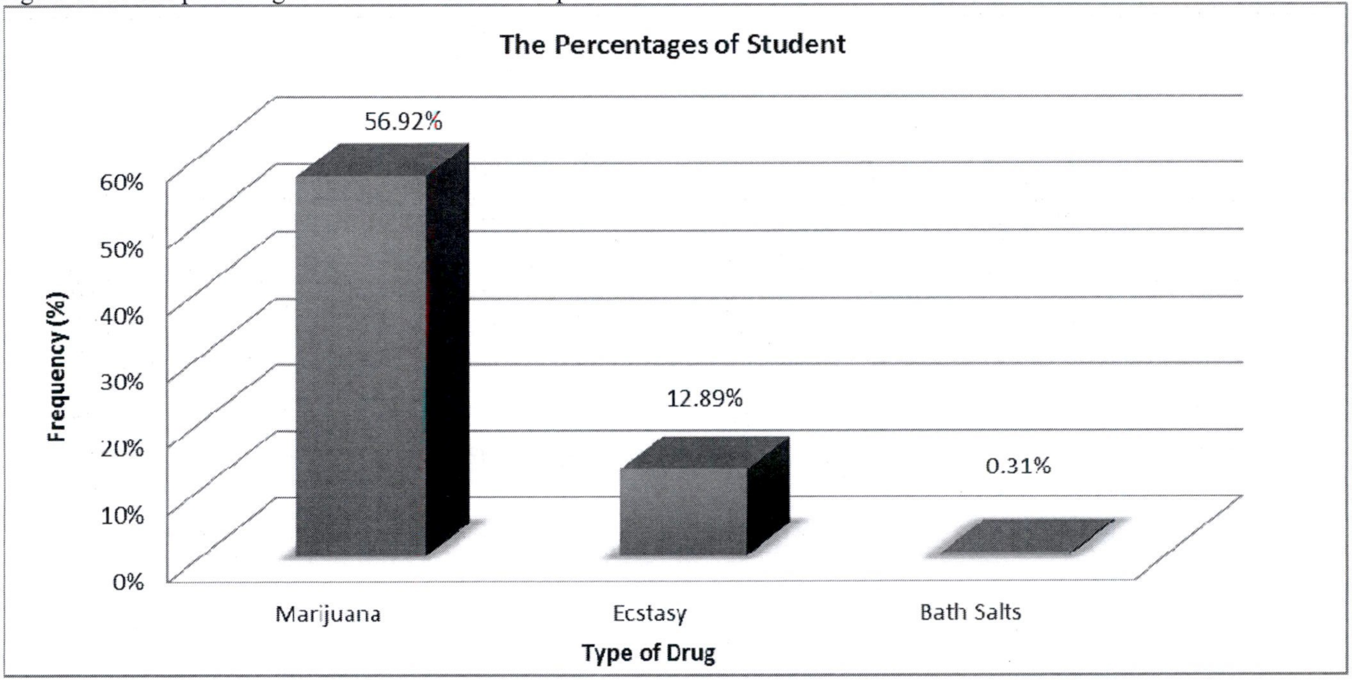

Figure 11-2. The preferred purchase method of US Students.

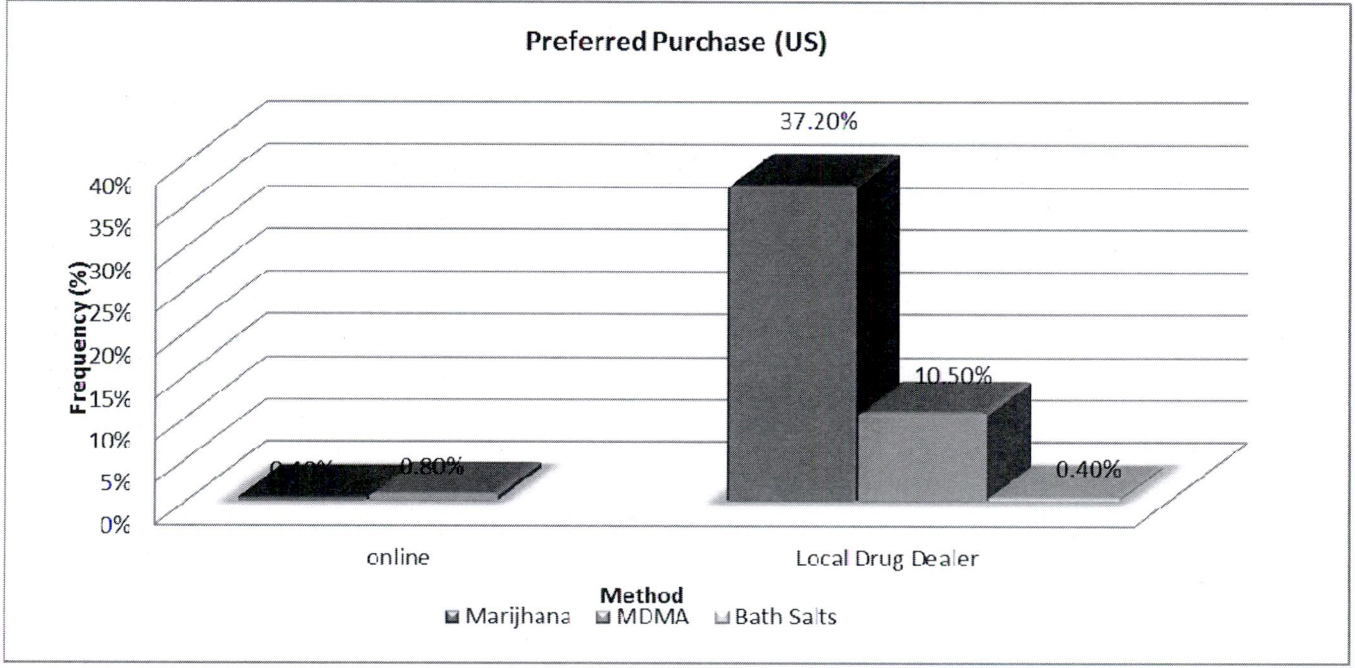

Figure 11-3. Preferred bath salts purchase methods difference between students in the US and UK

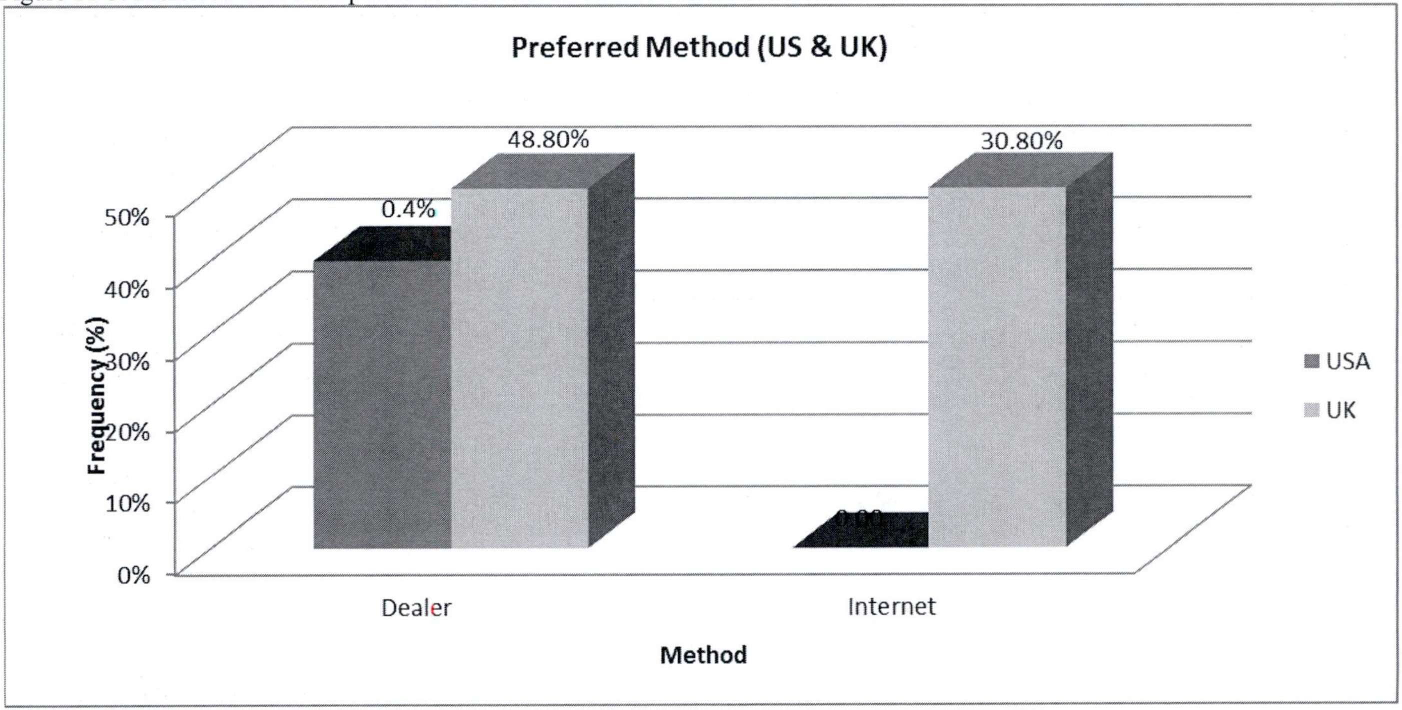

Figure 11-4. Future purchase methods of US students

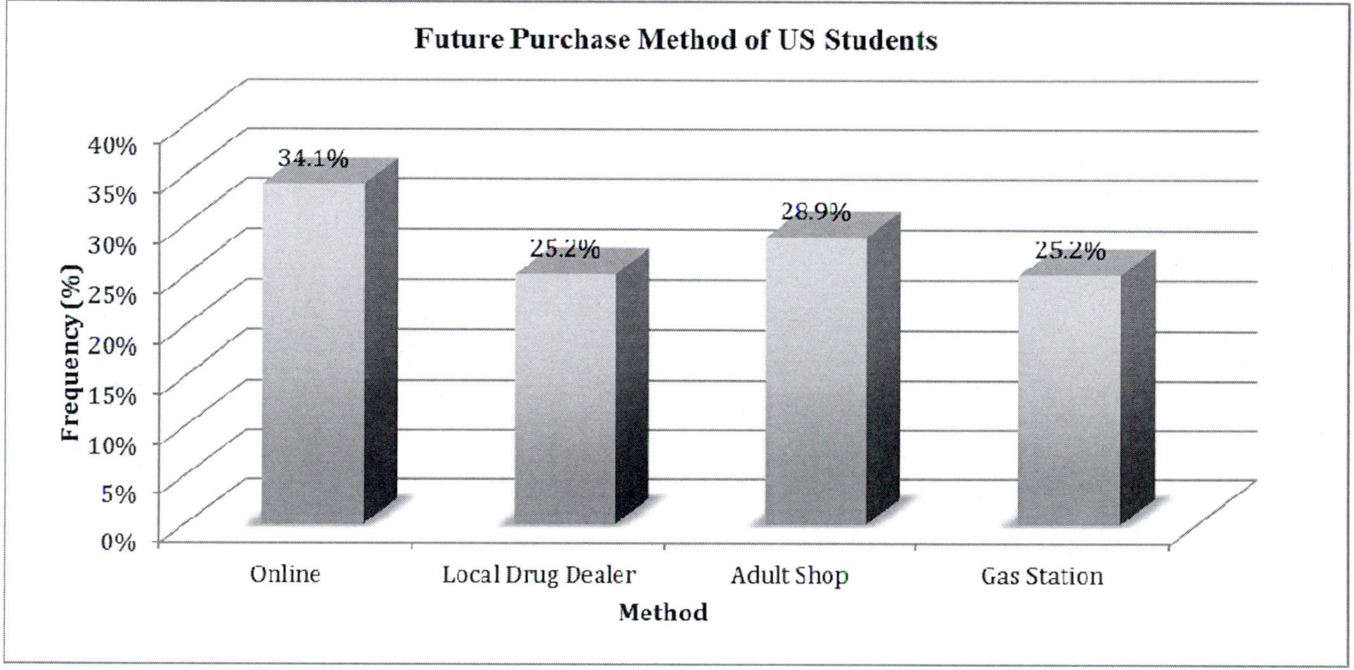

A case study was presented by Topping and Hern (2014) in which they discussed buying recreational drugs online with a 21-year-old student from Oxford University in London. In the interview, the student discloses that he started buying drugs online because it seemed safer, easier, and more reliable when compared to purchasing drugs on the street. He praises Silk Road as a source that provides reliable drugs (Topping and Hern, 2014).

It was interesting that Topping and Hern's participant reported that he felt safe when buying drugs off of Silk Road. By taking a Routine Activities Theory (RAT) point of view, one could wonder if the participant's perception of safety is false because he could potentially be putting himself at risk of identity theft or other cybercrimes by interacting the darknet world.

However, as the population in the UK showed an increased tendency of buying the drug via online, 34.1% (n=46) of the survey participants in the US were also willing to purchase bath salts via the Internet and adult shops (Figure 11-4). Winstock's (2014) research found that 14.3% of his respondents had actually purchased drugs online.

An aim of the present study was to see how the legal status of bath salts and its accessibility via the Internet impacted the increasing rate of the substance's abuse, and to see the students' perception of the drug. Even though the current preferred method to purchase bath salts is via a local drug dealer, the participants were willing to acquire bath salts via the Internet. As in the 2010 UK study, which stated an increasing rate of buying bath salts online among the substance users, the US drug users may also switch their purchase method from the traditional method to the Internet method as well.

BITCOIN AND THE DARKNET

As previously discussed in the payment methods analysis section, Bitcoin has been widely used among darknet market places. Ross Ulbricht gave credit to Bitcoin as the major factor in making his business possible. However, Bitcoin is not as private as one may think. Every Bitcoin transaction that happens in the payment network is recorded in the "blockchain." The blockchain is Bitcoin's way of keeping tabs on who has what coins and when so that they can try to combat counterfeiting and fraud. The transactions are recorded as addresses that are not really tied to someone's identity; the lack of being tied to a specific identity is the appeal for those that wish to use the currency for anonymous and illegitimate exchanges (Greenberg, 2013).

Ulbricht once disclosed to Andy Greenberg (2013) that his darknet site, Silk Road, increased the anonymity for its users by utilizing an internal tumbler for when sellers take their payments and a general mix for all withdrawals and deposits. He claimed that this made it impossible to link withdrawals and deposits and ensured difficulty in being able to see that an individual's withdrawal came from Silk Road. Sarah Meiklejohn, a computer science researcher at the University of California at San Diego, along with her colleagues from UCSD and George Mason University have conducted work that points to flaws in Ulbricht's claims of darknets' abilities in providing definite anonymity to users (Greenberg, 2013).

Meiklejohn and her colleagues have discovered a possible way to remove the anonymity factor in using Bitcoin. Meiklejohn and her colleagues found that looking into the blockchain can usually show who owns which Bitcoin addresses. The researchers used "clustering" methods and capitalized on clues in how bitcoins are usually grouped or segregated to identify thousands of addresses based on a few transaction tests they conducted. Based on data from 344 of their own transactions, the researchers were able to uncover the owners of over one million Bitcoin addresses (Greenberg, 2013). Meiklejohn also reported that by making 4 deposits and 7 withdrawals, she and her fellow researchers were able to identify 295,435 addresses belonging to the specific drug market (Greenberg, 2013).

Greenberg and some of his colleagues at Forbes conducted an experiment in which they purchased small amounts of marijuana from three different Bitcoin-based darknets to then have Meiklejohn see if she could trace their transactions. Greenberg provided Meiklejohn with their Bitcoin addresses in their account on Coinbase, a popular Bitcoin wallet service. He did this because, theoretically, the information he provided to her could be available to law enforcement by giving Coinbase a subpoena. With the information about the addresses, Meiklejohn was able to trace all of the transactions made by Greenberg and his colleagues, including those with Silk Road and two other markets similar to Silk Road, "Black Market Reloaded" and "Atlantis" (Greenberg, 2013).

Before an individual can use Bitcoins as currency in exchanges on darknets like Silk Road, the Bitcoins have to be deposited in the individual's account on the site. Meiklejohn was able to track down Greenberg's deposit to his account through a process by which she tied the deposit address provided to her with about 200 other addresses. Some of the 200 other addresses were discovered to be connected to Silk Road through her clustering analysis. Greenberg reported that after he had sent 0.3 Bitcoins to the Silk Road deposit address, the blockchain showed that his Bitcoins, along with little amounts of Bitcoins from the other addresses, which included the known Silk Road addresses, were grouped together in an account of 40 Bitcoin. Meiklejohn stated that this shows that whoever had control of the deposit address Greenberg used most likely had control of Silk Road addresses as well; this means that Greenberg's previous transaction could be proven to be a Silk Road deposit (Greenberg, 2013).

There are some limitations to the methods used in the experiment conducted by Meiklejohn and her colleagues. Coinbase and other similar Bitcoin services are able to be subpoenaed and may be able to connect Bitcoins to users' addresses and real names, meaning that a law enforcement agent looking into a similar case to that of the one Meiklejohn was using in her experiment would have access to the information that Meiklejohn was granted to have a starting place for her efforts. This being said, there are some alternatives to Coinbase and similar services that would not make it so easy on law enforcement investigations. An individual could send their Bitcoin purchases through other addresses that have been generated through the use of desktop-based wallet software. There are even Bitcoin laundry services, like Bitmax, Bitlaundry, and Bitcoinlaundry, which an individual can send their Bitcoins through that make tracking the transactions extremely difficult (Greenberg, 2013).

Meiklejohn and her team of researchers' work has provided some interesting and possibly highly effective ways in which Bitcoin can be used to ensure that anonymity is taken away from individuals. Meiklejohn's methods of tracing transactions and uncovering user identities in Bitcoin purchases need to be implemented in Law Enforcement methods in taking down darknet users that buy and sell illegal goods, like bath salts. In order to get around the limitations of Meiklejohn and her colleagues' work, more attention and research needs to be provided to similar forensic methods in regulating the sales and purchases of bath salts, and other drugs, through the use of the Internet.

TRANSNATIONAL EFFORTS OF THE UNODC)

Transnational coordinated responses are necessary in dealing with transnational organized crime, as seen with Silk Road. A transnational coordinated response is imperative to making sure that the crime networks do not just move their activities into countries that have weak cooperation and criminal justice responses, which could be an explanation for the rise of Silk Road 2.0 immediately following the shutdown of the original Silk Road by the Federal Bureau of Investigations (UNODC, 2014).

As previously discussed, the UNODC attempts to help law enforcement gain the knowledge and tools necessary in successfully regulating cybercrime at an international level. The UNODC does this by perpetually creating new tools to aid international cooperation in dealing with international organized crime. The UNODC has developed manuals, a mutual legal assistance request writer tool, an online directory of national authorities, a legal database, and best practices case law. The UNODC works with States parties to the Organized Crime Convention to help responses and prevention methods of organized crime across and between borders (UNODC, 2014).

The UNODC provides help to countries by working with their governments in designing specific intervention strategies. They do this by performing a technical needs assessment of the country, in which they consider existing strategies of national authorities, the legal system, operational procedures, existing approaches to interagency involvement, regional cooperation, human and technical resources, and cultural and political contexts. Upon specific requests, the UNODC)will also help countries take effective steps against or in prevention of organized crime in accordance with the United Nations Convention Against Transnational Organized Crime and the Protocols Thereto (UNTOC). The UNODC has aided in implementing the UNTOC in Central America, Asia, Africa, Latin America, and Europe (UNODC, 2014).

The development of technical assistance tools is a major factor in the UNODC's ability to help countries go against organized crime. In order to create effective tools, the UNODC utilizes experts with a diverse range of experience. The UNODC aims to produce tools that reflect perspectives that are diverse and come from common and civil law and from low and high resource countries. The Conference of Parties to the Organized Crime Convention instructed the UNODC to create practical assistance tools. The tools that the UNODC created included training manuals, handbooks, model laws, international cooperation tools, issue papers, digests of relevant case law and legal commentaries, and other materials that seek to enhance the ability of countries to implement and use the convention and its protocols (UNODC, 2014).

Discussion, Policy Implications and Call for Future Research

It is essential to address the importance of comprehensive and strict regulations on hallucinogenic drugs due to the risks of drug trafficking on the Internet. In this study, possible changes in the drug-sourcing trend from the physical world to cyber space were detected. In reality, drug trafficking via the Internet is occurring in many countries, even in the nations that have been considered to be "drug free zones." South Korea, for example, has been mostly immune to narcotic trafficking and abuse because of its extensive drug policy. However, in the last few years, the number of incidents of drug trafficking using the Internet has sharply increased. Attempts to smuggle narcotics such as marijuana and other drugs through international delivery services rose by 37% in number and 600% in value since 2012 (*The Korean Herald*, 2013). In circumstances where narcotics (both illegal and designer drugs) are freely traded internationally via the Internet, the US government and all the states also should be prepared to effectively regulate further online drug trafficking.

In terms of the essential formal capable guardianship perspective, law enforcement agencies need to be properly and adequately trained in how to successfully handle cases related to buying drugs like bath salts off of the Internet through darknets. Again, we come back to Silk Road; even though Ross Ulbricht had been arrested by law enforcement and Silk Road was shut down, others rose up after him to create Silk Road 2.0, which bounced back and became bigger than before. This proved just how resilient darknets that sell bath salts could be, even in the face of law enforcement. This resiliency could be due, in part, to the anonymity that the Internet and Bitcoin provide.

Chapter 12 - Formal Guardianship in the Social Control of Cybercrime

Earlier we covered the concept of capable guardianship in Routine Activities Theory. As a recap, guardianship can be defined in three categories: formal social control, informal social control, and target-hardening activities. I stress that target-hardening activities using computer security (digital guardian) is the key factor in minimizing computer-crime victimization.

This chapter will discuss formal social control. In both the physical world and in cyberspace, formal social control agents play important roles in reducing crime. However, formal social control has a relatively low impact on cybercriminal activities. Other than jurisdictional and technical issues, there is a more important issue in cyberspace—the public tends to view their cyber-activities as civil rather than criminal infractions. This public perception allows cybercriminals to escape control, processing, sanctioning, and criminal labeling.

Formal social controls simply mean our criminal justice system. They are the police, the courts, and the correctional system. In order to manage cybercrime, strengthening formal control agents is critical because they affect virtually every aspect of administering criminal justice and facilitate setting rules and regulations regarding information systems in cyberspace. In addition, formal social control process provides the enforcement that is necessary when cyber behaviors have been violated. Thus, it is important to know how laws and regulations can apply to cyberspace as one of our formal control agents.

This chapter briefly introduces various cyber laws. I personally believe that one of the most important areas is laws associated with intellectual property in cyberspace, because so many people download books, documents, music, movies, or programs without considering cyber laws and regulations. They may claim that "everyone is doing it," or "I did not know these activities are illegal," but although their actions were unintended, negative consequences can always happen; it is extremely important not to overlook our online behaviors.

INTELLECTUAL PROPERTY

Intellectual Property (IP) law is the branch of civil law that makes all innovation possible, and as you can probably imagine has very important implications for computing, information security, and cybercrime.

- Copyrights, trademarks, and patents/trade secrets are specific types of IP, each protected by federal laws that are grounded in legal rights established by the U.S. Constitution.
- Patent and copyright protections are specifically addressed in Article 1, Section 8 of the Constitution, which says that Congress has the power to promote the progress of science and the useful arts, by securing for limited times to authors and inventors the exclusive right to their respective writings and discoveries.

There are three types of Intellectual Property Law Protections:

1. Trademark
   Any word, name, symbol, color, sound, product shape, device, or combination of those used to identify goods and distinguish them from those made or sold by competitors.
2. Copyright
   Original works of authorship; the expression of ideas rather than the ideas themselves.
3. Patent/Trade Secret
   A legally enforceable right to exclude others from using an invention: confidential proprietary business or technical information that is protected as long as the owner takes certain security actions.

COPYRIGHT LAW

The Computer Software Act of 1980, the Semi-conductor Chip Protection Act of 1992, the No Electronic Theft Act of 1997, and the Digital Millennium Copyright Act of 1998 have all amended the primary copyright law passed in 1976 to address the potential for innovations in IT to facilitate copyright infringement (Clifford, 2011).

Collectively these laws make it illegal to use computers or other devices to copy original or reproduced works of authorship such as literature, illustrations, diagrams, photographs, musical or dramatic works, sculpture, motion pictures or other audiovisual works, architectural works, software, and so on. The laws also make it illegal to distribute these, or other expressions fixed in a tangible form, without the expressed permission of the legal copyright holders.

Digital Millennium Copyright Act of 1998 (DMCA) makes it illegal to manufacture, distribute, or sell technology that enables circumvention of copyright protections. However, the fair use doctrine provides narrow exceptions for legally reproducing copyrighted works without paying royalty fees to authors, artists, or their publishers.

In determining fair use, the law requires courts to consider:

- Why the material was copied and whether copying involved commercial motives,
- The nature of the works copied,
- The amount and proportion of materials copied, and
- The effect that copying the material had on its commercial value.

It is important to note that because courts decide fair use on a case-by-case basis, anything you copy that does not qualify as one of these exceptions may be construed as a violation of federal copyright law (Clifford, 2011).

FEDERAL LAWS AGAINST CYBERCRIME

Due to the multi-jurisdictional nature of the Internet, federal regulatory agencies enforce major cybercrime cases—such as potential computer abuse, cybercrime violations, and information security issues—and coordinate investigations with law enforcement agencies in cases involving suspected violations of regulations and crime laws.

Formal Control Agents: Government Regulations

1. **Securities and Exchange Commission (SEC)**
   - Established in 1929.
   - Was charged with the mission to prevent misrepresentation in corporate financial statements and in the sale and exchange of securities.
   - Regulates the procedures for the solicitation of proxies, enforces restrictions on insider trading, and oversees many aspects of security transactions.

2. **Federal Communications Commission (FCC)**
   - Established in 1934.
   - The FCC regulates interstate and international communications by radio, television, wire, satellite, and cable. As such, the commission is concerned with obscene, fraudulent, or other illegal or inappropriate broadcasts and communications carried out over the nation's IT communications network.
   - The FCC is a key regulatory agency for the prevention and control of cybercrimes.

3. **Federal Trade Commission (FTC)**
   - Established in 1903.
   - Over several decades, the mission of the FTC evolved to become among the most important bodies in the federal government for combating cybercrime.
   - This is accomplished through promotion of information security standards, spamming and identity theft fraud investigations, and regulatory oversight of corporations with regard to fair market practices.

4. **Federal Deposit Insurance Corporation (FDIC)**
   - Established in 1933.
   - The FDIC is very interested in scrutinizing financial institution rating systems, lending practices, and the veracity of financial information systems' security standards and practices.

- Since a substantial number of cybercrimes are also financial crimes and/or involve attacks on financial institutions, the FDIC is another key agency involved in protecting the country from cybercriminals.

5. **Federal Aviation Administration (FAA)**
   - Established in 1958.
   - Issues and enforces regulations and minimum standards covering manufacturing, operating, and maintaining aircraft and certifies pilots and airports that serve air carriers.
   - The FAA is very concerned with the security of information systems for controlling civilian, commercial, and military aircraft—all vital to the nation's critical infrastructure.

It is important to review key federal cybercrime laws and crime sanctions in order to understand the formal social control process in cyberspace (McQuade, 2006).

Please keep in mind the four primary purposes of federal laws based on preventing and controlling cyber-crime:

1. Protect individual privacy and provide access to government information
2. Secure federal government information and information services
3. Ensure national critical infrastructure availability and reliability
4. Define IT-enabled abuse and crime

HACKING & INTERNET FRAUD CATEGORY

The Computer Fraud Abuse Acts of 1986 (CFAA) prohibits unauthorized accessing of federal government computers or financial institutions that contain financial or credit data. The National Information Infrastructure Protection Act of 1996 included all "protected computers" connected to the Internet. The CFAA remains among the most important, evolving, and expansive federal anti-cybercrime statutes.

Hacking: Sanctions

Hacking into a computer system of a university funded by federal research grants is a felony under the CFFA—punishable by up to 20 years imprisonment.

The Mail, Bank, and Wire Fraud Acts

A close read of the statute (codified at U.S.C. Title 18, Section 1342) reveals that the Mail Fraud Act was the forerunner to federal prohibitions against identity theft, and, as amended, prohibits computer and telecommunications-enabled frauds involving delivery of goods via delivery services. The statute also prohibits transmitting an electronic signal, such as writings, signs, signals, pictures, or sounds in order to obtain money or property under false or fraudulent pretenses (Clifford, 2011).

The Mail, Bank, and Wire Fraud Acts: Sanction

Violators of this law are subject to fines and/or imprisonment not exceeding 20 years' incarceration.

Bank Fraud: Sanctions

A person has to knowingly execute, or attempt to execute, a scheme or document that results in defrauding a financial institution or obtaining money, funds, credit, assets, securities, or other property owned by, or under the custody or control of, a financial institution, by means of false or fraudulent pretenses, representations, or promises.

A person convicted of federal bank fraud may be fined up to $1 million, imprisoned up to 30 years, or both (Clifford, 2011).

COPYRIGHT CATEGORY

The No Electronic Theft Act of 1997 authorized imposition of criminal fines and incarceration for people convicted of intentionally distributing copyrighted works over the Internet. The NET Act legislation includes people (e.g., file sharers) who do not profit from unauthorized distribution of codes.

Copyright Law: Sanctions

Federal criminal penalties for violating copyright for altruistic purposes, as opposed to financial gain, were first authorized in the No Electronic Theft Act of 1997. Under this law, a violator may receive 5 years' imprisonment and be fined up to $250,000.

Criminal provisions for copyright violations involving intent to gain financially are codified in U.S.C. Title 17, Section 1204. Violators are subject to 5 years' imprisonment and a $500,000 fine for a first offense, up to 10 years in prison and a $1 million fine for additional offenses (Clifford, 2011).

ID THEFT CATEGORY

The Identity Theft and Assumption Deterrence Act of 1998 makes it illegal to create, transfer, possess, or use either a fake or someone else's real identification to commit, promote, carry out, or facilitate a crime involving the acquisition of money, property, or credit under an assumed name.

ID Theft: Sanctions

Persons convicted of identity theft or conspiracy to commit identity theft may be imprisoned for up to 20 years.

SPAM CATEGORY

The Controlling Assault of Non-Solicited Pornography and Marketing (CAN-SPAM) Act of 2003 represents the first U.S. national standard for the sending of commercial email, and requires the Federal Trade Commission (FTC)) to enforce its provisions (McQuade, 2006).

Spam: Sanctions

On December 18, 2004, U.S. District Judge Charles R. Wolle awarded a $1 billion judgment to Robert Kramer of Davenport, Iowa, for losses associated with 300 companies alleged to have sent 10 million spam messages per day per ISP customer—enough to make most people discontinue processing email.

Kramer's suit alleged violations of Iowa's Ongoing Criminal Conduct Act, which allows for damages of $10 per unsolicited spam message, and the federal Racketeer Influenced and Corruption Organizations (RICO) Act, which provides for triple damages (NBC News, 2004).

ONLINE CHILD PORNOGRAPHY CATEGORY

Communications Decency Act of 1996 (CDA) and Child Online Protection Act of 1998 (COPA) ban sexually explicit materials from online sites where children could easily find it.

Child Pornography: Sanctions

Anyone who distributes online obscene and potentially harmful content to minors could face a $50,000 fine and six months imprisonment.

Discussion 1:
A nationally known public figure who resides in Virginia sues a nonresident for defamation as a result of statements the defendant made on his Web site at a URL bearing the plaintiff's name. The defendant challenged the jurisdiction of the Virginia court, stating that he did not specifically target Virginia Web surfers. Using the Zippo standard, who will prevail? See Jerry L. Falwell v. Gary Cohn and God, Info Civ, Act. No 6:02CV0040 (W.D. Va. March 4, 2003).

Discussion 2:
Is it possible for the United States or any other country to completely follow the Council of Europe Cybercrime Agreement pertaining to the investigation of computer crime? Why or why not? Explain what changes would have to be made in order for the international standards to be met. Give specific examples from U.S. laws that meet standards set in the Council of Europe agreement.

PART VI

Digital Evidence, Criminal Procedure, and Forensic Investigation

The rapid transition from manual records to computer records in the business world is causing a major impact on the way law enforcement officers do their jobs. More and more computers are being discovered and seized during the execution of search warrants; however, most law enforcement officers lack knowledge concerning the processing of computer data and related evidence.

Besides the obvious use of computers for Internet fraud purposes, criminals use computers to store data relating to drug deals, money laundering, embezzlement, mail fraud, extortion, and a variety of other crimes. In addition to the simple storage of records, criminals also manipulate data, infiltrate private computers belonging to others, and illegally use telephone lines. In order to address the legitimate need for access to computers and the information they contain, law enforcement must develop an organized approach to examine investigative and intelligence information, and at the same time preserve the information for subsequent admission in court.

It is essential that experienced law enforcement officers, knowledgeable in the rules of evidence, preserve and process the evidence because proper documentation and expert testimony is necessary to effectively deal with the seizure and processing of computer-related evidence. For this reason, it is important that law enforcement officers become trained in this new forensic science. Many times the specialist must be present during the first moments of the raid. If a criminal has installed destructive programs or taken other defensive measures, only a trained person can recognize, defeat and document these extraordinary measures without destroying evidence.

Part VI introduces the general criminal procedure regarding the search and seizure of digital evidence. Additionally, specific computer crime investigative steps will be discussed using a sample of an actual computer crime case.

Chapter 13 - Principles of Digital Evidence: Search and Seizure Digital Evidence

Digital Evidence: the term was used by SWGDE (Scientific Working Group on Digital Evidence) and IOCE (International Organization on Computer Evidence) in October of 1999. Digital evidence is information and data of investigative value that is stored on or transmitted by an electronic device in binary form. Such evidence is acquired when information and/or physical items are collected or stored for examination purposes. The term evidence implies that the collector of evidence is recognized by the courts. The process of collecting is also assumed to be a legal process and should be appropriate for rules of evidence in that locality.

According to Casey (2000), the term "digital evidence" includes "any and all digital data that can establish that a crime has been committed or can provide a link between a crime and its victim or a crime and its perpetrator" (p. 1). Digital data is essentially a combination of numbers that represent information of various kinds, encompassing text, images, audio, and video. With the increasing use of technology and the Internet, digital evidence is becoming more substantial and important to investigative efforts.

Digital evidence is digital information that can prove the relationship between the crime itself and the suspect/victim. Data in the storage media, including hard drive or USB media, temporarily maintained information in the computer memory, data transferred through a network, and so on, are all included as digital evidence.

Digital evidence is invisible to the naked eye. It is easily modified and fragile and the original cannot be distinguished from the duplicated one. Digital evidence has massive material and various formats. It is transferred through wired or wireless networks.

There are many kinds of digital evidence found on the crime scene. The most conventional digital evidence is the computer system. Computer systems include; personal computers, web servers, messenger servers, game servers, file servers, database servers, and email servers. As we already know, a server is the computer system that provides a service to the client responding to the request from the client. The service includes; email, web, database, games, and so on.

Data storage includes the hard disk drive, the floppy disk, the compact disk, the digital versatile disk, the zip drive, the tape drive, the USB storage (also known as a "Flash Drive" or "Thumb Drive"), and the memory stick. These data storages could be found all around the crime scene and are very reliable sources of crime evidence.

Network devices include the router, the switch, the firewall, the intrusion detection system, and the intrusion protection system. Each network device may maintain login records or the network traffic and these are most valuable resources for the cybercrime investigation. With the advance of technology, new digital devices have been manufactured including cell phones, personal digital assistants, global positioning systems, MP3 players, portable media players, closed circuit television, and digital camcorders that are compatible with network devices. These devices use digital information in the data process so that we should fully understand what the digital media is like, how the data processes, and where we can find the exact information in them. Closed circuit television, also known as CCTV, also has the digital media to record and play the scene.

Carter (1995) proposed the following criminal justice cybercrime categories.

- C1. The computer as the target (e.g., computer intrusion, data theft, techno-vandalism, techno-trespass).
- C2. The computer as the instrumentality of the crime (e.g., credit card fraud, telecommunications fraud, theft, or fraud).
- C3. The computer as incidental to other crimes (e.g., drug trafficking, money laundering, child pornography).

C4. Crimes associated with the prevalence of computers (e.g., copyright violation, software piracy, component theft).

The United States Federal Guidelines for Searching and Seizing Computers (DOJ 1994) contains a solid set of guidelines and cybercrime categories. In this context, hardware refers to all of the physical components of a computer and information refers to the data and programs that are stored or transmitted while using a computer. The final three categories that refer to information fall under the forms of digital evidence.

1. Hardware as contraband or fruits of crime
2. Hardware as an instrumentality
3. Hardware as evidence
4. Information as contraband or fruits of crime
5. Information as an instrumentality
6. Information as evidence.

It is important to note that each of the categories has unique legal procedures that must be followed. In most cases, a warrant is required to search and seize evidence, but there are exceptions such as consent, exigency, and evidence in plain view. However, in some situations, privacy laws might protect the evidence.

HARDWARE

Hardware as Contraband or Fruits of Crime

The fruits of crime include property that was obtained by criminal activity, such as computer equipment that was stolen or purchased using stolen credit card numbers.

The main reason for seizing contraband or fruits of crime is to prevent and deter future crimes. When law enforcement officers decide to seize evidence in this category, a court will examine whether the circumstances would have led a reasonably cautious agent to believe that the object was contraband or a fruit of crime.

Hardware as an Instrumentality

Hardware as an instrumentality applies when computer hardware has played a significant role in a crime. For example, computer crackers often use hardware type sniffers to collect passwords that can then be used to gain unauthorized access to computers. Since the cracker utilizes a computer hardware that is specially manufactured or configured to commit a specific crime, it is considered to be an instrumentality.

When deciding whether or not a piece of hardware can be seized as an instrumentality of crime, it is important to note that "significant" is the operative word in the definition of instrumentality (Casey, 2000).

It is ultimately up to the courts to decide whether or not an item played a significant role in a given crime. So far, the courts have been quite liberal on this issue. For example, according to the Eastern District Court of Virginia, a computer with related accessories was an instrumentality because it contained a file that detailed the growing characteristics of marijuana plants (Casey, 2000).

Hardware as Evidence

The Federal Rule of Criminal Procedure 41(b) commands officials to "search for and seize any property that constitutes evidence of the commission of a criminal offense."

This category of hardware as evidence is necessary to cover computer hardware that is neither contraband nor the instrumentality of a crime. For example, if a scanner that is used to digitize child pornography has unique scanning characteristics that link the hardware to the digitized images, it could be seized as evidence (Casey, 2000).

INFORMATION

Information as Contraband of Fruits of Crime

Contraband information refers to information that the private citizen is not permitted to possess. A common form of information as contraband is encryption software. If a criminal is caught, but all of the incriminating digital evidence is encrypted, it might not be possible to decode the evidence and prosecute the criminal. Information as fruits of crime includes illegal copies of computer programs, stolen trade secrets and passwords, and any other information that was obtained by criminal means.

Information as an Instrumentality

Programs that computer crackers use to break into computer systems are the instrumentality of a crime. Computer programs that record passwords when a person logs into a computer can be an instrumentality and computer programs that crack passwords often play a significant role in a crime.

Information as Evidence

This is the richest category of all. Many of our daily actions leave a trail of digits. All service providers—such as telephone companies, ISPs, banks, and credit card companies—keep some information about their customers. For example, the U.S. Computer Assistance Law Enforcement Act, which took effect in 2000, compels telephone companies to keep detailed records of their customers' calls for an indefinite period of time.

If a suspect used encrypted email to communicate with another individual around the time a crime was committed, this might be considered sufficient probable cause to obtain a warrant to examine the email, or even search the second person's computer or residence.

In other words, our daily activities that are linked to any digital form (information) can be considered as evidence.

Understanding Digital Forensic Investigation

Criminal investigation is defined as "the process of legally gathering evidence of a crime that has been or is being committed" (Brown 2001, 3). The way evidence is gathered and processed in cybercrime cases is relatively similar to other criminal cases except the investigators need to confront the bulk of the actual evidence in electronic or digital format.

The cybercrime investigation can still be assimilated into a sound report for prosecution. The way in which a case is investigated is heavily influenced by the composition of the investigation team. In other words, cybercrime investigations use the same principles as traditional criminal investigations that do not deal with digital evidence.

Prior to the discussion of the forensic process, it is important to understand the term, digital forensics:

> *Forensic science is generally defined as the application of science to the law. Digital forensics, also known as computer and network forensics, has many definitions. Generally, it is considered the application of science to the identification, collection, examination, and analysis of data while preserving the integrity of the information and maintaining a strict chain of custody for the data. Data refers to distinct pieces of digital information that have been formatted in a specific way. Organizations have an ever-increasing amount of data from many sources. For example, data can be stored or transferred by standard computer systems, networking equipment, computing peripherals, personal digital assistants (PDA), consumer electronic devices, and various types of media, among other sources. Because of the variety of data sources, digital forensic techniques can be used for many purposes, such as investigating crimes and internal policy violations, reconstructing computer security incidents, troubleshooting operational problems, and recovering from accidental system damage* (Source: National Institute of Standards and Technology (2006), Guide to Integrating Forensic Techniques into Incident Response).

The whole area of computer forensics or digital forensics is a skillset that you acquire in order to investigate and analyze electronic data in the interest of determining potential legal evidence. Computer forensics enables the systematic and careful identification of evidence in computer related crime and abuse cases.

Forensic Staffing

Practically every investigation team needs to have some capability to perform computer and network forensics. Without such a capability, the investigation will encounter difficulty in determining what events have occurred within the computer systems and networks.

For example: Let's say investigators are working a case involving sourcing and distribution of illegal drugs via the Internet. Having seized the computer of the suspect, the investigator passes it on to the analyst for processing. The investigator tells the analyst that he believes that the suspect has been in contact with other small scale dealers using email and email chat but fails to tell the analyst that there's no information on how payments have been made and, in fact, the criminal has been exchanging funds via PayPal using the cover of a fake email account. Because the analyst is unaware that the method of payment is not known to investigators, he does not investigate any matters related to email or eBay. It's reasonable to say that the majority of the fault here lies with the investigator, not the analyst.

Although the example sounds like a simple case, it is almost impossible to resolve the case by one investigator. The primary users of forensic tools and techniques within an investigation team usually can be divided into the following three groups:

- *Forensic Investigators.* Forensic investigators are typically responsible for investigating allegations of criminal activities in law enforcement agencies. The forensic investigator is a skilled digital forensic analyst, who has an in-depth knowledge of surrounding circumstances of the case and the ability to apply the comprehensive knowledge directly within the forensic examination. Larger police agencies tend to have dedicated cybercrime units. It is important to note that objectives must be clearly stated during the investigation and that the forensic investigator needs to have as much background information on the case as possible. The forensic investigator typically uses many forensic techniques and tools. Investigators within private organizations might include legal advisors and members of the human resources department.
- *IT Professionals*. This group consists of technical support staff and system, network, and security administrators. They do not heavily use forensic techniques but tend to use tools specific to their area of expertise during their routine work (e.g., monitoring, troubleshooting, data recovery).
- *Incident Handlers*. This group responds to a variety of computer security incidents such as unauthorized data access, inappropriate system usage, malicious code infections, and

denial of service attacks. Similar to forensic investigators, incident handlers typically use a wide variety of forensic techniques and tools during their investigations.

Professor Edmond Locard, the founding father of modern forensic science, mentioned that

> "wherever he steps, whatever he touches, whatever he leaves, even consciously will serve as a witness against him." Not only his fingerprints or his footprints, but his hair, the fiber from his clothes, the glass he breaks, the tool-mark he leaves, the paint he scratches, the blood or semen he deposits. All of these, and more, can be a mute witness against him. This is evidence that does not forget, it's not confused by the excitement of the moment, it's not absent because human witnesses are, it's factual evidence that cannot be wrong, cannot perjure itself, it cannot be wholly absent. Only human failure to find it, study and understand it can diminish its value" (Paul et. al. 1954).

Generally summarized as "every contact leaves a trace," this principle holds fast in relation to digital evidence. Although an electronic or digital form of evidence is not easy to read or understand, every action performed on a digital device will leave a digital footprint. That footprint may be fragile and transient but it will exist.

Locard's principle in action

- The objective of the digital investigator is to locate and preserve the digital footprint without tainting it.
- Pre-Internet days: Data found on a computer system is sufficient evidence.
- Today: An outside influence such as hacking, Trojan horse, and viruses can easily manipulate the digital evidence.

All factors have to be taken into consideration by the examiner today and the evidence that may be tainted by unknown users must be considered. The digital forensic investigator has to locate and preserve the digital footprint without any contaminations.

During the pre-Internet days, the mere presence of data on the computer was sufficient evidence. Those days have passed. For example, the perpetrators might be located on the other side of the world when they commit the crime. IP tracing techniques are commonly used to determine the origin of criminal activities and it is now necessary to prove the histories of files found on a computer system to determine whether the real crime scene is located where the perpetrator performed the act or if it is the victim's location.

Prior to the Internet era, there was little possibility that the system had been accessed online by an unauthorized individual. Nobody at that time had heard of a Trojan horse and any virus activity would be contained in the standalone system. All these factors now have to be taken into consideration by the digital forensic investigator. Unfortunately, no longer is the contact that leaves a trace only in relation to the known user of the computer; the malicious outsider must now be discovered or discounted.

Operating Principles and Requirements for Forensic Investigation

Please note that the following information was derived from the British Association of Chief Police Officers.

Although computer forensics, as a discipline, has only existed for around 20 years, some universal operating principles have evolved. The wording of these principles used in this lesson is that of the British Association of Chief Police officers. The operating principals are widely used in other nations and professional associations.

Principle 1: If evidence is to be of any use to the prosecution, the evidence must be proved to be the original evidence. If an examiner were to change the data in any way, it would immediately and rightly become open to challenge by the defense.

Principle 2: In exceptional circumstances, where the person finds it necessary to access original data held on a computer or on storage media, that person must be competent to do so and be able to give evidence exploring the relevance and the implications of their actions.

Principle 3: The work undertaken should be properly documented and fully replicable by a person with similar skills.

Principle 4: The person in charge of the investigation has overall responsibility for ensuring that the law and these principles are adhered to.

Forensic examiners very rarely work on the original evidence item. There are, however, circumstances when this cannot be avoided. The operating principles emphasize that should a competent person, in this case a qualified examiner, need to work in any way on the original evidence, they should be able to clearly understand and express what, if any, changes have been made. When this was first stated, the cases in which original evidence was likely to be accessed were very rare.

This has changed somewhat with the advent of mobile telephones and in many cases the only way to extract data from a mobile telephone is to access the device itself. In these cases the examiner must be able to show that he/she has taken every reasonable precaution to prevent the device from accessing the mobile phone network whilst it was in his/her possession.

Digital Forensic Principles

The principle of digital forensics is that no action should change data in the computer or storage media. In a case of unavoidable access to the data, evidence should be created to be able to explain the reason for the access and the implication of the action to the data. An audit trail of all processes applied to digital evidence should be created and preserved. The officer in charge of the investigation has overall responsibility for the whole process.

Requirements for Understanding the Forensic Examination

As mentioned earlier, digital forensic investigators must have a comprehensive understanding of the technology. Although a deep knowledge of computers and other digital devices is not required for writing the forensic report, it is crucial to digest general knowledge of digital devices and media for effective forensic examinations.

Before attempting to collect or examine files, digital forensic investigators should have a reasonably comprehensive understanding of files and filesystems. First, the investigator should be aware of the variety of media that may contain files.

File Storage Media

The widespread use of computers and other digital devices has resulted in a significant increase in the number of different media types that are used to store files. In addition to traditional media types such as hard drives and floppy disks, files are often stored on consumer devices such as PDAs and cell phones, as well as on newer media types, such as flash memory cards, which were made popular by digital cameras.

Two Types of Digital Devices: Programmable vs. Non-programmable Devices

1. Programmable devices: A device utilizing an Operating System and other programs to run.
   Ex) A personal computer with MS Windows (Operating System) and word processor use an Operating System, software that allows other third party programs to run. Some of our telephones also have this facility but to a much more limited extent.
2. Non-Programmable Devices: For some devices, the manufacture controls the options available to the user, such as with a digital camera.
   Ex) A digital Camera

Most other digital devices are non-programmable. This does not mean that the user cannot direct the device to take certain actions or that the data may not be stored upon them; in fact, the device would be pretty useless if this were the case. It means, in effect, that the manufacturer controls the options available to the user. To clarify this, a personal computer may be loaded with Microsoft Windows or another operating system. The user may then choose to load and execute Word processing, graphics spreadsheets, communications, or any other type of program at will. The device is therefore programmable. By way of contrast, a digital camera may allow the setting of shutter speeds or aperture or even the use of preset image manipulation, like red-eye removal. A digital camera will not allow the user to load a program that turns it into a music player or a voice recorder; in the context in which we use the term, it is therefore non-programmable.

Personal Computers (PC)

The networking of the PC has many benefits in relation to the sharing of information and resources. From the investigative point of view, having many locations to store or hide data is the downside.

Computer Hardware Components

- **CPU**: A part of a computer performs data processing.
- **POST**: A diagnostic test of the computer's hardware for presence and operability during the boot sequence prior to running the operating system.
- **ROM** (read-only memory): This is a form of memory that can hold data permanently. ROM is nonvolatile memory, meaning the data remains when the system is powered off. Having these properties (read-only and nonvolatile) makes ROM ideal for files containing start-up configuration settings and code needed to boot the computer (ROM BIOS).
- **RAM** (random access memory): A computer's main memory is its temporary workspace for storing data, code, settings, and so forth. RAM is usually volatile memory, meaning that upon losing power, the data stored in memory is lost.

Two Types of Memory

1. **RAM (random access memory)**:

RAM (random access memory):

- The short-term, working memory of the computer
- The contents of the RAM will be lost when the power is down
- The contents of the RAM may be captured to the hard disk drive as a swap file
- The swap may be useful to the examiner because it may contain password information or complete documents
- The contents of the RAM are always changing (volatile memory).

In certain circumstances, the contents of the RAM may be captured to a hard disk in what's known as a swap file. The contents of this file may be of great use to the examiner. In the swap file, data may sometimes be found that has never actually have been saved to a disk such as password information or complete documents.

2. **Hard Disk Drive**

When one moves onto file servers, the volume of data to be examined gives real cause for concern. The file servers control many terabytes of data. The hard disk drive is generally of more interest to us in the context of digital evidence. The hard disk drive is a huge filing system. In addition to the more obvious contents such as documents, images, programs, and etc., there are many different items of data that enable a comprehensive picture of the previous use of the computer to be painted.

The sheer volume of data dictates that the search for and extraction of digital evidence must now be subject to a much tighter focus than it once was. Modern versions are far more powerful and have an ability to store a considerable amount of data. They can run cut down, but still powerful versions of PC software. If a tablet loses its data, there is always a ray of hope; most users synchronize the content of their tablet with a host PC. If it's possible to examine that PC, then the synchronized data may be recoverable.

Mobile/ Smart Phone

In only 10 years, the mobile phone progressed from being a luxury item to a necessity consumer item. Even the most simple and inexpensive mobile telephone has the capability to store address books, scheduling information, call records, and etc. Call records may provide excellent evidence, and of even more value is the SMS. The nature of the information users are willing to transmit using tech services may be quite astounding.

An individual is provided with the ability to substitute large gigabytes of internal storage with a smartphone. To gain a complete picture of the use of a mobile telephone, it is often necessary to obtain the billing records of that mobile telephone. Since the primary function of the mobile service provider is to make a profit, the service company certainly retains that important information for cybercrime investigations.

Digital Camera/ Video Camera

Digital cameras and video cameras provide first class evidence. High capacity memory cards, or sticks, can store any type of files. This capacity makes digital cameras and video cameras ideal mediums for transporting concealed data.

Miscellaneous Storage Devices

There is a wide range of devices that are not generally recognized as digital evidence, such as personal music players, game consoles, DVD recorders and domestic appliances.

Satellite Navigation Unit

Satellite Navigation Units have become extremely common and relatively inexpensive in a very short period of time. A Satellite Navigation Unit can contain crucial evidence relating to the movements of a suspect. Many miscellaneous storage devices have the facility to attach a memory card that may be the ideal place to conceal contraband data. There is a wide range of devices that are not generally recognized as items of evidential value, but today most electronic devices produce digital a signature, which may contain information of evidential value.

SEARCH AND SEIZURE OF DIGITAL EVIDENCE

For the most part in cybercrime cases, investigators need search warrants to search and seize evidence. To attain a search warrant, an officer needs to prepare an affidavit that describes the basis for probable cause.

Probable cause is a reasonable belief that a person has committed a crime. The affidavit must specify the area to be searched and the evidence being sought. The search warrant allows the officer only a limited right to violate a citizen's privacy. For example, if there is probable cause of digital evidence on a CD, this would not justify seizing every computer on the premises (Brenner and Schwerha, 2002). If the investigator wants to seize a computer and analyze it later, the probable cause statement should demonstrate the impracticality or danger of examining the computer on the premises and the need to confiscate and analyze it off-site (Volonino, Anzaldua, and Godwin, 2007, p. 56).

The Search Warrant Requirement

The Fourth Amendment has generally been interpreted to require that a search warrant contain a complete analysis and description of the place to be searched by law enforcement officers.

Here's a crucial question: What information should a law enforcement officer include during the search for digital evidence?

Consider the Fourth Amendment below:

> *The right of the people to be secure in their persons, houses, papers, and effects, against unreasonable searches and seizures, shall not be violated, and no Warrants shall issue, but upon probable cause, supported by Oath or affirmation, and particularly describing the place to be searched, and the persons or things to be seized* (U.S. Const. amend. IV).

Many cybercrime investigation training materials relating to the handling of digital evidence recommend following the phrase: "including but not limited to." It is believed that this wording will allow officers to show that they are looking for specific evidence but there is the potential for the suspect to have additional evidence that may not have been accounted for in the search warrant.

Thus, it is important that law enforcement officers provide a thorough list of every item that could potentially contain digital evidence and then include a statement concerning how digital evidence may take many forms and so there is the potential that the suspect may have additional pieces of technology that was not included.

In addition, it is also important that law enforcement officers who request a search warrant ensure that the signing judge understands what they intend to seize. Many cybercrime investigators recommend that all officers who request search warrants involving digital evidence and computers carry a pocket dictionary of computer terms. The judge may then be provided with these easy-to-understand definitions, should there be any doubt as to what the search warrant is calling for in terms of seizures (Moore, 2011).

Preplanning Associated with the Search Warrant

Please note that, pursuant to the search warrant, personnel must ensure they only seize computers that are covered by their search warrant.

ECPA

Investigators also need to consider whether the actions of their search warrant will affect any federal legislation. If the computer-related evidence to be seized is used in the transmission of emails or other electronic communications, there is the possibility that the Electronics Communication Privacy Act of 1986 (ECPA) may govern the actions of government agents. ECPA regulates the amount of information that law enforcement officers may obtain with certain levels of service. Currently, an officer needs the following level of service to obtain information about a potential suspect under the ECPA (Moore, 2011).

1.Subpoena—basic subscriber information (name, address, local and long distance telephone connection records, session times and duration, length of service, types of service used, telephone number or IP address, sources of payment, and the content of emails that are older than 180 days and have been previously opened by the owner)

Benefits:

If a suspect has a screen name that indicates the user is a MSN customer, using a subpoena drafted with this online identity the investigator could get the name, address, and billing information for the person who registered that screen name with MSN.

2. Court order—transactional information

Benefits:

The addresses of past email correspondents is beneficial to investigators, especially investigators who are handling an investigation involving child pornography or identity fraud. The list of past email correspondents will allow investigators to determine how many individuals in the public could have been exposed to the individual's behavior.

3. Search warrant—the actual content of email messages.

Benefits:

The use of a search warrant will allow for examination of email contents, as well as audit logs, addresses, and billing information.

The search warrant, while allowing for the greatest collection of evidence, is also the hardest level of service to obtain as it requires the investigator to complete a statement of underlying facts supporting the issuance of a search warrant. In this statement the investigator must show that a crime has been committed, that the individual who owns the account is linked to the crime, and that the electronic account contains information relevant to the investigation of the case. If investigators fail to consider the provisions of the ECPA, they may find their evidence inadmissible.

PPA

The Privacy Protection Act (PPA) is another piece of federal legislation that investigators should consider. The purpose is to protect unpublished materials—such as books and magazines, etc.—from having their materials released by law enforcement officers prior to making them available to the public.

If the materials are legal, then law enforcement officers are under a duty to return any publishing materials back to the owner as soon as possible.

Warrantless Search Doctrines and Technological Evidence

What should happen if law enforcement personnel determine that the option of using a search warrant is not available? If this is the case, it is up to the government to prove that the circumstances justified not using a search warrant in the situation.

Warrantless Consent Searches

There are several factors to consider when attempting to seize a computer or search a hard drive on the basis of consent. Does the individual granting the consent have a legitimate right to consent to the search?

In United States v. Smith (1998) the court found that a search of a suspect's computer was valid despite the fact that consent was granted not by the suspect, but by the suspect's girlfriend. It was the opinion of the court that there was evidence that the two individuals shared a common living space and therefore an expectation of privacy for the computer could be overruled by consent from either party. In addition, the court considered the fact that the computer files obtained were not password protected, which led to the belief that the files were accessible by anyone in the house.

Please note that absent a search warrant, there is the potential for the individual to revoke their consent, or, even worse, wait until trial and then claim that they attempted to revoke consent in the middle of an examination. There have been a variety of court decisions that discuss revoking consent, but the following court decisions from the state of Florida perhaps illustrate this concept best. Consent may be withdrawn by any of the following:

1. The individual may revoke consent verbally (State v. Hammonds, 1990).
2. The individual may revoke consent through an intentional act, such as grabbing the investigator's hand in order to stop the search of a Particular area (Jimenez v. State, 1994).
3. The individual may revoke consent to a search by fleeing from the search (Davis v. State, 1986).

Again, having a search warrant to search the contents of the computer will prevent a suspect from claiming any of these actions were attempted during the search of the computer.

Searches Based on Exigent Circumstances

Law enforcement personnel have long been granted use of an exigent circumstances claim to justify the warrantless seizure of evidence. However, exigent circumstances surrounding a seizure must be verified by indicating:

- That a reasonable person would believe that entry was necessary to prevent physical harm to law enforcement personnel or others in the surrounding area;
- That the warrantless seizure was necessary to prevent the destruction of valuable evidence;
- That the warrantless seizure was necessary to prevent the escape of a suspect;
- Or that the warrantless search was necessary to prevent any further consequences that could delay legitimate law enforcement efforts (United States v. Alfonso, 1985).

It is possible that the warrantless seizures of digital evidence under exigent circumstances could play a significant role in the future of high-technology crime investigation. Consider the example of United States v. David (1991). In David, law enforcement officers obtained a suspect's electronic date book without a search warrant. The court agreed with the actions of the officer, finding that in that situation there was sufficient proof that the suspect knew law enforcement personnel were after evidence within the device. In an attempt to prevent the information from being obtained, the suspect was deleting the evidence (Moore, 2011).

It is worth noting, however, that the court also agreed that the exigency ended the moment the date book was seized and there was no further danger to the integrity of the evidence. Law enforcement officers should consider the seizure of a technological device without a warrant to be a possibility, but the search of the same device should be conducted under the provisions of a valid search warrant.

SEIZURE OF EVIDENCE

The issue of legal authority to conduct a search depends upon whether the investigator is investigating a civil or criminal case. If the investigator is involved in a criminal case, the legal authority to conduct a search is under the local jurisdiction. Within the legal framework of a criminal investigation, the investigator needs a search warrant that specifies the scope of his/ her search, as mentioned in the previous lesson. It is important to keep in mind the guarantees provided by the Fourth Amendment to the U.S. Constitution. In this section, we review the search and seizure guidelines for cybercrime investigations.

Due to the characteristics of digital evidence, there are many controversial issues on the evidence's admissibility to the court. To prevent these issues, it is important to follow an adequate digital forensic process.

According to Volonino, Anzaldua, and Godwin (2007), the digital forensic seizure process has 3 stages. Let's first see what should be done in the seizure process. When we arrive at the site to execute a search and seizure warrant, we should look for the digital evidence at the site. Prior to conduct seizure process, we should acknowledge what types of the digital evidence should be searched and try to find out all important aspect of the investigation. Thus, collecting preliminary data at the site is crucial.

Stage 1. Collect Preliminary Data at the Site

Once the investigator has ascertained the legal authority and scope of the investigation, the next steps are to fully document the scene by taking pictures and then gathering initial information.

Prior to the evidence collection at the site, the investigator should be prepared to consider a number of important questions.

- What types of digital evidence am I looking for?
- Photographs, documents, databases, spreadsheets, financial records, email, etc
- What is the skill level of the suspect in question?
- The suspect's capability to alter or destroy evidence
- What kind of hardware is involved?
- IBM PC or MAC computer
- What kind of software is involved?
- Hacking tools, MS Office, FoxPro data, etc
- Do I need to preserve other types of evidence?
- Fingerprints, DNA, or trace evidence
- What is the computer environment like?
- Network, ISP, OS, usernames and passwords, etc.

Stage 2. Determining the Environment for the Investigation

After acquiring initial information, the next step is to determine whether to do the forensic work onsite or transfer the equipment to a trusted lab environment. There are various considerations to take into account. However, the primary consideration is always the integrity of the evidence. The best practice as a digital forensic investigator is to always do your examination in a trusted environment, such as a forensics lab.

Factors to consider when deciding where to conduct the examination should include:

- Integrity of the evidence collection process
  Is the evidence volatile enough that by waiting or transporting the evidence back to the lab I am going to risk losing it?

- Estimation of the time required to do an examination
  A short examination is usually worth doing onsite. If the investigation is extremely critical or appears that it may take some time, the best practice is to do this type of exam in the lab.

- Equipment resources
  Will the equipment you bring onsite be sufficient enough to handle the examination thoroughly and professionally? Can you bring the equipment from the lab or will that be impractical?

Integrity of the evidence collection process is the most essential factor.

Examples:

Operating System (OS)

- Booting a computer will cause the attributes of hundreds of files to be altered
- Potentially affect the overall evidential integrity of the drive
- The OS maintains records of the attributes of each file stored on the system, which includes the file name, the time and date that the file was created, modified and accessed.
- Booting a computer equipped with Microsoft Windows will cause the attributes of literally hundreds of files to be altered. This does not necessarily mean that the content of the file will be changed. However, it could potentially affect the overall evidential integrity of the drive.
- The operating system of a computer maintains a record of the attributes of each file stored on the system. These attributes include the name of the file, the time and date that the file was created, modified, or accessed.

The investigator often has to collect the digital information in a computer that is turned on. We can find a great amount of valuable information from the computer memory so we have to gather as much information as possible from the turned on computers. Because the contents of the memory can easily disappear when the computer is turned off to seize it, it is important to secure information in the memory. Usually, when we get information from the computer memory, the use of adequate equipment for securing specific volatile information is needed. During the examination process, you should record contents and current states of digital evidences in all processes. Because other people may get involved in the data process, detailed information of the examination process should be recorded to be helpful to the other people. Because the suspect most likely has a tendency to try to hide the critical information related to his/her wrongdoing, it is not such an easy job to find a lead to solve the case from the digital evidence.

However, the investigator should find out the information because the actual investigation will follow the acquisition of critical information that incriminates the suspect.

The amount of digital evidence is now getting bigger and bigger and it is quite a difficult job to process investigations of digital media with huge amounts of data.

There are two distinctive seizure patterns: the personal computer and the computer servers. The personal computer is a standalone computer generally operated by a single user.

1. When you seize a personal computer, you should collect digital evidences promptly because the data in the memory can be easily changed and removed. You should also collect other digital media like flash drives, digital camcorders, phones, and tablets as well as hard disk drives.
2. When you seize computer servers used by more than one user, you should consider the amount of data seized, the number of connected users, and the intricacy of computer manipulations. If there is more than one connected user, you should adopt a different strategy for search and seizure than the normal personal computer. For the most part, when you seize the server, you should collect data from the live system on-site through the network after consulting with the computer system administrator.

Stage 3. Securing and Transporting Evidence

When the cybercrime evidence is seized, many of the basic procedures are exactly the same as in the seizure of any physical piece of evidence.

The sequence of common steps is as follows:

1. Document the evidence,
2. tag it,
3. bag it, and
4. transport it to the forensics lab.

Document the Evidence

It is essential that the investigator should be able to demonstrate the location of the evidence throughout its time in the possession of the agency and who has had access to it. In many jurisdictions, it will be acceptable to group together certain items of a similar nature and from the same location. For example, it would be acceptable to have an exhibit comprising of 5 flash drives from a desk drawer, but it would not be appropriate to present an exhibit of 10 flash drives found in different locations at the same premises.

In common with other physical evidence, the location the item was found can be highly relevant to the investigation. It is very important to make detailed notes of what was found and where it was found. If possible, establish who has had and who has not had access to the computer.

When you begin your initial documentation, you should do the following:

- Locate all evidence to be seized.
- Record a general description of the room, including:
- Type of media found
- All peripheral devices attached to the computer(s)
- Make, model, and serial numbers of all devices (computers or others) to be seized
- What types of media devices are located in, near, or on the computer
- Note all wireless devices
- Make use of chain of custody forms

Each cable should be labeled and numbered with the corresponding number being marked on a label attached to the computer. This will make it much easier to reassemble the machine in the laboratory. In the case of computers, the machine should be photographed on site before any cables are disconnected. In addition to writing down this information, taking photographs of the scene would be the best way to preserve this type of documentation. It is also important that the investigator photograph the layout of the room and if it is a fairly large area, anything within 20 feet of the computers.

Tag the Evidence

The next step is to begin tagging all the items that are going to be transported back to the forensic lab. Since you are photographing everything, the tags serve as backup documentation and show a physical documentation audit trail. On these tags, you should note the time, date, location, and general condition of the evidence.

Bag the Evidence

After you have finished tagging all evidence items, each evidential item should be securely packed using Anti-Static packaging. Anti-Static bags can be purchased for hard drives, but even brown paper bags can be used. Plastic packaging can create static electricity, which in some circumstances could cause damage to the system. Small media, sticky notes, and USB drives can be placed into antistatic bags that are quite small. Larger items such as external hard drives or computers can be transported via antistatic boxes.

Transport the Evidence

Now you need to start looking at how to transport the evidence back to your lab. The tools and equipment you need for transport depend on the amount and types of evidence to be transported. Problems usually arise when there are delays and the evidence is exposed to environmental factors that could destroy or degrade it. When the equipment is being transported, it should be kept as far as is reasonably possible from electromagnetic sources such as police radios. Other factors such as high humidity, high heat, excessive vibration, and direct exposure to sunlight all have negative effects on the evidence. An air-conditioned vehicle with cargo tie-downs on antistatic mats would be the safest vehicle for transportation. Once you arrive at the forensics lab, document the time and date and complete the chain of custody forms. Store the evidence in a secure area where access is limited and controlled. Ideally, you should have a locked vault with labeled shelves or drawers to store and organize your evidence. It is vital that the original evidence remains unchanged from the moment it comes into the possession of law enforcement. There are a number of investigative guidelines that can greatly assist the investigator in achieving this objective.

Seeking the advice of a trained forensic practitioner

- The suspect may divulge more information when they are unsettled by the initial presence of the investigator.
- If the seizure of the computer equipment is to be part of a planned operation, then advice of an expert should be sought during the planning stage. Ideally, the forensic practitioner should be present at the time of seizure, or at least available to give advice by telephone.

The suspect should be physically separated from the evidence to be seized

- The suspect must be physically separated from the evidence to be seized under any circumstance and should not be allowed to touch any evidential item. It is extremely easy to construct a computer system that will cause a total destruction of evidential content by pressing only a few keys. Many criminals have been found to have such controls present on their computers.

Question the suspect with regard to any passwords used and as to the location of possible evidence

- Questioning the suspect with regard to any passwords used and the location of possible evidence often leads to a successful investigation. It is a basic investigative principle that the suspect may divulge more investigation when they are unsettled by the initial presence of the investigator. By the time the investigator is ready for a formal interview, the suspect will have had time to think and may be more reticent.

Making a thorough and detailed search

- A great deal of data can be stored on a tiny card or flash card. Although the severity of the case may be a deciding factor in the time that can be allotted, the search should be as complete as possible.

Favorite Physical Hidden Places For Evidence

Criminals often hide data CDs in a commercial music CD case, behind the original disk. It is essential to conduct a special search of the suspect's desk and the area close to it

- Ex) Look for notes stuck on the underside of the desk and for small portable memory devices held with gum to the underside of the desk or the back of a drawer
- Look for any cables that cannot be identified – they may connect to the remote storage device
- If a suspect has a network installed, follow any cables to establish whether there are more computer or storage devices
- Check every electrical outlet on the premises. What is plugged in? Wireless devices can be secreted well away from the computer.

Seize any paperwork or notes

People often make a written note of passwords and other relevant information

- Ex) The password on a sticky note was not seized by officers but the note was visible in the photographs of the scene and the password was able to be read
- If chargers or cables for mobile devices are present, seize them
- Switching on a modern computer causes many hundreds of files to be changed. Even worse, evidential data may have been destroyed.
- If a computer system is switched on, it should be powered down as soon as practicable (after photographing the screen) by removing the power cable from the machine. In the case of a laptop computer, the battery should be removed.
- Routine shutdown procedures can result in the erasure of temporary files that may be relevant to the investigation. In a

similar way to the user initiated processes mentioned above, routines can be constructed that will destroy data if certain key presses are not input at the time of shutdown.

Rules of Mobile Phones

- Mobile phones should be treated differently than computer systems
    - If the phone is switched on, it is better to leave it in that state.
    - Switching it off may invoke a security code (PIN number)
- Special bags are available that prevent the phone from connecting to the network
    - If a phone does connect, the calls or messages that may be received could result in the erasure of earlier items

A mobile phone should be immediately taken to the forensic lab, as it is possible that battery life is very limited.

Rules of PDAs and SatNav Devices

- PDAs and SatNav devices suffer from limited battery life
- The best practice is to leave them in whatever state they have been seized in
- Ensure that they are delivered to a competent examiner as soon as is practicable.
- SatNav should be enclosed in an anti-static bag and then placed in a sturdy metal box, thus avoiding, as much as possible, the reception of a satellite signal.

SUMMARY

This chapter addressed digital evidence principals and the search and seizure process. The search warrant should contain a thorough description of the various technological devices expected to be encountered at the scene of the search. Recognizing that there may be scenarios in which it is impossible to think of every possible type of technology that could be encountered, the courts have allowed some jurisdictions to utilize the phrase "including but not limited to." If the use of a warrant using such terminology is challenged, then the investigator who drafted the warrant could argue that their attempt to list every known technological device commonly encountered during an investigation of such a crime should prevent the appearance of a fishing expedition.

There may be certain situations in which an investigator may be unable to take the necessary time to draft a valid search warrant. Should such a situation arise, there has been precedent established that would allow for the warrantless search and/or seizure of technological and digital evidence. Currently, the best rule to follow in situations that involve a warrantless seizure is to use one of the established warrantless search doctrines to conduct a seizure of the evidence and then immediately seek out and obtain a well-drafted search warrant to search the internal portions of the evidence.

It is absolutely vital that the original evidence remain in an unchanged format the very moment it comes into the possession of law enforcement. The key component of methodical investigation is to set good policies and procedures that serve as guidelines. These policies and procedures are designed not only to delineate the process of an investigation but also to aid in the management of a computer forensics lab.

Discussion 1:
Please list devices that are important to digital evidence collection and why your selected devices are important to digital forensic investigations.

Before we start discussing the process itself, it's useful to spend a little time considering the philosophical principle of digital forensics, known as Locard's Principle.

Every action performed on a digital device will leave a "digital footprint." It may be fragile and transient but it will exist.

Discussion 2:
What information should a law enforcement officer include during the search for digital evidence and why?

Discussion 3:

Consider the way in which you would undertake a computer forensic search.

List the points that you consider most essential and explain why.

Chapter 14 - Principles of Digital Forensic Investigation

In the previous chapter, we examined the types of devices or media that may be seized and some of the factors to be taken into consideration at the time of seizure. In this chapter, we'll move on to the types of evidence that can be extracted and an overview of how this process takes place. The topic of securing data integrity will be discussed in this lesson as well. In terms of a cybercrime investigation, what are we looking for?

Examples

- Word processor documents
- Unlawful images
- Accounting data
- Email Messages
- Contact Information
- Call Records
- Text Messages
- Internet Usage Records
- Copied Intellectual Properties (Music, Video, Etc.)

This is really just the tip of the iceberg. Digital Forensic investigation consists of far more than data recovery. For a piece of data to be present on storage media, it must have been processed by a digital device.

The processing of digital evidence stored on a media device

- Involves creation, copying or downloading

- The search for digital evidence will focus on what is actually stored on internal or external media
- The investigator needs to trace the processing of all the evidence in order to establish its provenance
- The investigator must recognize the evidential significance of what they have found
- The investigator should be able to create a cohesive evidence collection
- The investigator must then go back and apply scientific methodology to demonstrate the scientific validity of that evidence

The search for digital evidence will focus on what digital evidence is actually stored on either internal media (for example, a hard drive) or external media such as a flash drive or CD. Having found the evidence, the investigator will then look for various traces of the processing of all the digital evidence in order to establish its provenance. The investigator must recognize the evidential significance of what they have found and be able to create a strong case based upon that evidence.

What, Why, When, How, Where, and Who

It is important to have six friends during the investigation, and their names are What, Why, When, How, Where, and Who.

What? What is on the computer or other device and how can it assist us in the pursuit of justice? This can be a word processing document, a graphic image, a spreadsheet, an e-mail, or any other type of data produced by a program. Other examples include programs, hacking tools, virus production programs, and steganography programs (steganography is a method of concealing data within an innocent looking file). A Smoking Gun can be stolen intellectual property or a catalog collection of child pornography. At the simplest level, the presence, or occasionally absence, of files can be critical evidence. Indeed, sometimes simply the presence of certain programs on a system may serve to prove at least the capability to perform certain actions.

In the forensic examination of digital device, fragments of previously existing files may be the most crucial factors.

Why? In reality, the presence of certain digital files is just the starting point for analysis. "Why" suggests motivation. Motivation may not be thought to be in the province of digital evidence. The retrieval, however, of such diverse data as bank statements, e-mail threads, or text messages may greatly assist in establishing motivation. For example, diverse data as bank statements, e-mail, or threads of text messages may greatly assist in telling us what the suspect was trying to do.

When. It may be crucial to the prosecution to establish when the suspect created or modified files or accessed a computer system. The digital investigator should delineate a reliable timeline that can clearly demonstrate the history of the evidential data. This may not be a simple task, as the computer literate suspect may go to considerable lengths to attempt to cover their tracks.

How. How data came to be on a computer or other digital devices may be a very subjective question, but in many cases, the important question is not whether the evidence exists, but how it came to exist. Excluding allegations of impropriety, challenges generally take the form of casting doubt as to the creator or user of the data.

Where. The location of data within the system can be vital evidence. Where is the evidence located? Where did it come from? Microsoft Windows utilizes a system creating a folder called, "temporary Internet files." Every image that is viewed on the Internet will be saved into this folder. If unlawful images are found only in the temporary Internet files folder, it may be possible to assert that there was a lack of intent. However, if a folder like "My Documents/Child Images/Boys/Six to eight" is found, the origin of the evidential matter can be extremely important. No version of windows, of which I am aware, automatically creates a folder entitled, "My Documents/Child Images/Boys/Six to eight." Establishing the origin of the evidential matter can also be extremely important for a cybercrime investigation.

Who. This is often a challenging issue in cybercrime cases. Whilst it is often possible to prove the existence of data on a system in the history of the evidence, it can be extremely difficult to prove beyond all reasonable doubt who really placed the evidence on the computer. It is sometimes necessary to resort to traditional investigative methods to establish who could, or could not, have had access to the computer. Consider the following examples;

DIGITAL FORENSIC PROCESS: SECURING DATA INTEGRITY

Data related to a particular event is identified, labeled, collected, recorded, and the integrity of the data is maintained during the collection of digital evidence. During the next phase, forensic and examination techniques and tools appropriate to the types of data that were collected during the collection process are used to identify and extract useful information while preserving the integrity of the data.

The examination may rely on both manual processes and automated tools. The following phase is the analysis. During the analysis, the results of the examination are analyzed to produce information to answer the questions that motivated the collection and examination. The last phase is the reporting of the findings of the analysis. The report may include the procedures, tools, the actions performed, guidelines, other forensic processes, what actions now may need to be performed, and directions for policy improvement.

The process of digital forensics includes these basic phases (Volonino, Anzaldua, and Godwin, 2007):

- Collection: Following procedures to maintain the integrity of the data in order to acquire, identify, label, and record pertinent data.
- Examination: The forensic processing of the data that was collected by utilizing both manual and automated methods to derive and assess relevant data. Examiners must maintain the integrity of the data during the examination process.
- Analysis: The use of legally justifiable techniques and methods to analyze the results of the examination in order to produce information that can help answer the questions of the case.
- Reporting: Reporting the results of the analysis. The report may include the procedures, tools, the actions performed, guidelines, other forensic processes, what actions may now need to be performed (i.e. securing vulnerabilities found, the examination of other data, and the improvement of security functions), and directions for policy improvement.

Evidence Collection: Integrity of Data

When you seize digital evidence at the crime scene, the first thing you should do is the forensic duplication of the digital evidence. The most important thing in dealing with digital evidence is maintaining the integrity of the digital media. Because digital evidence is easily modified by external impact, you should never be working on the seized digital media. You must work on the duplicate, not the original.

When you are having trouble seizing the hard disk drive in cases of seizing computer servers, you should collect data through the network by using the DD command or other imaging collectors. After forensic duplication, you should image the hard disk drive using forensic tools such as "Encase" and other tools found in forensic tool kits.

A disk image is a single file or storage device containing the complete contents and structure representing a data storage medium or device, like a hard drive. A disk image is usually created by creating a complete sector-by-sector copy of the source medium and thereby perfectly replicating the structure and contents of a storage device.

After creating the disk image, you can perform extra analyses against the disk image using forensic tools.

When you find the evidence, you can then categorize and document it for later processing. You should document all processes, including details of the steps and processes you worked on. You need to be cautious when handling digital evidences.

There are a number of forms that a forensic image might take. The examiner can either make exact clone copies to a similar hard drive or acquire the information into special files that can then emulate the original disk. The common factor is that the acquisition will employ write blocking hardware. As the name suggests, this allows all the content of the subject disk to be read but not allow any changes to that disk. Similar images may be obtained from other types of media such as memory cards, thumb drives, etc. It is also now possible to image the random access memory of a computer.

This may be undertaken in a proper forensic manner but requires very detailed notes to be taken. The examiner will be working on the original evidence and must be prepared to answer potentially difficult questions as to the consequences of his actions. Whether to use this facility or not is dependent upon the circumstances of the case and the skills of the examiner.

Forensic Images

A forensic image differs from a mere copy in that every bit and byte on the original disk or card is extracted. Using this methodology, files that have been deleted and fragments of files that have previously existed may be amenable to recovery. The image is verified using industry standard procedures that can identify any disparity of even one single bit. From this point onwards, the original machine is locked away and the image is analyzed. The analysis of the image takes place using specialized forensic software such as EnCase or FTK. The image does not need to be booted, it's started up for the examination to take place. Indeed, in its native format, the image is incapable of being booted. A bonus, though, is that it is possible, if required, to make any number of restored copies of the original drive without affecting its evidential integrity.

In the commercial sector, the ability to take a verifiable image of a computer in a particular moment of time is absolutely essential. For the purposes of business continuity, it may be totally impractical to take a computer offline for an extended period.

Most jurisdictions now accept a verified image, and thus, if the circumstances so dictate, the evidential computer can be returned to the user. A better solution, though, may be to retain the original drive and to restore the forensic image to a new drive, which is placed in the subject computer. This allows the machine to continue computer function as normal while retaining the original evidence for the legal process.

Although computer forensics, as a discipline, has only existed for about twenty years, some universal operating principles have evolved. The wording of these principles in this lesson is derived from that used in a British publication, the ACPO Good Practice Guide for Digital Evidence (Association of Chief Police Officers, 2012, p. 6). The operating principals are widely used in other nations and professional associations.

Principle 1 If evidence is to be of any use to the prosecution, it must be proved to be the original evidence. If an examiner were to change the data in any way, it would immediately and rightly become open to challenge by the defense.

Principle 2
In exceptional circumstances, where a person finds it necessary to access original data held on a computer or on storage media, that person must be competent to do so and be able to give evidence as to the importance of exploring, the relevance of the exploration to the case at hand, and the implications of their actions.

Principle 3
The work undertaken should be properly documented and fully replicable by a person with similar skills.

Principle 4
The person in charge of the investigation has overall responsibility for ensuring that the law and these principles are adhered to.

- Physical items: Items on which data objects or information may be stored and/or through which data objects are transferred.
- Data Objects: Data objects are objects or information of potential probative value that are associated with physical items. Data objects may exist in different formats without altering the original information.

As discussed in the previous chapter, digital evidence is valuable evidence but is often latent in the same sense as fingerprints and DNA evidence. Digital evidence is also fragile as it can be easily altered, damaged, and/or destroyed. Furthermore, it is sometimes time sensitive and can cross borders with ease and speed. For that reason, we should handle digital evidence carefully and in the same manner as forensic evidence is handled, with respect and care in order to preserve its value as evidence. This relates not just to the physical integrity of a device, but also to the digital data it contains.

- Original Digital Evidence: Physical items and the data objects associated with those items at the time of acquisition or seizure

Digital evidence is categorized; 1) original digital evidence and 2) duplicate digital evidence. At the times of acquisition or seizure, physical items and the data objects are associated with each other.

Second, duplicate digital evidence is an accurate reproduction of all data objects contained on an original physical item. To make duplicate digital evidence, the original evidence should be acquired in a manner that protects and preserves the integrity of the evidence.

- <u>"Why We Use Duplicate Digital Evidence":</u>
  Let's have a look at why we use duplicate digital evidence:

  1. To prevent alterations to the original media and preserve the data/values in their original state.
  2. To ensure that the data present on the seized media are available for examination.
  3. To assist in defending against allegations of loss or destruction of data caused by examination.
  4. To allow controlled alterations and recovery of the imaged media or data for better examination.

- <u>What is a Forensic Copy (Duplicate)?</u> Forensic copy is the technical term for the end product of a forensic acquisition of a computer's hard drive or other storage device. That end product is a bit-stream copy (duplicate), which is a bit-for-bit digital copy of an original digital document, file, partition, graphic image, entire disk, or similar object.

Making several forensic copies is recommended so if something happens to one copy, another backup is readily available. A drive can be imaged (duplicated) without anyone viewing its contents so privacy or confidentiality issues are not at risk.

A bit stream copy is the basis of all forensic work. Forensic images or clones of the original media should be captured by using hardware or software that is capable of capturing a bit stream copy from the original media to ensure no difference between them. That should be archived to media and maintained consistently according to departmental policy and applicable laws as in the manner of all forensic work.

For every bit stream copy used to make duplicates, we should take the following precautions.

- Hardware or software write-blockers are to be used to prevent the evidence from being modified.

- Properly prepared media should be used when making forensic copies to ensure there is no co-mingling of data from different cases.
- Methods of acquiring evidence should be forensically sound and verifiable.

> IN PRACTICE: Write Blocking and Protection
> Never turn on the PC without equipping write-blocking devices or software in place. Write-blocking devices prevent any writes to the drives attached and offer very fast acquisition speeds. The simple act of turning on the PC can possibly alter critical data. While booting up, Windows-based operating systems alter many date/time stamps in the system and the data/time stamps of documents.

Bit Stream Image File:

- The process of making an entire copy of target media such as a hard disk
    - It could be referred to as a physical image file
- The process of making a bit stream copy of selected files, folder and partition
    - It could be referred to as a local image file

There are generally two methods for making duplicate digital evidence from the original digital evidence. One method is to make an image file of the original digital evidence. An image file is a digital file, sometimes compressed, from which a bit stream duplicate of an original digital object can be reconstructed. In order to comply with the principles of computer based electronic evidence, an image should be made of the entire target device and saved to a drive as an image file for later restoration. But sometimes, we need to make a larger image file such as imaging a server that may be beyond the scope of our hardware tools or imaging server. No matter what method or which image file we take, we should verify the integrity of an image file and have documentation that is correct.

Bit Stream Drive Clone (Direct drive-to-drive Clone):

To make an exact copy of the original drive by using hardware or software tools and placing the original drive and the wiped target drive into one computer.

For making duplicate digital evidence from the original digital evidence, we can make bit stream drive clones. We also need to verify the integrity of the image file and have documentation that is correct just as an image file does. A drive-to-drive copy is essential when the examiner must make a bootable copy of the drive.

Hash / Verification:

To be as reliable as the original, the integrity of duplicate digital evidence should be verified. Hash is a technique for uniquely identifying identical files and one of the methods of verification we have. A hash is a digital fingerprint of a file or collection of data, represented as a string of binary data written in hexadecimal notation (Volonino, Anzaldua, and Godwin, 2007).

The most common uses for hashes are to:

- Identify when a chunk of data changes, which often indicates evidence tampering.
- Verify that data has not changed, in which case the hash should be the same both before and after the verification.
- Compare a hash value against a library of known good and bad hashes, seeking a match.

There are numerous algorithms for computing the message digest of data, but the MD5 and the Secure Hash Algorithm 1 (SHA-1) are the most common methods in computer forensics. They take input data of arbitrary length and generate 128-bit message digests. SHA-1 is a Federal Information Processing Standards (FIPS) approved algorithm and MD5 is not, so it would be best for federal agencies to utilize SHA-1 instead of MD5 if you have to choose only one.

MD5 and SHA-1 hash values for files can be created through the use of the Evidence Processor's hash analysis setting. This will allow them to be used later. When the Hash Analysis hyperlinked name is clicked, the Edit Settings dialog will appear. Edit Settings gives the option to check to run one or both of the hashing algorithms.

Digital signatures can be generated through the use of Message digest 5 (MD5 Algorithm). It is a one-way hash function, in that it produces a fixed string of digits (a message digest) from a message. The likelihood that two files that have dissimilar content will have the same hash value is about 2 raised to the 128th power. In other words, if the hash values of two files match, you can be pretty sure that the file contents match exactly. If it has changed so much as one bit, we will get a completely different value for that media.

Acquisition Hash / Verification Hash:

- Hashing of the original data, commonly referred to as an acquisition hash, should be done when an image of the data is created.
- A verification hash of the image is done after the completion of acquisition, but it is important to ensure that the integrity of the data has not been compromised before the image is analyzed.

Copy:

A copy process only copies active files, ambient data will not be copied. A copy is an accurate reproduction of information contained on an original physical item independent of the original physical item. You only get the data area with a copy. Slack space and free space are left within a copy.

Proper Preservation and Presentation of Digital Evidence:

The methods of recovering digital evidence may seem complex but if you follow the process correctly, the integrity and quality of the evidence can be secured. Operating systems and other programs frequently alter the contents of electronic storage, and this change may happen automatically without the user's awareness. In order to comply with the principles of computer based digital evidence, a copy image should be made of the entire target device.

Partial copying may be considered when the amount of data to be imaged makes a full capture impracticable. Investigators should be careful to ensure that all relevant evidence is captured if this approach is adopted. It is essential to display objectivity of evidence in the court, as well as the continuity and integrity of the evidence. It is also necessary to demonstrate how the evidence has been recovered, showing each process through which the evidence was obtained.

FILE STORAGE: USING DATA FROM DATA FILES

A data file (also called a file) is a collection of information logically grouped into a single entity and referenced by a unique name, such as a filename. A file can be of many data types, including a document, an image, a video, or an application. Successful forensic processing of computer media depends on the ability to collect, examine, and analyze the files that reside on the media.

This section provides an overview of the most common media types and filesystems methods for naming, storing, organizing, and accessing files. It then discusses how files should be collected and how the integrity of the files should be preserved. The section also discusses various technical issues related to file recovery, such as recovering data from deleted files. The last portion of the section describes the examination and analysis of files, providing guidance on tools and techniques that can assist analysts.

For a digital forensic investigation examiner, the understanding of the relationship between the file system and investigation is crucial.

- A stored computer file is just a collection of bytes.
  A stored computer file contains data but it does not have any information to identify its attributes or itself. It is no more than unidentified data on a disk in the absence of an indexing system. Operating systems utilize indexing systems and keep information about the file. The information includes the length, time attributes, starting position, and the name the file is stored under.
- The file itself does not keep identifying data:
  The identity of the file can be found via the identifying system. The name and time data will not be recoverable if the indexing system is corrupted or if an entry is overwritten. However, the data in the file may be recoverable.
  It is favorable to the investigation that information relative to a file that was deleted may be held in the indexing system for some time. The file may be recoverable along with its identity

if the index entry had not been overwritten and if the file data has not been overwritten.

- Operating systems reuse disk space.
  The area of the disk is marked as available for re-use if a file is completely deleted from the index (i.e. by utilizing an empty recycle bin on a Microsoft Windows device). This is usually referred to as being "**unallocated clusters**."
  There have been many instances in which the most important evidence was evidence that the suspect actually attempted to get rid of. In some cases, data such as a picture or document can be completely recovered but not the history of it. In these cases, the recovered data is still valuable to the investigation.
  There are types of files, such as a word processing document, that keep internal information about themselves. This information is known as metadata. Recovered e-mails may contain metadata about their previous transmission but what is not available is their history on the device they were taken from. Another example would be, in child pornography, an investigation may find a small number of indecent images of youths in the live file system, but they may be able to recover an overwhelming amount of images from unallocated clusters.

Filesystems

Before media can store files, usually the media has to be partitioned and formatted into logical volumes. Partitioning is the practice of reasonably dividing a media into sections that function as separate units. The selected filesystem determines the logical volume formatting (Volonino, Anzaldua, and Godwin, 2007).

The way that files are organized, stored, named, and accessed on logical volumes is determined by the filesystem. There are a large number of filesystems that contain different features and data structures, but they all share a few common traits.

- Filesystems utilize the concepts of directories and files in order to store and organize data. Directories are organizational structures that group files together. Directories can also contain other directories (subdirectories).
- They use data structure to locate files on media.

- Filesystems use one or more allocation units to store written data files to media.

These allocation units are called clusters by some filesystems (i.e. NT File System [NTFS] and File Allocation Table [FAT]) and they are called blocks by other filesystems (i.e. Linux and UNIX). A file allocation unit is a group of sectors, the smallest units that are able to be accessed on media.

Some commonly used filesystems are as follows:

- **FAT12**: FAT12 is used only on floppy disks and FAT volumes smaller than 16 MB. FAT12 uses a 12-bit file allocation table entry to address an entry in the filesystem.
- **FAT16:** MS-DOS, Windows 95/98/NT/2000/XP, Windows Server 2003, and some UNIX OSs support FAT16 natively. FAT16 is also commonly used for multimedia devices such as digital cameras and audio players. FAT16 uses a 16-bit file allocation table entry to address an entry in the filesystem. FAT16 volumes are limited to a maximum size of 2 GB in MS-DOS and Windows 95/98. Windows NT and newer OSs increase the maximum volume size for FAT16 to 4 GB.
- **FAT32:** Windows 95 Original Equipment Manufacturer (OEM) Service Release 2 (OSR2), Windows 98/2000/XP, and Windows Server 2003 support FAT32 natively, as do some multimedia devices. FAT32 uses a 32-bit file allocation table entry to address an entry in the filesystem. The maximum FAT32 volume size is 2 terabytes (TB).
- **NTFS:** Windows NT/2000/XP and Windows Server 2003 support NTFS natively. NTFS is a recoverable filesystem, which means that it can automatically restore the consistency of the filesystem when errors occur. In addition, NTFS supports data compression and encryption and allows user and group-level access permissions to be defined for data files and directories. The maximum NTFS volume size is 2 TB.
- **High-Performance File System (HPFS)** : HPFS is supported natively by OS/2 and can be read by Windows NT 3.1, 3.5, and 3.51. HPFS builds on the directory organization of FAT by providing an automatic sorting of directories. In addition, HPFS reduces the amount of lost disk space by utilizing smaller units

of allocation. The maximum HPFS volume size is 64 GB.

- **Second Extended Filesystem (ext2fs) :** ext2fs is supported natively by Linux. It supports standard UNIX file types and filesystem checks to ensure filesystem consistency. The maximum ext2fs volume size is 4 TB.
- **Third Extended Filesystem (ext3fs)** : ext3fs is supported natively by Linux. It is based on the ext2fs filesystem and provides journaling capabilities that allow consistency checks of the filesystem to be performed quickly on large amounts of data. The maximum ext3fs volume size is 4 TB.
- **ReiserFS:** ReiserFS is supported by Linux and is the default filesystem for several common versions of Linux. It offers journaling capabilities and is significantly faster than the ext2fs and ext3fs filesystems. The maximum volume size is 16 TB.
- **Hierarchical File System (HFS) :** HFS is supported natively by Mac OS. HFS is mainly used in older versions of Mac OS but is still supported in newer versions. The maximum HFS volume size under Mac OS 6 and 7 is 2 GB. The maximum HFS volume size in Mac OS 7.5 is 4 GB. Mac OS 7.5.2 and newer Mac OSs increase the maximum HFS volume size to 2 TB.
- **HFS Plus:** HFS Plus is supported natively by Mac OS 8.1 and later and is a journaling filesystem under Mac OS X. It is the successor to HFS and provides numerous enhancements, such as long filename support and Unicode filename support for international filenames. The maximum HFS Plus volume size is 2 TB.
- **UNIX File System (UFS) :** UFS is supported natively by several types of UNIX OSs, including Solaris, FreeBSD, OpenBSD, and Mac OS X. However, most OSs have added proprietary features, so the details of UFS differ among implementations.
- **Compact Disk File System (CDFS) .** As the name indicates, the CDFS filesystem is used for CDs.
- **International Organization for Standardization (ISO) 9660 and Joliet:** The ISO 9660 filesystem is commonly used on CD-ROMs. Another popular CD-ROM filesystem, Joliet is a variant of ISO 9660. ISO 9660 supports filename lengths of up to 32 characters, whereas Joliet supports up to 64 characters. Joliet also supports Unicode characters within filenames.

- **Universal Disk Format (UDF):** UDF is the filesystem used for DVDs and is also used for some CDs.
- *Source: National Institute of Standards and Technology (2006), Guide to Integrating Forensic Techniques into Incident Response*

Other Data on Media

As described above, filesystems are designed to store files on media. However, filesystems may also hold data from deleted files or earlier versions of existing files. This data can provide important information.

The following items describe how this data can still exist on various media:

- **Deleted Files:** A file is not usually erased from the media when it is deleted; the information in the directory data structure that locates the file gets marked as deleted. The file is still kept on the media but is just not itemized by the operating system. The OS now sees it as free space that can be overwritten. Any portion or the whole deleted file could be overwritten.
- **Slack Space:** Filesystems utilize file allocation units to keep files. If a file needs less space than the size of the allocation unit, the whole file allocation unit is reserved for that file. If the file allocation unit size is 32 KB and the file is 8 KB, the whole 32 KB is allocated to that file but only 8 KB is used, creating 24 KB of unused space. The unused space is called file slack. File slack may keep remaining data, like parts of deleted files.
- **Free Space:** The area on media that is not allocated to a partition. Free space includes unallocated blocks or clusters. Commonly included is the space on the media in which files or entire volumes were at one time but were deleted. Free space may retain some data.

Collecting Files

During data collection, the analyst should make multiple copies of the relevant files or filesystems, typically a master copy and a working copy. The investigator can then use the working copy without affecting the original files or the master copy. It is often important to collect not only the files, but also significant timestamps for the files, such as when the files were last modified or accessed. A later module describes the timestamps and explains how they can be preserved.

COPYING FILES FROM MEDIA

Files can be copied from media using two different techniques:

- Logical Backup. A logical backup copies the directories and files of a logical volume. It does not capture other data that may be present on the media, such as deleted files or residual data stored in slack space.
- Bit Stream Imaging. Also known as disk imaging, bit stream imaging generates a bit-for-bit copy of the original media, including free space and slack space. Bit stream images require more storage space and take longer to perform than logical backups.

The analyst should take a bit stream image of the original media, label the original media and securely store it if it will be needed later for prosecution. All analyses should be conducted utilizing the copied media so that the original is not modified and a copy of the original can be produced at anytime if needed. All steps to produce the copy should be documented. This will make it so that any analyst can generate an exact duplicate of the original media via the same procedures. Proper documentation can show that evidence was not mishandled during collection. Supplementary information should be documented as well; information like the hard drive model and serial number, media storage capacity, and information regarding the imaging software or hardware that was used (i.e. name, licensing information, version number, etc.). The chain of custody is preserved via these actions.

Examining Data Files

Dependent on the forensic tools that will be used to conduct the analysis, the bit stream images or logical backups may have to be restored to another media before the examination of the data can take place. There are a number of tools that have the ability to analyze data directly from an image file but there are others that need the image or back up to be restored to a medium. During the examination, data should be accessed as read-only to make sure that the data being examined is not changed and that it will produce consistent results for future runs. Write-blockers can be implemented to guard against writes from occurring on the restored image. After the restoration of the backup, if it is necessary, the analyst will start to examine the data and will conduct an assessment of the related data and files by locating all files, including hidden files, deleted files, and remaining pieces of files in free and slack space. It may be necessary for the analyst to then extract data from all or one of the files. This could be made more difficult through the use of password protection, encryption, or other measures.

Locating the Files

Locating the files is step one in the examination process. Many gigabytes of free and slack space that can contain thousands of file fragments and files can be captured by a disk image. Manually extracting data from free or slack space can be difficult and time consuming. There are a number of tools that can automate the process. These tools can extract the data from unused space, save it to data files and recover deleted files and files in recycling bins. Special slack recovery tools or hex editors can be used to show the contents of slack space.

Extracting the Data

The remainder of the examination process requires the extraction of data from some or all of the files. Analysts need to know what type of data the file contains in order to make sense of the contents of a file. File extensions are supposed to denote the nature of file contents. An example of this is how mp3 extensions indicate music files and jpg extensions indicate graphic files. But users can exclude a file extension or assign any file extension to any type of file, like naming a text file mysong.mp3. File extensions could even be concealed or unsupported on other operating systems, so analysts should not assume the accuracy of file extensions.

The type of data stored in many files can be identified by looking at their file headers. File headers contain information about a file and possibly metadata about the file contents. The figure below shows how the file header has a file signature that shows the type of data the file contains. The example shows a file header, FFD8, which suggests that this is a jpeg file. It is possible that a file header could be located in a file that is separate from the actual file data. A simple histogram showing the distribution of ASCII values as a percentage of all characters in a file is another technique to identify the type of data in a file. An example of this is how a spike in the 'space,' 'a,' and 'e' lines usually suggests a text file but consistency across the histogram suggests a compressed file. Other patterns suggest files that were modified via steganography or were encrypted.

Encryption causes challenges for analysts. Folders, volumes, individual files, or partitions may have been encrypted to make it so that no one else other than the individual that performed the encryption can access the contents without a passphrase or decryption key. The operating system or a third-party program could perform the encryption. It may be easy to identify an encrypted file but it is not as easy to decrypt it. By discovering the encryption programs installed on the system, examining the file header, or finding encryption keys (which are usually stored on other media), the encryption method could potentially be delineated. Often, it is impossible to decrypt because the authentication (i.e. passphrase) for decryption is not available or the encryption method is strong.

Using Forensic Software

Forensic software is used to examine the image that has been created of the original media. The procedures employed will be dependent upon the nature of the case. The dedicated software allows many ways in which data can be located and refined.

The most commonly used forensic software suites are:

- EnCase from Guidance Software
- Forensic Toolkit (or FTK) from Access Data
- Helix from e-fense

There are many forensic tools available to analysts that allow for the performance of a variety of processes to analyze applications and files, extracting data, reading disk images, and collecting files. Most analysis products let the analyst create reports and log errors that happened during the analysis. The analyst needs to know which processes should be run for the specific question they have about the data. An analyst could potentially have to provide a response or answer a question about the data.

A complete forensic evaluation may not be needed or possible in these cases. The forensic software should have the ability to accomplish data analyses and examinations in different ways and can be run efficiently and speedily from CD's, floppy diskettes, or forensic workstations. These are some of those that an analyst should be able to conduct using a number of different tools (Volonino, Anzaldua, and Godwin, 2007):

- Using File Viewers. It is important to use File viewers instead of the original source applications to scan or preview data. This is also a more efficient technique because native applications are not needed to view each type of file. A variety of tools exist that allow for viewing common file types. For viewing graphics, there are specialized tools. If the file viewers that the analyst has access to do not support a specific file format, the analyst can use the original source application. If the analyst does not have access to the original source application, he/she might have to research the file format and extract the data from the file manually.
- Uncompressing Files. Useful information or other compressed files may be found in compressed files. For that reason, it is imperative that the analyst locates and extracts compressed files. Uncompressing files should occur in the early stages of the forensic process to make sure that the contents of the compressed files are incorporated in other actions and searches. It is possible for compressed files to have malicious content, like compression bombs. Compression bombs are files that have been compressed dozens or hundreds of times that cause examination tools to fail or contain malware. There are methods to minimize compression bombs' impact, but there is no definite method to detect compression bombs before uncompressing files. Up-to-date antivirus software should be in use and the examination system should be standalone so that only that system is affected. An image of

the examination system should be generated so that, if necessary, the system can be restored.

- Graphically Displaying Directory Structures. Graphically displaying directory structures allows analysts the ability to gather general information about the contents of media, as in the type of software installed and the likely technical astuteness of the user or users that produced the data quicker and with more ease. Some products are specialized for Macintosh directory structures but most can display Linux, Windows, and UNIX.
- Identifying Known Files: It is important to find files of interest; however, unimportant files, like known operating system and application files, need to be eliminated from consideration. Validated hash sets, like validated manually created hash sets or those generated by NIST National Software Reference Library (NSRL) project, can be used as a way to identify known malicious and benign files. The MD5 and SHA-1 algorithms are usually used to create message digest values for known files.
- Performing String Searches and Pattern Matches.
  String searches aid in examining large amounts of data to find key words or strings. Developing concise sets of search terms for common situations can help the analyst reduce the volume of information to review.

One of the great benefits of this methodology is that instances of the keyword may be found in hidden locations or in the remnants of deleted files. When a keyword is located in a document, it is necessary for the investigator to examine that document using human eyes and a human brain to establish whether the hit is relevant to the case.

A reasonable example would be a case involving the manufacture of illegal drugs. Searching a computer for the words "drugs" or "narcotics" is likely to produce an awful lot of false hits. Using the names of the chemicals used in the manufacture of drugs or the current slang names for drugs used by people who use or supply them is likely to provide a far better result. If a computer is told to search for a word, it can identify this as only a collection of letters; it cannot establish any meaning or context. The collection of letters that form a short word may often be found within longer words and thus bring in many false positives when searched. It is possible, using special search techniques, to overcome this problem, but skill and experience is required to do so effectively.

In some cases, particularly those involving illegal pictures, forensic software is very useful in identifying all the picture files on the disk. This will include all those that have been hidden or deleted. Establishing whether a new image is an illegal one, though, depends on the examiner looking at the pictures one-by-one.

- Accessing File Metadata
  Details about any given file can be found in file metadata. Collecting metadata on a graphic file may show the creation date, the creator's identity, copyright information, and description. The metadata of graphics created by a digital camera could contain information on the make and model of the camera, the aperture, flash, and F-stop settings. Metadata may identify the author, when and by whom edits occurred, user-defined comments, and the organization licensed the software. Metadata can be extracted by special utilities.

ANALYSIS

After the examination has been completed, the next step is to perform an analysis of the extracted data. The analysis process interprets the result of the examination process and to tries to identify information relating to the arrest of the suspect. This process generally involves both forensic examiners and field investigators discussing the meaning of the documentation produced after the examination process.

As previously mentioned, there are many forensic software tools available that can be helpful in the analysis of different types of data. Knowing when an incident occurred, a file was created or modified, or an e-mail was sent can be critical to forensic analysis. For example, such information can be used to reconstruct a timeline of activities. Although this may seem like a simple task, it is often complicated by unintentional or intentional discrepancies in time settings among systems. Knowing the time, date, and time zone settings for a computer whose data will be analyzed can greatly assist an analyst.

WRITING THE REPORT

When you are writing the report, you should include the contents of the recovered data, as well as the analysis process in the report. This is needed to secure the appropriateness of the actions and steps during the investigation process. You should also keep the contents that are recorded during the investigation process and have not been included in the report. This is for the testimony because, in court, you might be asked. These contents may also be helpful in future investigations. Investigators involved in the investigation process may testify detailed explanations of the investigation process, appropriateness of the working process, and whether investigators are entitled to the specific working process, later in court.

SUMMARY

Analysts should examine copies of files, not the originals. During collection multiple copies of the wanted files or filesystems should be made, usually a working copy and a master copy. This makes it so that analysts can work on the working copy to ensure that the original files or the master copy is not affected. If preserving file times is necessary, or if evidence might be needed for prosecution or disciplinary actions, a bit stream image should be generated.

File integrity should be verified and maintained. During backups and imaging, write-blockers prevent a computer from writing to its storage media. Computing and comparing the message digests of files can verify the integrity of copied data. Images and backups should be accessed as read-only when possible and write-blockers can be used to prevent writing to the image file or backup or the restored image or backup.

File headers, not file extensions, should be used to identify file content types. Analysts should not assume that file extensions are accurate because users can assign any extension to a file. By looking at their file headers, the type of data stored in many files can be identified. To conceal actual file types, people can alter file headers, but this is not as common than altering file extensions.

Analysts should possess forensic toolkits for data analysis and examination. Various tools that provide the ability to conduct rapid reviews of data as in-depth analyses should be in the toolkits. The toolkits should allow applications to run efficiently and rapidly from forensic workstations or removable media such as CDs.

Discussion 1:
In your experience, what types of digital forensic evidence can assist in an investigation? Describe the usefulness of applying "What, Why, When, How, Where and Who" principles in the search for and extraction of digital evidence.

Discussion 2:
Please search the U.S. operating principals considering the local, state, and federal level.
Do these basic principles differ among the U.S. agencies? If so, how?

Discussion 3:
Computers are becoming smaller, faster, and more powerful. They are also integrated into more devices, systems, and infrastructure. Currently, it is possible to purchase a refrigerator with a built-in screen for World Wide Web access. Other home appliances are also available for incorporation into newly constructed or retrofitted "smart houses." What kind of security risks might these devices pose? As computers become more integrated into our daily lives, how does the job of computer crime law enforcement change? Provide two specific examples.

PART VII

Cybercrime Prevention Strategies

Chapter 15 - Macro & Micro Interventions Against Computer Crime

Government Efforts and Current Proposals against ID Theft and Internet Fraud

The effects of data breaches are one of the most salient issues in identity theft, phishing, and Internet fraud. This is due to the fact that one hacking incident in the business industry can cause substantial numbers of victims through the misuse of personal information. As we discussed, identity thieves target individuals as well as organizations. Although there is not sufficient empirical evidence or research examining relationships between data breaches and identity theft, the 2006 Identity Theft Survey Report and Gordon et al.'s research indicated that between 12 and 27 percent of identity theft incidents may result from data breaches. According to, Gordon et al's (2007) report using the U.S. Secret Service data of 517 identity theft cases, 37.1 percent of victims were financial industry organizations in the most frequent victim category, and personal information was misused in credit card frauds, loan frauds, check frauds, and illegal wire-transfers. The retail industry was also a major target for identity thieves, which consists of 21.3% of victimization. The stolen information was used as account fraud and fraudulent credit cards purchase. Gordon et al. also uncovered that 59 percent of the victims did not know the offenders.

It is naturally expected that if data breaches occurs in the business industry, most individual victims of identity theft do not know how and when their personal information was stolen. In this case, individual efforts toward identity theft prevention are likely to be in vain, thus strengthening the idea that corporate security with coordination of government efforts must be prioritized as a macro approach in prevention strategies against cybercrime.

Considerable effort has been made every year on a government level. A 2010 CRS Report for Congress addresses the importance of data breach notification requirements. Through breach notification requirements, people become immediately aware of victims of identity theft and rapidly take compensatory steps to mitigate the damage. Reporting requirements on business industries may spur businesses towards increasing their data security standards, which can minimize data breaches and any potential identity theft incidences.

Other government proposals are concerned with securing Social Security numbers (SSN) that are widely exposed to the risk of potential identity thefts in both the private and public sectors (CRS Report for Congress, 2010). The current proposals are listed below:

- Prohibiting states from displaying or electronically including SSNs on driver's license, motor vehicle registrations, or personal identification cards.
- Prohibiting the display of SSNs on Medicare cards
- Increasing restriction on the disclosure of certain forms of personally identifiable information, such as SSNs, in connection with federally funded grant programs
- Criminalizing the display, sale, or purchase of SSNs without consent from the individual, prohibiting the use of SSNs on government-issued payment checks, and banning inmate access to SSNs.
- Requiring the Commissioner of Social Security to provide the Secretary of Homeland Security with the personally identifiable information of individuals in the instance that the Commissioner determines that a SSN has been used with multiple names.
- Producing SSN cards made of tamper-proof material that contains a digital image of the cardholder.
- In addition, legislation introduced law enforcement and consumer notification systems in the Congress in order to enhance its effectiveness.

- Requiring consumer reporting agencies to report suspected identity theft to the U.S. Secret Service and the Attorney General, as well as requiring the Secret Service to report identity theft to the Federal Bureau of Investigation or the Department of Homeland Security if there are suspected terrorism or immigration elements.
- Requiring the Commissioner of Social Security to report suspected identity theft to the individual at risk as well as to the appropriate law enforcement authorities.
- Requiring the agency or business entity wherein the breach occurred to notify individuals whose personally identifiable information may have been compromised.

Assistance from the business industry appears to be a crucial key to investigate identity theft cases because they are the main resource that keeps investigative information. It is important to share the information with a mandated government agency. The effective collaborative work seems to be the best strategy to combat the crime victimization as a macro approach. Securing personal information within the government structure and establishing effective communication within all levels of law enforcement agencies would facilitate mitigating cybercrime victimization. More importantly, structured legal remedies for victims, who suffer from financial loss and serious emotional frustration, need to be offered by both private and public sectors.

INDIVIDUAL EFFORTS

In the United States, the Identity Theft and Assumption Deterrence Act of 1998 and the Fair and Accurate Credit Transaction Act of 2003 mainly facilitate victim assistance, complaint, and consumer education services for victims of identity theft or Internet fraud. Obtaining a credit report has been much easier than in previous times, so monitoring personal financial information online can be conveniently implemented, using a fraud alert service from private companies. However, this convenient online service is often associated with monthly fees that may hinder people to use the credit monitoring service. I personally believe that providing free service with a government sponsor would be a considerably effective method to prevent potential fraud victimization.

Education fundamentally alters the ways cybercriminals work. Teaching online users how the latest scams operate may weaken the ability of the scam to work, and therefore, can possibly lower the incidence of personal victimization in cyberspace. Proactive approaches to self-changing adequate online behaviors also need to be prioritized.

There are numerous educational materials that are available through government and business websites. The most common advice is if it seems too good to be true, it is too good to be true, so extreme caution would not be too extreme when you decide to purchase items or use any service on the Internet. In regards to phishing, con artists acquire mailing lists from social networking sites or web-based email accounts. The phisher sends users emails using a victim's email account to encourage the users to visit a website that discloses their personal information. In online auctions, con artists run large number of auctions for a short period (anywhere from 1 to 3 days) when compared to the average of at least seven days. Once victims have sent money in an online auction, the con artist disappears, later reemerging under a new user ID.

MICRO INTERVENTION AGAINST COMPUTER CRIME

The findings from my empirical study suggest that college students who overlook their computer oriented lifestyle in cyberspace or who neglect the presence of computer security software in their computer are likely to be victimized. The results revealed differential lifestyle patterns directly link with the occurrence of criminal victimization in cyberspace. In addition, this research supports the conclusion that the presence of computer security is the most crucial component to protect the computer systems from computer criminals. MaQuade (2006) stated that "Routine Activities Theory has important implications for understanding crimes committed with or prevented with computers, other IT devices, or information systems" (p. 147). In other words, computer-crime victimization can be significantly minimized through abiding by adequate online lifestyle and equipping computer security technology. This section presents the importance of establishing the computer crime prevention program, which is mainly derived from the suggested research findings.

The findings suggest that establishing prosocial views of promoting adequate online lifestyle and utilizing efficient computer security will contribute to a reduction in computer-crime victimization. Even though self-directed decisions by computer users for acquiring adequate online lifestyle and installed computer security on their computers have become increasingly important, contemporary criminal justice crime prevention programs tend to neglect the importance of these issues. In addition, while the number of computer users is increasing every day, structured computer-crime prevention programs are not fully available to online users. Computer-crime prevention programs, however, can be logically categorized as school-based crime prevention programs. In fact, some colleges and universities currently offer introductory and specialized courses in computer crime and information security issues (McQuade, 2006). The primary goal of the computer-crime prevention program is to minimize potential computer-crime victimization based in an educational setting. The school should be the setting for initial exposure and training in this program because many school crime prevention programs already offer specific guidelines that establish responsibilities for students in the classroom and the community at large. Gottfredson et al. (1993) asserted that "interventions to establish norms and expectations for behavior" are some of the most effective strategies in the school crime prevention program (p. 145). This statement matches the general strategy and goals of the computer-crime prevention program. Numerous studies suggest that social context factors have a significant influence on crime victimization. In other words, when we educate students with an adequately structured computer-crime prevention program, the beneficial outcomes should be expected by establishing individuals' appropriate online lifestyle and building their own protections during the usage of computers.

Duke (1989) emphasized that a school environment that promotes shared values and expectations can positively influence behaviors. Changes in the school and classroom environment can clarify behavioral norms through school and discipline management intervention (Gottfredson et al., 2004). These existing effective school programs establish norms and adjust expectations for illegal or delinquent behaviors. In terms of computer-crime prevention application, the combination of computer security awareness programs and school campaigns against computer crime would facilitate changing individual online lifestyle via the social environment at school if the program is adequately constructed and implemented. McQuade (2006) asserts that a major opportunity to minimize computer crime through enhanced information security is via "public awareness, formal education, and professional training" (p. 487). The program should not only address specific methods such as general knowledge of information security and valuable tips to avoid crime victimization to help prevent computer crime, but also it should emphasize law and regulations relating to cybercrime to facilitate the acquisition of solid ethical standards for students.

The computer-crime prevention program must offer students efficient practices for safeguarding information, including the

> use of strong passwords and effective password management, frequent updating of antimalware definitions; installation and use of software or hardware firewalls; regularly downloading security and other patches for operating systems and applications; installation and frequent use of antispyware and antiadware applications; backing up data systematically and in different ways; using antikeylogger, encryption, and digital signature technology. (McQuade, 2006, p. 453)

In addition, the program must employ adequate online lifestyles by alerting the individual to online risk-taking behaviors that allow students to transform the constructed general online practices into their personal lifestyles. Furthermore, the program should emphasize law and regulations on computer crime with the goal of reinforcing ethical norms and expectations for computer users' behaviors.

As computer technology evolves every day, the level of complexities related to computer crime and information security management changes (McQuade, 2006). There are only a few empirical studies available regarding the issue of computer crime. Thus, it is essential to develop and research computer crime related topics in order to manage future computer crime. As noted in the RAT literature, motivated offenders and suitable targets frequently collide in cyberspace. This happens because target suitability in cyberspace is a fully given situation due to the fact that personal information on the computer naturally carries valuable information into cyberspace that constantly attracts computer criminals. In addition, as technology advances and computer criminals become more sophisticated, law enforcement is likely to find prevention difficult. Fortunately, informal social control agents are slowly recognizing the seriousness of computer crime, even if they are not actively operating in our cyber society. Thus, implementation of computer-crime prevention programs should become a part of building strong informal social control agents to strengthen existing effective guardianship through an effective education method.

It is also important to recognize that effective computer-crime prevention cannot be accomplished solely through the proposed program. A formal system of capable guardianship is also necessary to protect computer users from computer crime. Australian law enforcement strategy on computer crime emphasized issues such as "training and education; development and retention; and information and intelligence exchange" (Etter, 2001, p. 9). Carter and Katz (1997) point out that "decision makers in business, government, and law enforcement must develop policies, methods, and regulations to detect incursions, investigate and prosecute the perpetrators, and prevent future crimes" (p. 12). Fortunately, government has a fundamental interest and role in preventing computer crime by collectively working with both private and nonprofit sectors, and international agencies.

As a macro approach, changing social perceptions toward computer abusers is also essential. The media generally do not provide detailed coverage of computer crime and often paint hackers' activities in a positive light. *The New York Times* reported that "bright youngsters who breach computer security should receive commendation, not condemnation" (1987, p. 121). Because there is little stigma attached to their activities, hackers rarely think of themselves as real criminals, even though they may be prosecuted and convicted of committing computer crimes.

Therefore, it is necessary to change both the social and individual environments for those who are in a position to engage in these activities in order to manage future computer crime. This goal can be accomplished through the implementation of an effective computer-crime prevention programs by informing effective cyber security, encouraging safe online lifestyles, increasing the level of formal and informal guardianship, and eliminating favorable or ambiguous perceptions about computer criminals.

FUTURE DIRECTIONS ON COMPUTER CRIME PREVENTION PROGRAM

Prevention is the preferred strategy for dealing with crime, but there are few cyber-crime prevention programs in existence. Few existing cyber-crime prevention programs have been empirically evaluated. The policy implication section briefly introduced a computer-crime prevention program, which was mainly derived from Routine Activities Theory.

In order to construct an effective computer crime prevention program, it is imperative to reflect on other theoretical perspectives that would convey positive effects on deterring potential computer crime. Recent criminological literature links illegal computer crime activities to social learning processes (Akers, 1985; Hollinger, 1988, 1991, 1992; Skinner & Fream, 1997).

Skinner and Fream (1997) tested the relationship between the theoretical elements of social learning and the behaviors of cyber-criminals. The researchers (1997) posited that the nature of computer crime requires that individuals learn not only how to operate computer equipment, but also to master specific procedures, programming, and techniques for using the computer for illegal activities. The researchers (1997) examined five types of computer criminal activities for verifying this argument: (a) knowingly using, making, or giving to another person a "pirated" copy of commercially sold computer software; (b) trying to guess another's password to get into his or her computer account or files; (c) accessing another's computer account or files without his or her knowledge or permission just to look at the information or files; (d) adding, deleting, changing, or printing any information in another's computer files without the owner's knowledge or permission; and (e) writing or using a program that would destroy someone's computerized data (e.g., a virus, logic bomb, or Trojan horse).

The results of a multivariate regression analysis support social learning theory as an explanation for computer crime in general (Skinner & Fream, 1997). Skinner and Fream (1997) found that one of the most significant predictors of committing computer crime is interacting with friends who engage in illegal activities. If a student wants to learn how to use a computer for illegal activities, his friends, who have successful experience in these activities, are likely to offer advice and assistance. Friends are also generally willing to share technical information and allow others to acknowledge new-found games, programs, or techniques.

Skinner and Fream (1997) also found that family members significantly influence students' learning about the behavior of pirating software. Siblings and parents often distribute illegal copies of new programs and games in the family setting, if they have access to them. Interestingly, the research findings indicated that teachers who not only ignored piracy but who also strongly support it through their words and actions increased the frequency of piracy and violation of any type of computer crime among students (1997).

Guided by social learning theory and research, the proposed program can be driven upon the experience of empirically validated school-based crime prevention programs. The primary goal of a computer crime prevention program is to facilitate the acquisition of solid ethical standards for general students, computer science students and computer professionals to acquire before they become cyber-criminals. The school is the setting for initial exposure and training in ethics, but the process is expected to continue in the workplace. The researcher suggests a potentially efficient strategy to deter future cyber-crimes through a well-constructed computer ethics program.

Ethics programs have been broadly utilized in various fields in our society. Most law enforcement training in the United States includes ethics training in order to provide "a clear definition of proper and improper conduct; mechanisms for detecting and sanctioning improper conduct" (Kappeler, 1998, pp. 216-217). Colleges and universities in the United States have Institutional Review Boards (IRB) in order to ensure that research is conducted in an ethical manner.

Computer professional associations such as the Association for Computing Machinery (ACM) and Association of Information Technology Professionals (AITP) have codes of ethics that establish expected behaviors and responsibilities for computer users and computer professionals (Harris, 2000, p. 1). Their codes of ethics share three major principles: "1) to maintain competence, 2) to disclose conflict of interest, and 3) to maintain confidentiality of information" (Harris, 2000, p. 1). The codes of ethics also contain sufficient ethical guidelines and regulations for computing practices. These codes of ethics, however, do not have any legal weight since both AITP and

ACM are private membership organizations (Harris, 2000). Therefore, abiding by computer ethics becomes optional for computer users, and this option facilitates opportunities for computer crime and abuse (Harris, 2000). A mandated computer ethics program, followed by continuing reinforcement, is necessary to instill and maintain, within the next generation of computer users, appropriate guidelines for cyber behaviors.

Thus, establishing the mandated ethics program is vital for constructing pro-social views of cyber-crime among students. The sixth proposition of differential association states that individuals become criminals as the result of an excess of definitions favorable to violating the law over definitions unfavorable to violating the law (Sutherland, 1947). If individuals repeatedly observe that illegal computer activities are beneficial to them or others, they are more likely to engage in those activities.

In addition, computer ethics classes must address law and regulations relating to cyber-crime. Akers (1985) posited that social behavior responds to rewards and punishments. Any given behavior is likely to continue or to increase if it is followed by more rewards than punishments (Akers, 1997). The theory proposes that criminal and delinquent behavior is acquired, repeated, and changed by the same process as conforming behavior. In other words, when individuals observe more punishments than rewards, through consequences of their actions, they will likely discontinue the specific behaviors.

Instruction should include studies of court cases and convictions of cyber-crime from the Department of Justice. In addition, the class will examine existing government legislation on cyber-crime. By examining criminal law and court cases, students will understand the potential negative consequences of engaging in cyber-crime. One example of course content is listed below:

> In the fall of 1998, Congress passed the Identity Theft and Assumption Deterrence Act. This legislation made identity theft a new federal offense and prohibited:
>
> > Knowingly transfer[ring] or us[ing], without lawful authority, a means of identification of another person with the intent to commit, or to aid or abet, any unlawful activity that constitutes a violation of Federal law, or that

> constitute a felony under any applicable State or local law (18 U.S.C. #1028[a][7]).
> Under general most circumstances, the offense carries a maximum term of 15 years' imprisonment, a fine, and criminal forfeiture of any personal property used or intended to be used in committing the offense or gained through the offense (Benner and Schwerha, 2002).

Social learning theorists hold that the learning process depends on priority, intensity, and duration (Akers, 1997). Skinner and Fream (1997) assert that the more college students associate with peers who are engaging in illegal computer activity, the greater the frequency of the behavior. The three tenets of the social learning process, priority, intensity, and duration, are the crucial elements in the proposed mandated ethics program. The proposed mandated ethics program should be implemented in the first year of college, followed by multiple training sessions before and after employees formally initiate their profession. In this way, the ethics course will be a more effective method to prevent computer crime. In addition, after graduation from college, students will naturally receive reinforcement through professional training sessions after they are hired by a company. Thus, the proposed ethical training should continue during the transition from college to the professional training setting, and would continue to increase and reinforce individuals' ethical standards.

The mandated ethics program is intended to intervene before individuals associate with new peers who encourage them to engage in illegal computer activities. Through the social learning process, individuals will eventually recognize the importance of abiding by ethical standards, policies, and procedures for computer usage as a student and computer professional. Furthermore, the mandated ethics course should change an individual's beliefs and attitudes so that they do not develop positive definitions about computer crime. In sum, when the future computer crime prevention program truly take both routine activities theoretical perspectives and the components of social learning perspectives into consideration, positive effects should be expected.

Chapter 16 - Cyberterrorism: Criminal Patterns and Countermeasures

This chapter was mainly constructed based on the Korean Institute of Criminology's research report (2012) dedicated to cyberterrorism.

After the attacks on September 11th, 2001, terrorism has evolved into a new form, more networked, diverse, and intricate. Cyberterrorism has received greater attention globally due to the recent cyberattacks against European countries and the United States.
DDoS (Distrubuted Denial of Service) attacks and the hacking of national government agencies initiated by China prove these threats are real. Examples of direct forms of cyberterrorism are DDoS attacks, the Stuxnet worm, hacking and the use of botnets. Other forms of cyberterrorism are the utilization of the Internet for traditional activities such as, recruitment, propaganda, training, education, financing, command & control, and the procurement of supplies. The United Nations Office on Drugs and Crime (UNODC) defined this type of activity as "the use of the Internet for terrorist purposes." Cyberterrorism is globally recognized as fundamental threats to national security as well. A violation of the safety of cyberspace, comprising computer systems and networks, can be considered as serious as an attack as in the physical realm.

Definition of Cyberterrorism

There is a controversial definitional issue of cyberterrorism; and so, it has many definitions. Cyberterrorism can be generally seen as an "act of disrupting critical infrastructure such as energy, transportation and public facilities by using cyber tools for the purpose of threatening the government or its people. Cyberterrorism utilizes software and networks in cyberspace to commit an act of terror" (Yoon and Morris, 2012).

The Center for Strategic and International Studies (CSIS) defines cyberterrorism as:

> *"The use of computer network tools to shut down critical national infrastructures (e.g., energy, transportation, government operations) or to coerce or intimidate a government or civilian population."*

Alternatively, the National (US) Conference of State Legislatures has defined cyberterrorism as:

> *"... the use of information technology by terrorist groups and individuals to further their agenda. This can include use of information technology to organize and execute attacks against networks, computer systems and telecommunications infrastructures, or for exchanging information or making threats electronically..."*

Infrastructure attacks also include targeting a computer system that contains critical data in order to disable or destroy it. The USA Patriot Act of 2001 defines critical infrastructure as "systems and assets, whether physical or virtual, so vital to the United States that the incapacity or destruction of such systems and assets would have a debilitating impact on the security, national economic security, national health or safety, or any combination of those matters."

However, in order to charge the person responsible for the act of cyberterrorism, the identification of the person who actually committed the cyberterrorist act is required. It is nearly impossible to identify the person responsible if the attack originated from a different country. Other than the activities listed above, the USA Patriot Act of 2001 additionally requires serious financial loss of at least $5,000, physical injury to any person, and a threat to public health or safety or damage affecting a computer system used by or for a government entity in furtherance of the administration of justice, national defense, or national security (Moore, 2011).

Cyberterrorism is a type of cyber-attack A cyber-attack can be either cyberterrorism or cybercrime depending on the circumstances concerning national security or the social norm. As discussed in chapter 1, cybercrime can be generally defined as criminal behaviors that use computing technology connected with the Internet as a tool. Cyber-violence may involve the sharing or distribution of bomb-making guides, warfare strategies, or information to assist an individual's learning of hacking techniques that could later be used in a criminal activity.

There is an overlap between the results and the acts of cybercrime and cyberterrorism. There are many crimes committed in cyberspace that would be considered a cybercrime, but if the crime was committed by a terrorist, it would constitute cyberterrorism. In addition, Moore (2011) addresses the importance of understanding proper classification of cyberterrorism because many cybercrimes can be labeled as cyberterrorism.

Cyber-warfare means an act of aggression through the use of the Internet by a state. The fact that a state is the aggressor can mean much more serious consequences; however, it is very similar to cyberterrorism in form. Terrorists' use of the Internet should be examined as a form of cyberterrorism. Between the variations in definitions, cyberterrorism condenses many forms of cybercrimes, which may or may not constitute cyberterrorism. These include any type of criminal activity that transpires in cyberspace including general forms of malicious computer hacking and/or cyber-attacks. Such acts of terrorism may be direct (e.g., attacks on infrastructure) or indirect through the generation of revenue via cybercriminal techniques (e.g., credit fraud and identify theft).

There is concern of a surprise cyber-attack on the critical infrastructure that would, with a single event, be catastrophic in the U.S. In fact, there may have already been cyber-attacks and attempts on the critical infrastructure in the U.S., but none have been linked to terrorist organizations. Some argue that the fear of cyberterrorism on the critical infrastructure is based largely on a lack of education about the topic and media portrayals of terrible events.

However, many reports indicate that China has attempted to build a unit of computer hackers with the intention to launch cyberattacks against the U.S., and China has already launched successful attacks against U.S. information systems in recent years.

CYBERATTACK TOOLS.

Two primary cyber-terror-attacks are Stuxnet Worm and DDoS.

The Stuxnet Worm is speculated to have been originally developed as a 'cyber weapon' to attack the centrifuge in Iran's nuclear reprocessing plant at Natanz, Iran. The Stuxnet Worm used a weakness in the Microsoft Windows operating system to spread and attack Siemens industrial computers in the United States and Germany. Due to the complexity of this computer virus, there were suspicions that there was state intervention (U.S. and Israel) in its creation. James Lewis of the Center for Strategic and International Studies defined the Stuxnet Worm incident as the first case of cyberwarfare.

A Distributed Denial-of-Service (DDos) attack overloads computer resources or stops a network by exhausting bandwidth of the network. If this attack succeeds, the victimized computer system or network is rendered inoperable.

TYPOLOGY OF CYBERTERRORISM

Category	Definition and Explanation
Information Attacks	Cyberterrorist attacks focused on altering or destroying the content of electronic files, computer systems, or the various materials therein.
Infrastructure Attacks	Cyberterrorist attacks designed to disrupt or destroy the actual hardware, operating platform, or programing in a computerized environment.
Technological Facilitation	The use of cyber communications to send plans for terrorist attacks, incite attacks, or otherwise facilitate traditional terrorism or cyberterrorism.

Category	Definition and Explanation
Fundraising and Promotion	The use of the Internet to raise funds for a violent political cause, to advance an organization supportive of violence political action, or to promote an alternative ideology that is violent in orientation

(Source: Ballard, J. D., Hornik, J. G., & McKenzie, D., "Technological facilitation of terrorism Definitional, legal and policy issue," In Ozeren, Suleyman, "Cyberterrorism and International Cooperation: General Overview of the Available Mechanisms to Facilitate an Overwhelming Task," Reponses to Cyber Terrorism, Centre of Excellence Defense Against Terrorism, Ankara: Turkey IOS Press, 2008, p. 74)

Besides information attacks and infrastructure attacks, terrorists can use the Internet for a number of other activities such as communication, planning and support functions, data mining, propaganda, and fundraising and financial activities.

Technological Facilitation

In terms of technological facilitations of terrorist groups, cyber communication technology has dramatically shortened transmission time from one member to the next. Web forums, social networking sites, video conference chatting software, and voice-over-internet-protocol (VIOP) can all be used by terrorist organizations to enhance their efficiency in communication. In addition, IT largely facilitates terrorists' planning activities and support functions.

The Use of the Internet by Al Qaeda

Since 2008, civic groups against terrorism in the U.S. saw Al Qaeda's activities on the Internet, especially using social networking sites, as a problem and started making official complaints.

For example, Awais Younis, a 25-year-old man born in Arlington, Virginia, was arrested for disseminating threatening messages throughout the U.S. At that time, Younis threatened on his Facebook account that he would deploy explosives. According to a document from the Joint Terrorism Task Force of the FBI, Younis had written technical details of making pipe bombs, and expressed his intentions to deploy three to four pipe bombs in subway cars in the Washington D.C. transit system area. His selection of these particular targets was because these locations were where the most commuters would have been located and the deployment of the bombs may not have been visible.

Another example is Zachary Adam Chesser, who was prosecuted for expressing threats in cyberspace. One of the charges against Chesser was that he not only expressed threats, but also solicited terrorist acts from others. This solicitation was posted on his blog and Internet bulletin boards. He uploaded 200 books related to "Jihad, Islam and War" on social networking sites and also uploaded a book about "making preparations" for terrorism. The prosecution also found, in evidence discovered on the Internet, that Chesser had connections to Al Qaeda, and this charge was also added to his case.

Al Qaeda tends to use the Internet to share political messages and rally supporters, which clearly indicates a potential threat to the nation. However, the protection of the freedom of speech in the First Amendment of the U.S. Constitution can make complications. Currently, the First Amendment guarantees safety against the violation of essential elements of freedom of speech, but expressions on the Internet that express provocation, propagation, inducement, and conspiracy of terrorism are exempt from First Amendment protections.

1. Technological Facilitation: Communication

Online communication is an area not firmly regulated by the authorities and hence, it remains one of the most common ways that terrorists make use of the Internet; websites, forums, blogs, emails, instant messaging, voice over IP, etc. are as frequently used by terrorists as by everybody else. Online communication facilitates exchanging information between terrorists and terrorist organizations and plays an important role in communicating with the media and the public in general.

Digital cryptography has, in recent years, become very easy to learn. It is now very easy for a person to hide information in a digital file (e.g., an image) that appears to be harmless. Many freely available software programs exist that can easily encrypt messages and information, which can be accessed via the Internet, decrypted, and utilized for the purposes of a terrorist attack.

In fact, data encryption use by terrorist organizations was reported in conjunction with the September 11, 2001 attacks on the United States. One report suggested that Al Queda used intelligence hidden via encryption on pornographic websites and sports chat rooms. Such information could have been accessed by any person at any time, but the massiveness of the files stored digitally makes it almost impossible to search for terrorist related information.

In addition to the more general communication, the Internet provides a wide array of options for global networking and recruitment. Due to widely available Internet technology, the Internet recruitment of new terrorist members has become a fully organizational activity and has been increasingly characterized by individuality and self-recruitment.

2. Technological Facilitation: Planning Activities and Supporting Functions

- Instructions for attacks and activities can be downloadable, open to the public in forums, and often very easy to follow.
- Training through guidebooks or handbooks (e.g. "Terrorist's Handbook," "Mujahadenn Poisons Handbook," "How to make Bombs") is freely available on the Internet.
- Supporting functions (communication, propaganda, coordination, administration, etc.) during attacks between individuals and organizations.
- Involving voluntary assistance from "outsiders" as a reaction to the attacks and/or political situation.

Instructions for less sophisticated attacks and activities, such as how to launch a DoS attack, make simple bombs, etc., are freely available on the Internet, easily accessible, and easy to follow. Interactive tutorials, guidebooks, and various online training opportunities create a perfect virtual training camp or open university to all interested counterparts. The Internet also plays a role in supporting activities such as communication, propaganda, coordination, administration, etc. during attacks between individuals and organizations.

Additionally, as mentioned above, the online environment makes it relatively easy to involve voluntary assistance from outsiders, and hence, magnify the effect and consequences of the attacks.

3. Technological Facilitation: Data Mining

- Researching information, contacts, and backgrounds for terrorist activities and targeting analyses
- Often using open sources for information (e.g. Google Earth, Google Maps, Microsoft Virtual Earth, NASA WorldWind etc.)
- P.W. Brunst: The combination of all unclassified information available on the Internet adds up to something that must be classified

Data mining is strongly interlinked with planning and supporting terrorist activities. The amount of information freely available on the Internet can be surprising. Open sources like Google Earth or NASA WorldWind provide more information than traditional maps. Moreover, researching the background of persons, targets, and security measures merely involves a few clicks.

Fundraising and Promotion

Terrorist groups also use digital technology for the purpose of disseminating propaganda intended to garner support from individuals. Promotions involve any use of cyber communications technology to promote the cause of a terrorist group, to recruit members, to solicit information, or to generate revenue (e.g., fundraising). Most major terrorist organizations have an Internet presence and can use digital technology as a tool, just as would any legitimate business.

1. Online Propaganda

- **The Internet is a low-cost, fast, and global medium:**
  - Presenting terrorist beliefs and spreading information about specific organizations, history, leaders' profiles, their

views, beliefs, aims and ambitions.
- Publicity (newsletters, videos, photos, etc.)
- Threats
- Usually via terrorist websites
- According to the US Department of State, 4,500 terrorist websites were known to exist in 2005.

The Internet is a low-cost, fast, and global medium presenting terrorist beliefs and spreading information about specific organizations' histories, leaders' profiles, their views, beliefs, aims, and ambitions. Successful and wide-spread propaganda not only promotes terrorism, but may also include threats to perform new acts and create fear among the public.

The main tools for propaganda are terrorist websites and various freely disseminated newsletters, videos, photos, etc.

2. Fundraising and Financial Activities

- To raise funds for their activities directly via Websites (e.g. donations of money and other items, profits from e-stores, etc.)
- To engage in resource mobilization through illegal means (e.g. credit card fraud, the use of electronic communication and encryption in drug trafficking, scam emails, etc.)
- The online environment offers anonymity for supporters.

Financing has been the most worrisome part of terrorists using the Internet. Funds for terrorist activities can be raised directly via websites; e.g. donations of money and other items, profits from e-stores, and/or engaging in cybercrime activities.

CYBERTERRORISM CASE STUDIES

The number of threats posed by cyber incidents and the growing vulnerability of modern information societies to such offenses is alarming. In recent years, international communities have witnessed a new wave of politically motivated cyber-attacks that have underlined the need to tackle cybercrime in national legislation. Additionally, these incidents have raised the issue of the necessity of a comprehensive approach to cyber security in general.

This section introduces 4 major cyber-attacks such as Estonia (2007), Lithuania (2008), Georgia (2008), and Sony (2014), and describes the background, targets, means, and effects of the attacks.

Estonia 2007: Background

The first case study focuses on the cyber-attacks on Estonia in 2007. Estonia is a small and highly IT developed country in Northern Europe. The state offers its citizens a wide availability of more than one thousand different electronic services and the Internet is actively used both in public and private spheres. Signing documents by electronic signature and voting in online parliamentary elections is common for Estonians. In Estonia, 95% of all banking operations are carried out electronically. These are just a few examples that illustrate the extensive use of and at the same time dependence on Information and Communication technologies (ICT).

The relocation of the Soviet Bronze Soldier in 2007 created political tensions that resulted in riots in the streets that soon turned into riots in cyberspace.

Estonia 2007: Targets

The main targets of the attacks were information distribution channels of both public and private sectors. The websites of public institutions, such as the president, government, parliament, ministries, state audit office, etc., as well as public and private e-services like banks and media were under assault. Additionally, ISP's and the websites of some of the political parties were attacked.

The cyber-attacks hit off with an emotionally charged phase that was characterized by relatively simple attacks. This included simple, openly distributed instructions in various Internet forums as well as the launch of DoS attacks and website defacements.

The next phase of the attacks was much more sophisticated. The use of large botnets and professional coordination was observed. The effects of the DDoS attacks were more severely noticed by users outside Estonia, as a large amount of foreign connections were cut off in order to cope with the excessive traffic. At the most active moment, 58 websites were shut down at once. Additionally, a heightened use of mass unsolicited email was detected against government email servers and individual email accounts.

The Estonian cyber-attacks quickly gained international attention and started an open debate on the spectrum of cyber incidents, national responses, relevant legal framework, and the growing vulnerability of modern information societies. The attacks proved, once again, that cyber threats are a cross-border issue and concern various jurisdictions. In addition, the attacks underline that a successful investigation requires international cooperation. The origin of the attacks remains unclear as the involvement of computers from 178 countries was reported.

Lithuania 2008: Background

The second case study describes cyber-attacks against Lithuania in 2008. Lithuania, a country situated in Eastern Europe, is a modern information society with ICT deployment statistics steadily growing. In 2007, the country had 48% of the population using the Internet and various online public services. A comprehensive IT regulatory framework has been in place since 2002.

June-July 2008: political discontent against a law amendment coinciding with cyberattacks

In 2008, Lithuania faced numerous cyber-attacks after the parliament adapted a law amendment concerning the freedom of speech and the freedom of assembly and the amendment was condemned by the Russian Federation.

Lithuania 2008: Targets:

The main type of attack reported was the defacement of websites. The original content of nearly 300 websites was replaced with communist images related to the Soviet Union. The defaced websites included both public and private institutions, such as the chief institutional ethics commission, Lithuanian social democratic party, etc. In addition, the attackers also used Internet forums and blasted email spam highlighting their manifesto and exploited the vulnerabilities of one ISP.

The Lithuania case is significant because the public institutions were warned about the possible attacks but did not manage to inform the private sector of the threat in time. The attacks also indicated the connection between political decisions and cyber-attacks. Defacement is considered to be a criminal offense under the Lithuanian penal code, but since the origin of the attacks was unclear, the investigation led to a dead end.

Moreover, the attacks raised the issue of the service level agreement for e-services because governments in countries with a high degree of cyber vulnerability need to consider additional guarantees for the smooth operations of their information infrastructure.

Georgia 2008: Background:

The third case study presents cyber-attacks against Georgia in 2008. Georgia is situated in the Caucasus region south of Russia. The country holds less than 10% of active Internet users and lacks nation-wide information society services and has a relatively weak IT regulatory framework. In addition, Georgia's information infrastructure relies heavily on its neighboring countries. Notwithstanding the low dependence on ICT, the country encountered cyber-attacks in 2008. The uniqueness of this case lies in the fact that the cyber-attacks fell within the timeframe and context of a broader armed conflict between the Russian Federation and Georgia.

Georgia 2008: Targets:

The targets of the cyber-attacks are similar to the previous two cases; the websites of public institutions, government sites, as well as newspapers, media agencies, and banks were under attack. The main means of attack were defacement and DdoS attacks. Several websites were defaced as to include pictures of twentieth century dictators such as Adolf Hitler. Additionally, instructions to launch the attacks, malicious software, and email addresses for spamming were distributed in blogs and forums.

The Georgian cyber-attacks took place at the time of a nationally declared state of war and were, hence, not the priority of national security. Nevertheless, the well-coordinated information blockade changed the usual belief that only highly developed IT societies were vulnerable to cyber threats. From a legal perspective, it can be concluded that the case covers the interrelation of three different fields of law: law of armed conflict, criminal law, and the legal relation of ICT infrastructure.

Sony Hack 2014: The Interview Case:

On November 22, 2014, Sony's computer system was hacked. Skulls appeared on employees' screens along with a threatening message to expose prime confidential Sony data. An unknown hacker group, Guardians of Peace, claimed that they were behind the cyber-attack. Sony's private company information such as confidential emails, employees' social security information, and bosses' salaries had been exposed to the public. In addition, Sony's new and unreleased movies were also stolen and shared through p2p websites.

Speculation about North Korea's involvement in the cyber-attack was derived from their initial threat in June to Sony about the upcoming release of the comedy movie *The Interview*. The comedy is about two journalists who were granted an interview for their television talk show with the North Korean leader Kim Jung-eun, but were then recruited by the CIA to assassinate him.

The significance of the hack intensified after the "Guardians of Peace" claimed they would commit 9/11-type attacks on movie theaters showing the Sony film. The cancellations of the film's New York premiere led Sony to announce that they were not going to release the film on December 25th, 2014 as planned. However, Sony later allowed a theatrical and online release of the movie at Christmas, which took in $15 million and was downloaded more than two million times in its first few days.

The timetable of the incident is listed below:

- 22 November: Sony computer systems hacked, exposing embarrassing emails and personal details about stars
- 7 December: North Korea denies accusations that it is behind the cyber-attack, but praises it as a "righteous deed"
- 16 December: "Guardians of Peace" hacker group threatens 9/11-type attack on cinemas showing film; New York premiere canceled
- 17 December: Leading US cinema groups say they will not screen the film; Sony cancels Christmas Day release
- 19 December: FBI concludes North Korea orchestrated hack; President Obama calls Sony cancellation "a mistake"
- 20 December: North Korea proposes joint inquiry with US into hacks, rejected by the US

- 22 December: North Korea suffers a severe Internet outage
- 23 December: Sony confirms a limited Christmas Day release for *The Interview*
- 2 January: The US imposes sanctions on North Korea in response to the cyber-attack.

Similarities:

Cyberattacks are fast, cheap, and moderately destructive, but no one would plan to fight using only cyber weapons. They are not destructive enough to damage an opponent's will and capacity to resist. Cyberattacks will not defeat a large and powerful opponent. In most scenarios involving state actors, these attacks will not be "cyber only" incidents unless an opponent makes major miscalculations or unless their tolerance for risk is high, and risk tolerance may be a function of their belief that the action is covert (and thus less likely to trigger a damaging response).

The four case studies share a number of similarities: First, the attacks were launched due to political and social motivation. Second, the attacks were carried out mostly via the same means; defacement, DDoS attacks, online propaganda, and etc. Third, the targets remain more or less the same, covering both public and private spheres. Additionally, all of the attacks appear to be coordinated and instructed and the attackers were never identified. It should be highlighted that the responses to the attacks required the cooperation of public and private institutions as well as international organizations.

Strategic Plan against Cyberterrorism

As discussed in this chapter, the recent trend of cyberattacks indicates an alarming rise in political motivation, and it is almost impossible to identify the attacker(s). The successful defense would be the sum of political, legal, and technical measures, which can be facilitated through establishing international information exchanges and international cybersecurity policies. This lesson was derived from Yoon and Morris's recommendations written in Cyberterrorism: Trends and Response.

When you construct your future strategic plan, it is important to consider the two alternatives below:

Strategic Plan

1. Although it is difficult to focus on a specific target due to complexities of interactions in cyberspace, law enforcement agencies must expand their technological capability to monitor targeted terrorist organizations.
2. While there are positive changes in law enforcement agencies, such as establishing information reception capabilities and improving information sharing across all agencies, there is still room for improvement. This requires international cooperation between government agencies.

International Cooperation

The Council of Europe has made it compulsory to 1) establish measures for swift and smooth international cooperation on criminal cases for effective punishment of cyberterrorism, 2) international and domestic support for the investigation, prosecution and detection of cyberterrorist acts, and 3) swift and fair international cooperation.

The United Nations Convention Against Transnational Organized Crime is intended to regulate serious crimes, such as hacking, DDoS attacks, and the use of threat and extortion for economic profit. 147 counties have signed and completed the ratification process. In the case of cyberterrorism, close cooperation is necessary among the involved nations to track down the suspect(s) of hacking or DDoS crimes. The suspect of either hacking or DDoS attacks is likely to be an intelligent criminal who can delete all traces of his involvement, and there is also the possibility that various system access logs and service user logs can be deleted after a certain duration of time. Thus, immediate tracking of the suspect is very important.

The G8 High Tech Crime 24/7 Network, a multinational network of law enforcement agencies that has a total of 49 country-members, was established for the purpose of persistent cooperation in investigations of transnational cybercrimes. Recognizing that the formal system of international cooperation processes through official diplomatic channels takes too much time and is inappropriate for investigations of transnational cybercrimes, this system has adopted a cooperation process that uses informal contacts (phone, email, fax, etc.) to request judicial assistance first and then goes through the official channels later, which gives it the unique advantage of swiftness.

The common element between the perpetrators and the protectors is that they use the same tools. No matter where the perpetrator is, the tools that they use to commit cyberterrorism are the same tools that security experts use and software developers create.

In light of this fact, international cooperation on sharing known flaws and exploits in hardware and software with the appropriate officials and security experts becomes one of the most essential safeguards against cyberterrorism. In other words, the security experts and IT developers can study the means to hack and experiment with their own computer systems and fix them up before any cyberterrorists or cybercriminals can exploit them for their purposes. Utilizing available venues where IT developers, security experts and government officials can convene and share flaws and exploits and prevent their use would be a very important step against cyberterrorism.

Law Enforcement Training

Crimes such as cyberterrorism that occur in cyberspace are different from traditional crimes. Beyond the absence of physical evidence and eyewitnesses, the concept of a crime scene can be largely ambiguous for cyberterrorism events. Similar to cybercrimes, cyberterrorism creates a "fractured crime scene" in that the attacker may be physically located in one country, route his attack through a server in a different country, which finally produces harm in a third, target country.

Cyberterrorsim requires a fresh response from law enforcement officers trained in both terrorist behavior and information technologies. However, such training is not commonplace in the U.S. It has been suggested that the federal government should provide support to local departments in a number of ways. The primary needs of most departments are funding for cyberterrorism initiatives, specialized training programs, and equipment. Supplying local law enforcement with the financial support they need, developing training on effective counter-cyberterrorism procedure, and providing the technology to detect and investigate cyberattacks present invaluable resources for a local department's preparedness.

The federal government can also facilitate the investigation of cyberterrorism by promoting alliances between local law enforcement and Internet Service Providers (ISP). Permitting ISPs to use the latest technologies to record connection histories can provide vital information to law enforcement investigations of cyberterrorist incidents. Promoting ISPs to share this information with local departments following such an attack represents an important opportunity available to the federal government in combating cyberterrorism. The Cyber Security Enhancement Act of 2002, a subsection of the Homeland Security Act, offers legal protection for ISPs that cooperate in this manner with investigations.

Federal law enforcement also needs to collaborate with state and local law enforcement in the investigation of cyberterrorism and apprehension of cyberterrorists. Cybercrime training programs are designed to teach law enforcement officers how to detect and respond to digital evidence. These training initiatives are primarily located among the FBI's 16 Regional Computer Forensic Laboratories (RCFLs) led by the RCFL National Program Office (NPO). The NPO was established in 2002 to manage the creation of a nationwide RCFL program, whose responsibilities include digital evidence examination related to investigations of cyberterrorism, online child pornography, white collar crimes, as well as a number of other cybercrimes (Regional Computer Forensics Laboratory, 2012). According to the Department of Justice's 2011 Annual Report for the FBI's Regional Computer Forensic Laboratories program, over 32,000 individuals were trained by the RCFL between the year 2004 and 2011 period. As a result, an estimated one in every three U.S. law enforcement agencies employs at least one officer who has attended a RCFL sponsored cyber training.

The National Cyber Forensics & Training Alliance (NCFTA) is another major agency dedicated to help fight cyberterrorism. The NCFTA was created in 1997 to combine expertise, communication, and resources by facilitating the assistance of law enforcement agencies, private industry, and academia. The initiatives enact international cooperation via internship programs to foster a greater knowledge of cybercrime investigation. In 2010, investigators from the Ukraine, Lithuania, Netherlands, Australia, Great Britain, and Germany attended a 90-day internship program to share knowledge and assist investigations. Training on an international framework is seen as necessary to combat the fundamental global source of cyberterrorism. The NCFTA has been addressed by President Barack Obama's administration as an "effective model" in national cyber security. It is important not to overlook cooperation with private enterprises, which can offer not only the best subject matter expertise, but also some of the most significant intelligence to the alliance.

Global Cooperation in Law Enforcement

The world views that U.S. federal law enforcement should strive for organizing international alliances to combat cyberterrorism; one such organization is the United Nation's International Multilateral Partnership Against Cyber Threats (IMPACT). While IMPACT is not aligned specifically to fight cyberterrorism, their 144-country membership creates a network of international agencies, corporations, academics and field experts that serves to assist in the recognition and response to cyber threats. The collected information from the reliable global resources can help increase the identification of cyberterrorist events and provide "best practices" in response to such instances. Further, the FBI reports collaboration with various nation-states including Canada, the United Kingdom, Columbia and Ukraine to provide international cooperation in the investigation of cyberattacks; a resource that could easily be utilized in the event of cyberterrorism.

Prevention Efforts from State/Local and Federal Law Enforcement Agencies

The response and investigation of cyberterrorist attacks is one aspect of law enforcement's role in combating cyberterrorism. The prevention of cyberterrorist attacks represents a proactive approach that can greatly minimize the terrorists' threats. Increasing the rate of successful identification of cyberterrorists via information sharing, and publicizing the punishment of cyberterrorist activity may provide some deterrent effect. However, responses that focus on the prevention and early detection of cyberterrorism will potentially have a larger impact on cyberterrorism threats.

- Prevention at the Federal Level
  Some argue that the main preventive role of the federal government should be increasing international communication on cyberterrorism. IMPACT, the multinational organization addressed above, is a UN-sponsored organization working with national governments, private corporations and field experts designed to assist these entities share information so

that they can lead the development of strong cyber protection on a global scale. The US federal government representatives to this coalition can transfer the lessons learned from other countries to agencies and corporations within its borders. Likewise, threats encountered within the U.S. can serve to educate the global IMPACT partners and promote greater global cybersecurity, ultimately hampering cyberterrorist's agendas.

- Prevention at the State/ Local Level
  The greatest effect of minimizing the cyberterrorism threat within the state and local level would be active community engagement to be aware of potential cyberterrorist activity on the Internet. Local and state law enforcement should inform their citizens to be alert of suspicious online activity and encourage them to report such behavior to a dedicated unit. Ideally, law enforcement would train a community network on how to recognize potential cyberterrorist groups and to report the suspicious activities or groups to law enforcement. This type of effort would increase the reporting of potential terrorist activities online.

Educating the Public and Corporate Entities on the Cyberterrorism Threat

Educating the general public can be an effective strategy to minimize the potential risks. Another aspect of civilian education is concerned with providing general knowledge of cybersecurity. Informing the public of the importance of securing home wireless networks by the simplest means, by employing strong password protection for Internet access, can potentially minimize the risk of cyberterrorist attacks. Furthermore, the national government should mandate ISPs to require passwords for every wireless router they provide and encourage them to disseminate the most recent technologies in cybersecurity.

Historically, government agencies have encountered a problem of partnering in cyberterrorism initiatives with private companies due to their fear of sharing valuable information to competitors, negative press associated with cyberattacks, and the discovery of vulnerable infrastructure. Nevertheless, the suggested collaboration represents a vital endeavor since private companies run nearly the entire US critical infrastructure.

Corporate entities should adopt the newest authentication technologies to strengthen control over their own networks. The practice of corporate entities locating vulnerabilities within their business networks and finding ways to strengthen their online presence against the threat of attacks needs to be systematically established. InfraGard, an FBI program, provides such a service to over 50,000 private and public entities within the U.S. The FBI program offers private corporations and individuals with information on the techniques of cyberterrorist activity and advice on how to minimize their victimization risk. Through local chapters led by an FBI Special Agent Coordinator, interested individuals in both the private and public sectors can coordinate with fellow community members on how to proceed in dealing with cyberterrorist attack events within their area. This type of collaboration serves to decrease the threat of cyberterrorism, increase information sharing on cyberterrorist events and minimize the harm caused by cyberterrorists.

Ideally, corporations should be proactive and build safe networks with security being of principal importance from the start. Corporations should train their employees on the threat of cyberterrorism and instruct them to practice secure and adequate online behaviors at their workspace. Furthermore, corporations should be encouraged to report cyberterrorism events and to seek prosecution.

SUMMARY

Even though terrorists have not yet taken responsibility for any Internet attacks that have caused great damage, they have been increasingly using the Internet for propaganda, financing, communication, data mining, planning, and support to fulfill their purposes.

Due to the characteristics of cyber-terrorism as progressively becoming a virtual movement in using cyberspace as a strategic battle ground, awareness of the threats posed by the use of the Internet for terrorist purposes needs to be raised as global societies are highly dependent on the Internet and various electronic services. Special attention should be paid to the possibility of attacks against critical infrastructure as they can have the most alarming outcome.

The case studies presented illustrate the alarming rise in politically motivated cyber-attacks that involve cross-border investigation. The global community should pay more attention to cyber-security policies and prepare their national legislation for politically motivated cyber-attacks in order to effectively regulate such offenses. The defense of such attacks demands national efforts in both the private and public sectors, together, with international cooperation and is the sum of political, legal, and technical measures.

Discussion 1:
Cybercrime and cyberterrorism events share many commonalities. Discuss differences and similarities based on the U.S. legal guidelines.

Discussion 2:
What recommendations would you make for dealing with cyberterrorism and cyberterrorist prosecution?

Discussion 3:
Historically, government agencies have encountered a problem with partnering on cyberterrorism initiatives with private companies. What types of recommendations would you make to promote the relationship between the private and government sectors?

Discussion 4:
What types of recommendations would you make for dealing with other cybercrimes such as online child porn, dating violence, cyberstalking, etc.? Please pick one cybercrime other than cyberterrorism and discuss the prevention strategies reflecting the recommendations in this chapter.

Discussion 5:
Do some online research to discover training programs, conferences, and other opportunities for investigators and prosecutors to learn more about cybercrime and information security issues. Briefly describe three examples with regard to who sponsors the training, what it covers and costs, and when and where criminal justice and information security professionals may attend.

Appendix - Cybercrime Incident Reports (January 5th - January 17th)

Category:	Date:	Case Summary:
Keylogging, Hacking, Federal Wiretapping	Posting Date: 5 January 2014 Committed: 22 April 2013	Title: "The County Sheriff who Keylogged his Wife" Miles J. Slack was a County Sheriff from Clay County, West Virginia. He was going through a divorce and was concerned with his wife's relationship with an "unnamed individual." Slack went into his wife's workplace, the Clay County Magistrate Court, after business hours and installed a keylogger on her work PC to record her e-mails, instant message chats, and usernames and passwords she used. Slack's wife would enter financial details of defendants convicted in court, including the credit cards they used to pay fines. Slack was caught in 3 weeks, on May 6, because a Supreme Court technician found the keylogger. When questioned by State Police, Slack "pretended not to know what a keystroke logger was"; a court filing called this "a response unworthy of a law enforcement officer. " Several months later he resigned and pled guilty to federal wiretapping. Slack argued that he only wanted his wife's information, not the courts and requested probation. Slack's wife also requested leniency. December 19, Slack was sentenced to 2 Yrs. of probation and a $1,000 fine. Judge Copenhaver said, "You have lost your position as sheriff, lost your career in law enforcement… That alone is enough."
Malware, ATM	Posting Date: 6 January 2014	Title: "Planning to Rob a Windows ATM? Ditch the Sledgehammer and Bring a USB Stick" Cybercrooks have created malware that creates a backdoor on ATM's using

		bootable USB sticks. They cut a hole in the plastic ATM chassis to access the USB port and then patch up the hole. The ATM can then be rebooted and the malware is installed. The malicious code was used to screw with functions normally restricted to engineering diagnostics. A 12-digit code was used to access an alternative interface. In order to prevent their street crews from going rogue and to stop rival gangs from going after their ATMs, the masterminds coded a challenge-response access control into the software. The attack on an unnamed Brazilian bank's ATMs was presented by two security researchers at the Chaos Communication Congress in Hamburg last month (December, 2013). Tillman Werner & partner. Tillman Werner, from security upstart CrowdStrike, explained that the malware used was not designed to intercept credit or debit card data. Werner says that disabling the "boot from USB" functionality on ATMs would be enough to frustrate this scam. ATM thefts using this technique surfaced last year and have remained isolated.
NSA, Privacy, Spying	Posting Date: 7 January 2014	<u>Title: "Secretive US Spy Court Once Again Ok's NSA Phone Record Collection"</u> The court that Ok's the National Security Agency's snooping has given the agency permission to keep collecting phone records even though there is current debate whether it is legal. A spokesman for the Office of the Director of National Intelligence, Shawn Turner, said that the government filed an application with the Foreign Intelligence Surveillance Court (FISC) to keep collecting telephony metadata in bulk, and as of Friday (Jan. 3rd?), the FISC renewed the authority. On December 13th, Judge Richard J. Leon of the District of Columbia ordered the

		agency to stop collecting data on two plaintiff's personal phone calls and to destroy what they had. He said that it was likely unconstitutional and against the Fourth Amendment. He's the only voice against it so far. The government appealed his decision. On Friday (Jan. 3rd?), the Department of Justice (DOJ) filed an appeal of Justice Leon's decision on behalf of President Barack Obama, Attorney General Eric Holder, and NSA Director General Keith Alexander in the US Court of Appeals for the District of Columbia Circuit. DOJ defended phone records program with how FISC judges approved it. Turner stated that 15 FISC judges approved the data collection 36 separate times in the last 7 years. In December, Judge William Pauley III of the US District Court for the Southern District of New York ruled on behalf of the NSA against the American Civil Liberties Union (ACLU), and found that their collection of phone records are legal. Last week, the ACLU appealed Judge Pauley's decision. FISC stated that it's "open to modifications" to improve privacy; and civil liberty protections "while still maintaining operational benefits." In mid-December, the President's Review Group on Intelligence and Communications Technologies recommended that the NSA keep collecting data but that the data be kept in private hands for "quires and data mining" only by court order.
Botnet, Malware, Microsoft, Security Threat, SophosLabs	Posting Date: 7 January 2014 Date on	Title: "Have We Seen the End of the ZeroAccess Botnet?" Microsoft took positive action against the ZeroAccess botnet in early December. Now, Microsoft declared the authors have "decided to surrender control of the botnet." Last version of each plugin seeded into the network had surrender

	TimeStamps of plugins: 7 December 2013	message: "WHITE FLAG." No new plugins being pushed into the P2P network and no new droppers released onto the internet: size of Botnet decreasing.
Ransomware	Posting Date: 6 January 2014 CryptoLocker issue: October 2013 Discussions of PowerLocker began: November 2013	Title: "Researchers warn of new, meaner ransomware with unbreakable crypto" Security researchers (Group called: "Malware Must Die") found evidence of a new piece of malware (called "PrisonLocker" and "PowerLocker") that might be able to take gigabytes' worth of data hostage. Discussions of this Malware have been in underground crime forums since November. This malware seems to be inspired by CryptoLocker – big issue in October, used uncrackable encryption to lock up computer files until hundreds of dollars paid. PowerLocker could be more dangerous because could be sold as a DIY malware kit for a $100 license. Powerlocker may also have more features: ability to disable task manager, registry editor, and other administration functions built into the Windows operating system, may contain protections to prevent it from being reverse engineered. Powerlocker uses keys based on Blowfish algorithm to encrypt files. Each key is locked and can only be unlocked by a 2048-bit private RSA key. Antivirus provider (Trend Micro) said new CryptoLocker versions have self-replicating abilities that allowed it to spread through USB thumb drives.
Malware, Gaming, Trojan	Posting Date: 6 January 2014	Title: "*World of Warcraft* users hit by account-hijacking malware attack" WoW players' accounts hijacked by a Trojan even when protected by two-factor authentication ("Authenticator") that sends temporary password to players'

		smartphones even after password change. Malware posing as installer of "Curse" (legitimate add-on that helps players manage other WoW add-ons) on unofficial sites. Steals account info and authenticator password as player enters them. Appears identical to real thing. (WoW developer) Blizzard officials have given warning of this. Fake "Curse Client" was coming up in searches for "curse client" on major search engines. Antivirus providers are in process of updating products to detect and remove malicious add-on Make sure address matches the official provider "Curse.com"
Hacking, Australia	Posting Date: 8 January 2014 Update: 9 January 2014	<u>Title: "Teen reported to police after finding security hole in website"</u> Joshua Rogers, 16 from Victoria, Australia found basic security hole (by using an SLQ-injection vulnerability, a common vulnerability that exists in many websites) in Government website ("Metlink" run by Transportation Department) and reported it. He was able to see info (full names, addresses, home & mobile phone numbers, email addresses, dates of birth, and a 9-digit extract of credit card numbers) on about 600,000 public transport users who made purchases through Metlink. Rogers contacted the site after Christmas to report security issue but didn't hear back for 2 weeks, so he contacted *The Age* (Newspaper in Melbourne) to report it. *The Age* contacted the Transportation Department for comment & the department reported Rogers to the police. Rogers hasn't been contacted by the police (as of 1/9/14) and had only heard he had been reported by the writer of the story for *The Age*.

SCADA, Hackers, Security	Posting Date: 10 January 2014	Title: "Hackers gain 'full control' of critical SCADA systems" Russian Researchers found over 60,000 exposed control systems online. Supervisory control and data acquisition (SCADA) Industrial control systems running energy, chemical and transportation systems. From home solar panel installations to critical national infrastructure. Home systems at risk too. Positive Research chief technology officer Sergey Gordeychik and consultant Gleb Gritsai detailed vulnerabilities in Siemens. Siemens WinCC software – used in industrial control systems including Iran's Natanz nuclear plant that was targeted by the US Stuxnet program. Siemens released patches to address the flaws. Vulnerabilities existed in the way passwords were encrypted and stored in the databases, allowed access to Programmable Logic Controllers using attacks as easy to launch and dangerous. Vulnerability was also in cloud SCADA platform Daq Connect – allowed attackers running a demonstration kiosk to access other customer installations. SCADA Strangelove identified over 150 zero day vulnerabilities affecting ICSes, PLCs and SCADA systems. Most prevalent vendors – Tridium, NRG Systems and Lantronix. Most common devices crawled using search engines – Windcube solar smartgrid system, the IPC CHIP embedded device, and the Lantronix SLS video capture platform. Researchers reported exposed devices to computer emergency response teams like the European infosec Agency (ENSIA).
Hacking, Data Loss, Privacy	Posting Date: 11 January 2014	Title: "Target's data breach MUCH bigger than first thought – now more than 100,000,000 records"

	Initial Incident: Late 2013 (Between Black Friday & Christmas)	Target – victims of enormous data theft of both customers and non-customers ("guests"). 40,000,000 payment card records taken by cybercriminals – card numbers, expiry dates, and more. 70,000,000 records separate of payment card data – names, mailing addresses, phone numbers or email addresses (PII-personally identifiable information). Target warns that Earnings per share (EPS) for shareholders will probably end up $1.30-$1.30 down from previous prediction of $1.50-$1.60. Warns of sales decline of 2%-6% for the rest of the quarter.
Safety, Statistics, Privacy, Security Threats	Posting Date: 13 January 2014	Title: "Half of the UK people are not protecting themselves online, says government" 94% of people surveyed see it as their personal responsibility to ensure a safer internet experience. However: 44% always install security software on new equipment 37% download updates and patches for PCs when prompted – (21% do it on mobile devices) 30% use complex passwords to protect online accounts 57% don't always check websites are secure before making purchases UK Government launched £4 million campaign – "Be Cyber Streetwise" to raise awareness of cyber security. Cyber Streetwise website provides tricks and tools "Threat Hunter" Game help spot threats on your desk Sophos is helping Cyber Streetwise with content, advice, tips and tools. Educate people on how to:

		1. Use strong, memorable passwords 2. Install antivirus software on new devices 3. Check privacy settings on social media 4. Shop safely online by always ensuring to check online retail sites are secure 5. Download software and application patches when prompted
Hacking, Google, Security Threats, Vulnerability, YouTube, AdSense	Posting Date: 13 January 2014 Hacking period: around June 2012 up until 11 September 2013	<u>Title: “Hacker Hijacked Youtube Channels to Milk AdSense for Money”</u> U.S. Man, Mathew A. Buchanan admitted he and his accomplices got into YouTube accounts via Google’s password reset recovery process and set the YouTube channels up with AdSense to milk them of at least $55,897. Gained access through a vulnerability to AOL employees’ email accounts. Buchanan has “modest” education (Associates degree in general studies from Montgomery College) and only professional experience is of working at grocery store at age 16. 2 Methods to take over Google accounts: 1. “Wrote a script that searched YouTube and returned publicly available account names associated with popular videos that hadn’t been monetized with AdSense. The script identified 200,000 of these accounts. They then submitted bogus password resets on the account names, exploiting a flaw that revealed a Google account holder’s primary email address during the password reset process. After finding 2. the primary email address, the conspirators then got at victims’ accounts by guessing their security question answers or by using password-cracking software.”

		3. "The second method involved exploiting secondary email addresses. Some Google users had concocted what they thought were nonexistent email accounts during the Google account registration process because they couldn't be bothered to open a genuine secondary account. While some of those email accounts were truly nonexistent, some of the accounts in fact were controlled by Buchanan, including dog@yahoo.com, dog@aol.com, bill@aol.com, pat@aol.com and lucas@yahoo.com. The conspirators submitted bogus password resets on the primary email address, and then they picked up the temporary passwords that were delivered to the secondary email addresses under their control. They would lock the victims out of their accounts. Buchanan & friends would then link the YouTube channels to their AdSense accounts making it so that advertising money would go to them instead of the victims. Buchanan will be sentenced March 28th & looking 5 years in prison.
Hacking	Posting Date: 12 January 2014 Hacking occurred during the 2013 Holiday Season	Title: "Neiman Marcus, Target weren't the only holiday hack victims" Reuters report reports at least 3 other U.S. retailers "with outlets in malls" were hacked during the 2013 holiday season, not publicly disclosed. They speculate that it was the same individuals that hit Target (they think they're from Eastern Europe). Reuters speculates that the attacks used techniques similar to those used on Target (one of which being a RAM scraper – "enables cyber criminals to grab encrypted data by capturing it when it travels through the live memory of a computer, where it appears in plain text").

Hacking, Cyberattack, Malware	Posting Date: 14 January 2014	Title: "Icefog hackers hit 'large US oil company' with evolved Java attack" Kaspersky Labs found new Java-focused variant of the "Icefog Malware" targeting some high-profile companies and government agencies, including "a very large American independent oil and gas corporation" while monitoring previously shut down Icefog command and control servers in a blog post that is harder to track than the original IceFog attacks. Found 8 IPs for 3 victims of Javafog, all in the US (one being the oil & gas co.). Kaspersky found 72 different C&C servers and were able to sinkhole 27. Installs malware in victim's system that lets it communicate with C&C servers. The module writes a registry value so that it is automatically started by Windows. It does not copy itself to that location. Then it enters a loop where it keeps calling its main C&C function.
Child Pornography, Abuse, CSEM	Posting Date: 16 January 2014 Operation Endeavour: began in 2012 Arrest & Rescue: in October 2012	Title: 29 Arrested in international case involving live online webcam child abuse" Organized crime group that facilitated live streaming of on-demand child sex abuse in the Philippines dismantled by joint ops (Operation Endeavour) of U.K.'s National Crime Agency (NCA), the Australian Federal Police (AFP), U.S. Immigration and Customs Enforcement (ICE), and Philippine National police (PNP). NCA, AFP, and ICE are members of the Virtual Global Taskforce – works to combat online child sexual exploitation. 29 international arrests – 11 were part of the facilitation group in the Philippines. 15 children in the Philippines ages 6-15 identified and safeguarded from sex abuse. Over £37,500 ($60,000) from payment for the live abuse from customers. Some of the facilitators were family members of the children. Northamptonshire, U.K. police

		discovered some videos on a routine home-check of registered sex offender, Timothy Ford & contacted NCA found more customers and associates which started a world-wide law enforcement investigation
Encryption, Sentencing, Terrorism, National Security	Posting Date: 17 January 2014 Originally Caught: In April 2012	Title: "Jailed Terrorist gets extra time for refusing to divulge USB stick password" British man, Syed Hussain age 22, from Luton, in jail for terrorist activity – discussing an attack on a local Territorial Army base headquarters with 3 other men (planned to send a homemade bomb ato the site by a remote controlled toy car). Hussain sentenced 4 more months for not giving up password on his memory stick. His lawyers said he couldn't remember code due to stress. 11 months after the deadline given by police to provide code, they told him that they were opening a new investigation: alleged credit card fraud by Hussain. This made him remember code and they found contents on USB stick relevant to investigation on fraud but not to the terrorism or national security.
Espionage, NSA	Posting Date: 17 January 2014 Dishfire in operation: from at least May 2008	Title: "NSA Sweeps up hundreds of millions of text messages daily" (Codename: "Dishfire"): NSA collect and store around 200 million text messages worldwide per day for metadata including location data, credit card info and contacts. Paul Lee, director of telecoms research at Deloitte, predicts that 50 billion messages will be sent daily across the globe in 2014. British spies were given access to the metadata but not the actual content of messages sent to and from British citizens.

Botnet, Internet of Things	Posting Date: 17 January 2014 Incident occurred: 23 December 2013 – 6 January 2014	Title: "Is your refrigerator *really* part of a massive spam-sending botnet?" Ars & Proofprint. Botnet of over 100,000 smart TVs, home networking routers, PCs, and other internet-connected consumer devices recently took part in sending 750,000 malicious e-mails & phishing messages worldwide over 2 week period. No more than 10 emails initiated from any IP address – difficult to block attack based on location. ("Thingbots"). Thingbots exploit default administration passwords that hadn't been changed and other misconfigurations. Able to take over devices running older versions of Linux operating system by exploiting critical software bugs. Skepticism of Proofprint's findings

References

2002 Internet fraud report. (2003). Retrieved June 1, 2007, from http://www .ic3.gov/media/annualreports.aspx

2004 Australian computer crime and security survey. (2005). Retrieved June 1, 2007, from http://www.auscert.org.au/render.html?it=2001

2004 IC3 Internet crime report. (2005). Retrieved June 1, 2007, from http://www .ic3.gov/media/annualreports.aspx

2005 FBI computer crime survey. (2006). Retrieved November 6, 2006, from http://www.fbi.gov/publications/ccs2005.pdf

2008 Computer Crime & Security Survey. (2009). Retrieved September1, 2009, from http://www.atl-htcia.org/files/csi2008.pdf

2008 IC3 Internet crime report. (2009). Retrieved September1, 2009, from https://www.ic3.gov/media/annualreports.aspx

2009 IC3 Internet crime report. (2010). Retrieved September1, 2009, from https://www.ic3.gov/media/annualreports.aspx

2010 IC3 Internet crime report. (2011). Retrieved September1, 2009, from https://www.ic3.gov/media/annualreports.aspx

2011 IC3 Internet crime report. (2012). Retrieved July 11, 2014, from https://www.ic3.gov/media/annualreports.aspx

2012 IC3 Internet crime report. (2013). Retrieved July11, 2014, from https://www.ic3.gov/media/annualreports.aspx

2013 IC3 Internet crime report. (2014). Retrieved August 1, 2015, from https://www.ic3.gov/media/annualreports.aspx

2014 IC3 Internet crime report. (2014). Retrieved August10, 2015, from https://www.ic3.gov/media/annualreports.aspx

2014 Consumer report. (2014). Retrieved August10, 2015, from http://www.consumerreports.org/cro/magazine/2014/07/your-secrets-aren-t-safe/index.htm

Aaron, Greg, and Rod Rasmussen. *Global Phishing Survey 2H2010: Trends and Domain Name Use.* Anti-Phishing Working Group, 2011.

Acoca, B. (2008). Scoping Paper on Online Identity Theft. Proceedings of the OECD Ministerial Meeting on the Future of the Internet Economy, Seoul, Korea.

Adams, P. (1998). Network topologies and virtual place. *Annals of Association of American Geographers, 88*(1), 88-106.

Agnew, R. (1992). Foundation for a General Strain Theory of Crime and Delinquency. *Criminology* 30:47-87

Agnew, R. (1995). Controlling delinquency: Recommendations from general strain theory. In H. Barlow (Ed.), *Crime and public policy* (pp. 43-70), Boulder, CO: Westview

Agnew, R. and White. H.R. (1992). An Empirical Test of General Strain Theory. *Criminology* 30:475-99.

Akers, R (1997). Criminological theories: Introduction and evaluation (2nd ed.). Los Angeles: Roxbury.

Akers, R. L. (1985). *Deviant behavior: A social learning approach* (3rd ed.). Belmont, CA: Wadsworth.

Akers, R. L., & Sellers, C. S. (2004). *Criminological theories: Introduction, evaluation, and application* (4th ed.). New York: Oxford University Press.

Al-Motarreb, A. Al-Habori, M.& Broadley, K. J., (2010) Khat chewing, cardiovascular diseases and other internal medical problems: the current situation and directions for future research. *Journal of Ethnopharmacology.* 132(3):540-8

Anderson, Keith. Who are the Victims of Identity Theft? The Effect of Demographics. *Journal of Public Policy and Marketing 25*, 2006: 160-171.

Anwar, S., & Loughran, T. A. (2011). Testing a bayesian learning theory of deterrence among serious juvenile offenders. Criminology, 49(3), 667-698. doi:10.1111/j.1745-9125.2011.00233.x

Archer, R. P. (2009). Fluoromethcathinone, a new substance of abuse. *Forensic Science International*, *185*(1-3), 10-20.

Asia News Network. (2013, June 20). Alarm bells ring as drug smuggling rises in South Korea" *The Korean Herald.* Retrieved July 20, 2014 from http://www.nationmultimedia.com

Associated Press. (2013, January 31). *Hoaxer was in love with Manti Te'o.* Retrieved

Association of Chief Police Officer (2011). ACPO Good Practice Guide for Digital Evidence. Retrieved November, 2013, from http://www.acpo.police.uk

Barber, R. (2001). Hackers profiled: Who are they and what are their motivations? [Electronic version] *Computer Fraud and Security, 2001*(2), 14-17. doi:10.1016/S1361-3723(01)02017-6

BBC (2015, January 2). Sony cyber-attack: North Korea faces new US sanctions. Retreived January 5, 2015 from http:,,www.bbc.com.

BBC News (2010, November 23). Digital Vaccine Needed to Fight Botnets. Retrived January 21, 2012 from http://www.bbc.co.uk

Bennett, R. (1991). Routine activities: A cross-national assessment of a criminological perspective. *Social Forces 70*(1), 147-163.

Bernburg, J. G., & Thorlindsson, T. (2001). Routine activities in social context: A closer look at the role of opportunity in deviant behavior. *Justice Quarterly, 18*, 543-567.

Birkbeck, C., & LaFree, G. (1993). The situational analysis of crime and deviance. *Annual Review of Sociology 19*(2), 113-37.

Blizzard Entertainment. (2010). *About Blizzard Entertainment.* Retrieved May 1, 2010, from http://us.blizzard.com/en-us/company/about/

Brauer, J. R. (2009). Testing social learning theory using reinforcement's residue: A multilevel analysis of self-reported theft and marijuana use in the national youth survey. Criminology, 47(3), 929-970. doi:10.1111/j.1745-9125.2009.00164.x

Brenner, S. W. & Schwerha, J. J., IV (2002). Transnational evidence gathering and local prosecution of international cybercrime. *John Marshall Journal of Computer and Information Law*, 20, 347-394.

Brenner, S. W., & Koops, B. (2004). Approaches to cybercrime jurisdiction. *Journal of High Technology Law*. Retrieved February 3, 2013, from http://www.jhtl.org/docs/pdf/JHTL_Brenner_Koops_Article1.pdf

Britz, M. T. (2004). *Computer forensics and cyber crime*. New Jersey: Pearson Prentice Hall.

Brown, M.F. (2001). *Criminal investigation: Law and practice* (2nd ed.). Boston: Butterworth-Heinemann.

Burgess, R. & R. Akers. (1966). A differential association-reinforcement theory of criminal behavior. *Social Problems* (Vol. 14, pp. 128-47). Berkeley: University of California Press.

Burke, T., & Dickey, J. (2013, January 16). *Manti Te'o's dead girlfriend, the most* Retrieved January 10, 2014,

from Deadspin.com: http://deadspin.com

Ottawa police seek girl, 17, in teen-pimp case, urge parents to monitor social media. (2012, June 12). *Canadian Press*. Retrieved from http://www.thestar.com

Carter, D. (1995) Computer crime categories: how techno-criminals operate, *FBI Law Enforcement Bulletin*, 64 (7): 21-26

Carter, L. D., & Katz, J. A. (1997). *Computer crime: An emerging challenge for law enforcement*. Retrieved November 20, 2004, from http://www.sgrm.com/_art11.htm

Casey, E. (2000). *Digital evidence and computer crime.* London: Academic Press.

Castells, M. (2002). *The internet galaxy: Reflections on the Internet, business, and society*. Oxford, United Kingdom: Oxford University Press.

Castells, Manual. *The Internet Galaxy: Reflections on the Internet, Business, and Society.* Oxford, United Kingdom: Oxford University Press, 2002.

Cernkovich, S. A., & Giordano, P. C. (1992). School bonding, race, and delinquency. *Criminology*, *30*(2), 261-291.

Chapple, C. L. (2005). Self-control, peer relations, and delinquency. *JQ: Justice Quarterly*, *22*(1), 89-106.doi:10.1080/07418820420003336 54

Chatterton, M. R., & Frenz, S. J. (1994) Closed-circuit television: Its role in reducing burglaries and the fear of crime in sheltered accommodation for the elderly. *Security Journal*, *5*(3), 133-139

Choi, K. (2008). Computer crime victimization and integrated theory: An empirical assessment. *International Journal of Cyber Criminology*, 2(1), 308-33.

Choi, K. (2010). Cyber-Routine Activities: Empirical Examination of Online Lifestyle, Digital guardians, and Computer Crime Victimization. In Jaishankar, K. (ed), *Cyber Criminology: Exploring Internet Crimes and Criminal behavior.* Boca Raton, FL, USA: CRC Press: Taylor and Francis

Choi, K. (2010). *Risk Factors in Computer-Crime Victimization.* El Paso, TX: LFB Scholarly Publishing

Choi, K, Earl, K. Park, A., & Della Guistina, J. (2014). Use of Synthetic Cathinones: Legal Issues and Availability of Darknet, *VFAC (Virtual Forum Against Cybercrime) Review,* 9-10, 2014.

Chua, Cecil Eng Huang, and Jonathan Wareham. "Parasitism and Internet Auction Fraud: An Exploration." *Information and Organization 18*, 2008: 303-333.

Clarke, R. V. (Ed.) (1992) *Situational crime prevention: Successful case studies.* Albany, NY: Harrow and Heston.

Clarke, R. V., & Homel, R. (1997) A revised classification of situational crime prevention techniques. In S. P. Lab (Ed.), *Crime prevention at the crossroads* (pp.17-30). Cincinnati, OH: Anderson.

Clifford, R. D. (Ed.). (2006). *Cybercrime: The investigation, prosecution and defense of a computer-related crime* (2nd ed.). Dunham, NC: Carolina Academic Press.

Clifford, R. D. (Ed.). (2011). *Cybercrime: The investigation, prosecution and defense of a computer-related crime* (3rd ed.). Dunham, NC: Carolina Academic Press.

Cohen, L. E., & Cantor, D. (1980). The determinants of larceny: An empirical and theoretical study. *Journal of Research in Crime and Delinquency, 17*(1), 140-159.

Cohen, L. E., & Felson, M. (1979). Social change and crime rate trends: A routine activity approach. *American Sociological Review, 44*, 588-608

Cohen, L. E., & Felson, M. (2004). Routine activity theory. In F. Cullen & R. Agnew (Eds.), *Criminological theory: Past to present* (3rd ed., pp. 433-451). New York: Oxford University Press.

Cohen, L. E., Felson, M., & Land, K. (1981). Social inequality and predatory criminal victimization: An exposition and a test of a formal theory. *American Sociological Review*, *46*, 505-524.

Cohen, L., Kluegel, J., & Land, K. (1981). Social inequality and predatory criminal victimization: An exposition and test of a formal theory. *American Sociological Review*, 46: 505-524.

Copes, Heith, Kent R. Kerley, Rodney Huff, and John Kane. "Differentiating Identity Theft: An Exploratory Study of Victims Using a National Victimization Survey." *Journal of Criminal Justice 38*, 2010: 1045-1052.

Corrado, R., Roesch, R., Glackman, W., Evans J., & Leger, G. (1980). Lifestyles and personal victimization: A test of the model with Canadian survey data. *Journal of Crime and Justice 3*(1), 125-149.

CSI/FBI. "Computer Crime and Security Survey." *FBI.* 2005. http://www.fbi.gov/publications/ccs2005.pdf (accessed November 6, 2009).

Cullen, F. T., and R. Agnew. (2003). *Criminological Theories: Past to Present*, Los Angeles: Roxbury Publishing. December 7, 2013, from Parenting today's kids: http://parentingtodayskids.com

Denning, D. (1990). Concerning hackers who break into computer systems. Proceedings of the 13th National Computer Security Conference, Baltimore, MD, 653-664.

Denning, D. (1999). *Information warfare and security*. Boston: Addison Wesley.

Dhamija, R, Tygar, J. and Hearst M., "Why Phishing Works (doi: 10.1.1.60.9112)." *CHI '06.* SIGCHI, 2006. 581-590.

Duke, D. L. (1989). School organization, leadership, and student behavior. In O.C. Moles (Ed.), *Strategies to Reduce Student Misbehavior* (pp. 19-46). Washington, DC: US Department of Education.

Eck, J. (1995). Examining routine activity theory: A review of two books. *Justice Quarterly, 12*,783-797.

Etter, B. (2001). *The forensic challenges of e-crime, current commentary No.3*. Adelaide, Australia: Australasian centre for Policing Research.

Evans, T., Cullen, F. T., Burton Jr., V. S., Dunaway, R., & Benson, M. L. (1997). The social consequences of self-control: Testing the general theory of crime. *Criminology*, *35*(3), 475-504.

Felson, M. (1986). Routine activities, social controls, rational decisions and criminal outcomes. In D. Cornish and R. Clarke (Eds) *The reasoning criminal* (pp. 302-327). New York: Springer Verlag.

Felson, M. (1998). *Crime and everyday life: Insights and implications for society*, (2nd ed.). Thousand Oaks, CA: Pine Forge Press.

Finklea, K. (2010). *Identity Theft: Trends and Issues.* Congressional Research Center.

Finklea, Kristin. *Identity Theft: Trends and Issues*. Congressional Research Center, January 5, 2010.

Fishbien, R. (2013, November 24). *Model suing Match.com says catfishing scam led to*

Flanagan, W., & McMenamin, B. (1992). The playground bullies are learning to type, Forbes, 150, 184-189. Retrieved April 25, 2010, from http://www.mindvox.com/cgi-bin/WebObjects/mindvox.woa/wa/staticpage?pagename=Media/Forbes1.html

Furnell, S. (2002). *Cybercrime: Vandalizing the information society*. London: Addison Wesley.

Garofalo, J. (1987). Reassessing the lifestyle model of criminal victimization. In M Gottfredson & T. Hirschi (Eds.), *Positive criminology* (pp. 23-42). San Francisco: Sage.

Gibbs, J. J., Giever, D., & Higgins, G. E. (2003). A test of the Gottfredson and Hirschi general theory of crime using structural equation modeling. *Criminal Justice and Behavior, 30*, 441-458.

Goldstein, A. (1994). *The ecology of aggression*. New York: Plenum Press

Goodman, M. (2001). "Making Computer Crimes Count." *FBI Law Enforcement Bulletin*, Vol.70, Issue 8: 10-17.

Goodman, M. D., and S.W., Brenner (2002), 'The Emerging Consensus on Criminal Conduct in Cyberspace, *UCLA Journal of Law and Technology*, 3

Gordon, G. R., Donald J. Rebovich, D. J., Choo, K-S., and Gordon, J. B,. *Identity Fraud Trends and Patterns: Building a Data-Based Foundation for Proactive Enforcement.* Center for Identity Management and Information Protection, 2007.

Gordon, M. P., Loef, M. P., Lucyshyn, W., & Richardson, R. (2004). *CSI/FBI computer crime and security survey*. Los Angeles: Computer Security Institute.

Gottfredson, D. C., Gerstenblith, S. A., Soule, D. A., Womer, S. C., & Lu, S. (2004). Do afterschool programs prevent delinquency? *Prevention Science, 4,* 253-266.

Gottfredson, D. C., Gottfredson, G D., & Hybl, L. G, (1993). Managing adolescent behavior: A multiyear, multischool study. *American Educational Research Journal, 30*(1), 179-215.

Gottfredson, M. R. (1984). *Victims of crime: The dimensions of risk. Home Office Research Study No.18*. London: Her Majesty's Stationer.

Gottfredson, M. R. (1986). Substantive contributions of victimization surveys. In Michael Tonry & Norval Morris (Eds.), *Crime and justice: An annual review of research,*. Chicago: University of Chicago Press.

Gottfredson, M.R., & Hirschi, T. (1990).A general theory of crime. Palo Alto, CA: Stanford University Press.

Gover, A. R. (2004). Risky lifestyles and dating violence: A theoretical test of violent victimization. *Journal of Criminal Justice 32*(2), 171-180.

Grabosky, P. (2000, March). *Cyber crime and information warfare.*

Grabosky, P., & Smith, R. (2001). Telecommunication fraud in the digital age: The convergence of technologies. In D. Wall (Ed.) Crime and the Internet. London: Routledge.

Greenberg, A. (2013, September 5). Follow the bitcoins: How we got busted buying drugs on silk road's black market. *In Forbes.* Retrieved from http://www.forbes.com

Guardian News (2014, April 14), Global Drug Survey Findings: more people buying drugs online in the UK. Retrieved October 4, 2014 from http://www.theguardian.com

Guardian News (2014, December 2), Pornography law bans list of sexual acts from UK-made online films. Retrieved January 11, 2015 from http://www.theguardian.com

Harris, A. (2000), IS Ethical Attitudes Among College Students: A Comparative Study, Proceedings *of ISECON 2000* (Philadelphia, PA), pp. 801-807.

Hay, C., & Forrest, W. (2008). Self-control theory and the concept of opportunity: The case for a more systematic union. *Criminology, 46*(4), 1039-1072. doi:10.1111/j.1745-9125.2008.00135.x *heartbreaking and inspirational story of the college football season, is a hoax.*

Helewitz J. (2005). *Cyberlaw: Legal Principles of Emerging Technologies*. N.J. Pearson/ Prentice Hall.

Hidelang, M. J., Gottfredson, M. R., & Gaffalo, J. (1978). *Victims of personal crime: An empirical foundation for a theory of personal victimization.* Cambridge, MA: Ballinger.

Higgins, G. E. (2005). Can low self-control help with the understanding of the software piracy problem?. *Deviant Behavior*, *26*(1), 1-24. doi:10.1080/01639620490497947

Higgins, G. E. (2007, January). Digital piracy, self-control theory, and rational choice: An examination of the role of values. International Journal of Cyber Criminology, 1(1), 33-55.

Higgins, G. E., Wilson, A. L., & Fell, B. D. (2005). An application of deterrence theory to software piracy. *Journal of Criminal Justice and Popular Culture, 12*(3).

Hinduja, S. (2010). Criminal Justice and Cyberspace. In G. Higgins (Eds.), *Cybercrime* (pp. 133150). New York: McGraw-Hill.

Hinduja, S., & Patchin, J. W. (2007). Offline consequences of online victimization: School violence and delinquency. Journal of School Violence, 6(3), 89-112.

Hinduja, S., & Patchin, J. W. (2010). Bullying, Cyberbullying, and Suicide. *Archives of Suicide Research*, 14(3).

Hinduja, S., & Patchin, J. W. (2010). Lifetime cyberbullying victimization and offending rates. In Cyberbullying Research Center. Retrieved March 12, 2012, from http://www.cyberbullying.us/research.php

Hirschi, T. (1969). *Causes of Delinquency*. Berkeley: University of California Press.

Hirschi, T., & Gottfredson, M. (1993). Commentary: Testing the general theory of crime. *Journal of Research in Crime and Delinquency,* 30, 47-54.

Hoffer, J. A., & Straub, D. W. (1989). The 9 to 5 underground: Are you policing computer crimes. *Sloan Management Review, 30*(4), 35-44

Holladay, J. (2010) Cyberbullying *Teaching Tolerance* Retrieved January 2012 from http://www.tolerance.org

Hollinger, R. (1998). Computer hackers follow a guttman-like progression. *Social Sciences Review*, 72, 199-200.

Holt, T. (2009). Lone hacks or group cracks: Examining the social organization of computer hackers. In F. Schmalleger and M. Pittaro (Eds.), *Crimes of the Internet* (pp. 336355). New Jersey: Pearson.

Holt, T. J., Bossler, A. M., & May, D. C. (2011, June 18). Low self-control, deviant peer associations, and juvenile cyberdeviance. American Journal of Criminal Justice. doi:10.1007/s12103-011-9117-3

Hu, L., & Bentler, P. M. (1995). Evaluating model fit. In R. H. Hoyle (Ed.), *Structural equation modeling: Concepts, issues, and applications* (pp. 76-99). Thousand Oaks, CA: Sage.

Hussain, R. (2011). Cyberspace task force for child protection. International Journal of Academic Research, 3(2), 1001-1007.

Huus, K. (2011, December 28). Bullied girl's suicide has ongoing impact. NBC News. Retrieved from http://usnews.nbcnews.com

Identity Theft (2007) *Bureau of Justice Statistics.* U.S. Government Printing Office.

Identity Theft: The Aftermath (2008) *Identity Theft Resource Center.*

Immorlica, N., Jain, K., Mahdian, M., & Talwar, K. (2005). Click fraud resistant methods for learning click-through rates. In X. Deng & Y. Ye (Eds.), *Lecture Notes in Computer Science* (pp. 34-45). Springer Berlin Heidelberg.

Ingraham, C. (2014, October 3). The online illicit drug economy is booming. Here's what people are buying. *The Washington Post.* Retrieved from http://www.washingtonpost.com

Ingram, J. R., & Hinduja, S. (2008). Neutralizing music piracy: An empirical examination. Deviant Behavior, 29(4), 334-366. doi:10.1080/01639620701588131

International cooperation (2014). In *UNODC.* Retrieved from https://www.unodc.org/unodc/en/organized-crime/international-cooperation.html

Internet Fraud Complaint Center. (2003). *IFCC 2002 Internet fraud report.* Washington, DC: U.S. Government Printing Office.

James, D., Adams, R. D., Spears, R., Cooper, G., Lupton, D. J., & Thompson, J. P. (2011). Clinical characteristics of mephedrone toxicity reported to the UK National Poisons Information Service. *Emergency Medicine Journal*, *28*(8), 686-689.

Jenson, G. F., Erickson, M. L., & Gibbs, J. P. (1978). Perceived risk of punishment and self-reported delinquency. *Social Forces*, *57*(1), 57-78. doi: 10.1093/sf/57.1.57

Johnson, B., & Friedman, M. (2013, December 5). *Bill that would outlaw 'cyber harassment' approved by N.J. Senate.* Retrieved December 7, 2013, from nj.com: http://www.nj.com

Jones-Brown, D. (1997). Promises and Pitfalls of Mentoring as a Juvenile Justice Strategy. Social Justice, 24(4), 212-246

Jordan, T., & Taylor, P. (1998). A sociology of hackers. *Sociological Review, 46*(4), 757-780.

Jordan, T., & Taylor, P. (2004). *Hacktivism and cyberwars: Rebels with a cause?* London: Routledge.

Kabay, M. E. (2001). *Studies and surveys of computer crime*. Norwich, CT: Department of Computer Information Systems.

Kaplan, D. (2000). *Structural equation modeling: Foundations and extensions*. Thousand Oaks, CA: Sage.

Kappeler, V. E., Richard D., and G. Alpert. 1998. *Forces of Deviance: Understanding the Dark Side of Policing*, 2nd ed. Prospect Heights, IL: Waveland Press.

Karmen, A. (2006). *Crime victims*. Thousand Oaks, CA: Thomson Higher Education

Kaspersky Virus News. (2013, December 1). *Number of the year: Kaspersky Lab is detecting 315,000 new malicious files every day.* Retrieved August 1, 2015, from http://www.kaspersky.com/about/news/virus/2013/number-of-the-year

Kennedy, L. W., & Forde, D. R. (1990). Routine activities and crime: An analysis of victimization in Canada. *Criminology* 28, 137-151.

Kent, K.et al., National Institute of Standards and Technology (2006). *Guide to Integrating Forensic Techniques into Incident Response.*

KIRO News Seattle. (2010, October 15). *Man charged in prolific cyberstalking case; police search for more victims.* Retrieved December 7, 2013, from kirotv.com: http://www.kirotv.com

Kline, R. B. (1998). *Principles and practices of structural equation modeling*. New York: Guildford Press.

Knetzger, M.,, and Muraski, J., (2008). *Investigating High-Tech Crime.* New Jersey: Pearson.

Kowalski, M. (2002). *Cyber-crime: Issues, data sources, and feasibility of collecting police-reported statistics.* Ottawa: Statistics Canada.

Kresse, W., Watland, H. and Lucki. J. (2007) *Identity theft: Findings and Public Policy Recommendations.* Institution for Fraud Prevention.

Kubic, T. (2001, June 12). *The FBI's perspective on the cyber crime problems*. Washington, DC: Congressional Testimony, Federal Bureau of Investigation.

Kubic, T. (2001, May 23). *Internet fraud crime problems*. Washington, DC: Congressional Statement, Federal Bureau of Investigation.

LaGrange, T. C., & Silverman, R. A. (1999, February). Low self-control and opportunity: Testing the general theory of crime as an explanation for gender differences in delinquency. *Criminology*, *37*(1), 41-72. doi: 10.1111/j.1745-9125.1999.tb00479.x

Laub, J. H. (1990). Patterns of criminal victimization in the United States. In A. J. Lurigio, W. G. Skogan, & R. C. Davis (Eds.), *Victims of crime: Problems, policies and programs.* Newbury Park, CA: Sage.

Laub, J. H. (1990). Patterns of criminal victimization in the United States. In A. J. Lurigio, W. G. Skogan, & R. C. Davis (Eds.), *Victims of crime: Problems, policies and programs.* Newbury Park, CA: Sage.

Laycock, G. (1985) *Property marking: A deterrent to domestic burglary?* London: Home Office.

Lipton, J. (2011). Combating Cyber-victimization. Berkeley Technology Law Journal, 26, 1104-1155.

Lynch, J. P. (1987). Routine activity and victimization at work. *Journal of Quantitative Criminology 3,* 283-300.

Lyng, Stephen (1990). Edgework: A social psychological analysis of voluntary risk taking. *The American Journal of Sociology 95*, 851-886.

Marcum, C., Higgins, G., and Ricketts, M. (2010) "Potential Factors of Online Victimization of Youth: An Examination of Adolescent Online Behaviors Utilizing Routine Activity Theory," *Deviant Behavior* 31: 381-410.

Massachusetts General Laws. 94C MGL 32L. Retrieved November 1, 2014 from https://malegislature.gov

Massey, J., Krohn, M., & Bonati, L. (1989). Property crime and the routine activities of individuals. *Journal of Research in Crime and Delinquency 26*, 378-400.

Matsueda, R. L. (1982). Testing control theory and differential association: A causal model approach. *American Sociological Review*, *47*, 489-504. Retrieved March 3, 2013

Matsueda, R. L., & Heimer, K. (1987). Race, family structure, and delinquency: A test of differential association and social control theories. *American Sociological Review*, *52*(6), 826-840. Retrieved March 3, 2013

Maxfield, M. G., & Babbie, E. (2008). *Research methods for criminal justice and criminology* (5th ed.). Belmont, CA: Thomas Wadsworth.

McMullan, J., and Perrier, D. (2007). The Security of Gambling and Gambling with Security: Hacking, Law Enforcement and Public Policy. *International Gambling Studies.*

McQuade, S. C. (2006). *Understanding and managing cybercrime.* Boston:Pearson/Allyn and Bacon.

Meier R., & Miethe, T. (1993). Understanding theories of criminal victimization. *Crime and Justice 17*, 459-499.

Melvin, S. P. (2005). *Cyberlaw and E-Commerce Regulation: An Entrepreneurial Approach.* Thomson South-Western College/West.

Mendoza, M. (2014, March 7). Cyberbully law proposed after girl's suicide. *SF Gate*.

Miethe, T., & Meier, R. (1990). Criminal opportunity and victimization rates: A structural-choice theory of criminal victimization. *Journal of Research in Crime and Delinquency 27,* 243-266.

Miethe, T., Stafford, M., & Long, J. S. (1987). Social differentiation in criminal victimization: A test of routine activities/ lifestyle theories. *American Sociological Review 52*(2), 184-194.

Mitchell, W. J. (1995). *City of bits: Space, place and the Infobahn.* Cambridge, MA: MIT Press.

Moitra, S. D. (2005) Developing policies for cyber crime. *European Journal of Crime, Criminal Law and Criminal Justice*, *13*(3), 435-464.

Moon, B., Blurton, D., & McCluskey, J. D. (2008). General strain theory and delinquency. Crime & Delinquency, 54(4), 582-613. doi:10.1177/0011128707301627

Moon, B., McCluskey, J. D., & McCluskey, C. P. (2010). A general theory of crime and computer crime: An empirical test. *Journal of Criminal Justice*, *38*, 767-772. doi:10.1016/j.jcrimjus.2010.05.003

Moon, B., Morash, M., & McCluskey, J. D. (2012). General Strain Theory and School Bullying: An Empirical Test in South Korea. *Crime & Delinquency*, *58*(6), 827-855.doi:10.1177/ 0011128710364809

Moore, R. (2005). *Cybercrime: Investigating high-technology computer crime*. Philadelphia: LexisNexis Group.

Moore, R. (2011). *Cybercrime: Investigating high-technology computer crime* (2nd ed). Boston: Elsevier/Anderson Publishing.

Morris, D. (2005). Tracking a computer hacker. Retrieved May 1, 2010, from http://www.usdoj.gov/criminal/cybercrime/usamay2001_2.htm

Mustaine, E., & Tewksbury, R. (1998). Predicting risks of larceny theft victimization: A routine activity analysis using refined lifestyle measures. *Criminology 36*, 829-857.

National and State Trends in Fraud and Identity Theft: January – December 2006. *Federal Trade Commission.* 2007.

National Center for Victims of Crime, (2004). Cyber stalking. Retrieved Feb. 18, 2006, from http://www.ncvc.org/ncvc.

National Conference of State Legislatures. (2012). *Substituted cathinones (a.k.a. "bath salts") enactments*. Retrieved from http://www.ncsl.org/issuesresearch/justice/substituted-cathinonesenactments.aspx

National Institute on Drug Abuse (2012) Drug Facts: Synthetic Cathinones ("Bath Salts"). Retrieved from http://www.drugabuse.gov/sites/default/files/drugfacts_bath_salts_final_0_1.pdf

National White Collar Crime Center (2002) *Identity Theft*. Retrieved May 15, 2003, from http://www.nw3.com

NBC News (December 18, 2004). ISP awarded $1 billion in anti-spam lawsuit. Retrieved October 4, 2010 from http://www.nbcnews.com

New York Times (2011, June 23). Guilty Plea in Theft of Data About iPad Owners. Retrieved January 21, 2012 from http://bits.blogs.nytimes.com/

New York Times (2011, June 23). Latvians Arrested in Scareware Scam. Retrieved January 21, 2012 from http://bits.blogs.nytimes.com.

New York Times (2011, May 8). There's No Data Sheriff on the Wild Web. Retrived January 21, 2012 from http://www.nytimes.com.

New York Times (June 3, 2011). E-mail Fraud Hides Behind Friendly Face. Retrieved January 21,2012 from http://www.nytimes.com.

Newcombe, R., (2009) *Mephoedrone: the use of m-cat (Meow) in Middlesbrough* Retrieved May, 2014 from http://www.lifeline.org.uk

Newton, J. (2013, October 21). An arrest in San Francisco reveals an unpoliced corner of the Internet. *Time Magazine*. Retrieved October 1, 2014 from http://content.time.com

NJN Network (2009, June 26). Canadian Snowbirds Victim of Identity Theft in Car Scam. Retrieved January 21, 2012 from http://njnnetwork.com.

NY man's suicide. Retrieved November 29, 2013, from Gothamist: http://gothamist.com

Ogilvie, E. (2000), Legislating Policing and Prosecuting Stalking Within Australia, *Research and Public Series,* Australian Institute of Criminology, Canberra.

Osgood, D. W., Wilson, J. K., O'Malley, P. M., Bachman, J. G., & Johnston, L. D. (1996). Routine activities and individual deviant behavior. *American Sociological Review. 61*, 635-655.

Paper presented at the Transnational Crime Conference convened by the Australian Institute of Criminology in association with the Australian Federal Police and

Paper presented at the Transnational Crime Conference convened by the Australian Institute of Criminology in association with the Australian Federal Police and Australian Customs Service.

Parker, D. B. (1998). *Fighting computer crime: A new framework for protecting information*. New York: Wiley.

Paul, L., Kirk, C., and Muehlberger, W. (1954). Crime Investigation---Physical Evidence and the Police Laboratory. Journal of Criminal Law, Criminology, and Police Science 44 (6), 832-834.

Pew Research Center, Internet & American Life Project [Washington DC, 2013].

Piazza, P. (2006, November). Technofile:Antisocial networking sites. *Security Management*, 1-5.

Power, M. (2013, April 26). The hidden dangers of legal highs. *The Guardian*. Retrieved October 1, 2014 from http://www.guardian.co.uk

Poyner, B. (1991). Situational crime prevention in two parking facilities. *Security Journal, 2*, 96-101.

Prosser, J. M. & Nelson, L. S. (2012) Review article: the toxicology of Bath Salts: a review of synthetic cathinones. *Journal of Medical Toxicology*. 8(1), 33-42

Ramasastry, A. (2004). *Cable News Network (CNN).com. Can Utah's new antispyware law work?* Retrieved January 16, 2007, from http://www.cnn.com/2004/LAW/06/03/ramasastry.spyware/index.html

Ramoz, R., Lodi, S., Bhatt, P., Reitz, A. B., Tallarida, C., Tallarida, R. J., et al. (2012) Mephedrone ("bath salt") pharmacology: insights from invertebrates. *Neuroscience*. 208:79-84

Ramsey, J., Dargan, P. I., Smyllie, M., Davies, S., Button, J., Holt, D. W. & Wood, D. M. (2010) Buying 'legal' recreational drugs does not mean that you are not breaking the law. *QJM: International Journal of Medicine*. 103(10):777–783.

Roncek, D. W., & Maier, P. A. (1991) Bars, blocks, and crimes revisited: Linking the theory of routine activities to the empiricism of hot spots. *Criminology, 29*, 725-753.

Rosoff, S. Pontell, H. and Tillman, R. (2010) *Profit Without Honor.* New Jersey: Pearson.

Sampson, R. J., & Laub, J. H. (1993). *Crime in the making: Pathways and turning points through life.* Cambridge: Harvard University Press.

Sampson, R. J., & Woodredge, J. D. (1987). Linking the micro- and macro-level dimensions of lifestyle-routine activity and opportunity models of predatory victimization. *Journal of Quantitative Criminology*, 3, 371-393.

Schifano, F., Albanese, A., Fergus, S., Stair, J. L., Deluca, P., Corazza, O., et al. (2010). Mephedrone (4-methylmethcathinone; 'meow meow'): chemical, pharmacological and clinical issues. *Psychopharmacology*, doi: 10.1007/s00213-010-2070-x

Schifano, F., Davey, Z., Corazza, O., Furia L. D., Farre, M., Flesland, L. & The Psychonaut Web Mapping Research Group. (2009). *Mephedrone report.*

Schmid, A.P. & Jongman, A. J., (2005). *Political Terrorism: A New Guide to Actors, Authors, Concepts, Data Bases, Theories, & Literature. New Brunswick*, NJ: Transaction Publishers.

Shaw, C.R., & McKay, H.D.(1942). *Juvenile delinquency and urban areas.* Chicago: University of Chicago Press.

Shaw, L. (2013, January 18). What is catfishing and why you should care. Retrieved

Sherman, L. W., Gartin, P. R., & Buerger, M. E. (1989). Hot spots of predatory crime: routine activities and the criminology of place. *Criminology, 27*(2), 27-55.

Shetty, S. (2005, April 13). *Introduction to spyware keyloggers.* Retrieved May 1, 2010, from http://www.symantec.com/connect/articles/introduction-spyware-keyloggers

Shoemaker, D. and Kennedy, D. (2009). Criminal profiling and cyber-criminal investigations. In F. Schmalleger, & M. Pittaro (Eds.), *Crimes of the Internet* (pp. 456-476). Upper Saddle River, NJ: Prentice Hall

Shoemaker, D.J. (2000). *Theories of delinquency: An examination of explanations of delinquent behavior*, New York: Oxford University Press.

Skinner, W. F., & Fream, A. M. (1997). A social learning theory analysis of computer crime among college students. *Journal of Research In Crime & Delinquency*, *34*(4), 495-518.

Smith, R.(2010). "International Identity Crime." *Cindy Smith, Sheldon Zhang, and Rosemary Barberet (Eds.), Routledge Handbook of International Criminology.* London and New York: Routledge.

Smith, S. J. (1982). Victimization in the inner city. *British Journal of Criminology,* 22(2), 386-402.

Spiller, H. A., Ryan, M. L, Weston, R. R., & Jansen, J. (2011). Clinical experience with and analytical confirmation of "bath salts" and "legal highs" (syntheticcathinones) in the United States. *Clinical Toxicology*. 49, 499–505

Spradley, J. P. (1979). *The Ethnographic Interview*. New York: Hancourt Brace Jovanovich College.

Stack, S., Wasserman, I., & Kern, R. (2004). Adult social bonds and use of internet pornography. Social Science Quarterly (Blackwell Publishing Limited), 85(1), 75-88. doi:10.1111/j.0038-4941.2004.08501006.x

Stalder, F. (1998). *The logic of networks: Social landscapes vis-à-vis the space of flows*. Retrieved November 26, 2005, from http://www.ctheory.net/ text_file.asp?pick=263

Standler, B. R. (2002, September 4). *Computer crime*. Retrieved April, 25, 2010, from http://www.rbs2.com/ccrime.htm

Standler, B. R. (2002, September 4). *Computer crime*. Retrieved February 6, 2005, from http://www.rbs2.com/ccrime.htm

Stolp, S. T. (2011). *Cathinone Analogs (AKA "Bath Salts") and California Regulation.*
Retrieved May, 1, 2014 from http://www.cdph.ca.gov

Sutherland, E. (1947). *Principles of criminology* (4th ed.). New York: Harper & Row.

Sykes, G., & Matza, D. (1957). Techniques of Neutralization: A theory of delinquency. *American Sociological Review*, 22, 664-670.

Symantec Corporation. (2010). *Corporate profile*. Retrieved May 1, 2010, from http://www.symantec.com/about/profile/index.jsp

Taylor, P. A. (1999). *Hackers: Crime in the digital sublime*. New York: Routledge.

Taylor, W. R., Caeti, J. T., Loper, D. K., Fritsch, J. E., and Liederbach, J (2006). *Digital crime and digital terrorism*. New Jersey: Person Education.

Thomas, D., & Loader, B. (2000). Introduction–Cybercrime: Law enforcement, security and surveillance in the information age. In D. Thomas & B. Loader (Eds.), *Cybercrime: Law enforcement, security and surveillance in the information age*. London: Routledge.

Tiernan, B. (2000). *E-tailing*. Chicago: Dearborn.

Tikk, E., Kaska, K., and Vihul, L., (2010) *International Cyber Incidents: Legal Considerations*. CCD COE Publications Tallinn

Tilley, N. (1993b) *Understanding car parks, crime and CCTIV: Evaluation lessons from safer cities*. London: Home Office.

Topping, A., Hern, A. (2014, April 13). UK buying more legal and illegal drugs online, survey finds: Global drug survey (gds) finds users moving from dealers to internet, while extent of alcohol use remains 'very worrying.' In *the Guardian*. Retrieved November 1,2014 from http://www.theguardian.com

Turgeman-Goldschmidt, O. (2008). Meanings that hackers assign to their being a hacker. *International Journal of Cyber Criminology*, *2*(2), 382-396.

UNODC (United Nations Office on Drugs and Crime). *The Use of the Internet for Terrorist Purposes*. Draft No.3, Vienna, Austria: United Nations Office on Drugs and Crime in collaboration with the United Nations Counter-Terrorism Implementation Task Force. 2012.

Viacom International Inc. (2014). Catfish: The TV Show. Retrieved January 10, 2014, from MTV.com: http://www.mtv.com/shows/catfish/

Vold, G.B., Bernard, T. J., & Snipes, J. (2002). Theoretical criminology (5th ed.). NewYork: Oxford University Press.

Volonino, L., Anzaldua, R., Godwin, J., Kessler, C.(2007). *Computer Forensics: Principles and Practices*. Pearson/ Prentice Hall (2007).

Wall, D. (2001). Cybercrimes and the internet. In D. Wall (ed.) *Crime and the*

Wall, D. S. (2005). The Internet as a conduit for criminals. In A. Pattavina (Ed.), Information technology and the criminal justice system (pp. 77–98). Thousand

Washington Post (2008, August 26). Data Breaches Have Surpassed Level for All of '07, Report Finds. Retrived January 21, 2012 from. http://www.washingtonpost.com.

Webb, B., & Laycock, G. (1992) *Reducing crime on the London underground: An evaluation of three pilot projects.*. London: Home Office.

Wiatrowski, M. D., Griswold, D. B., & Roberts, M. K. (1981, October). Social control theory and delinquency. *American Sociological Review*, *46*(5), 525-541. Retrieved March 3, 2013

Williams, F. P., & McShane, M. D. (1999). *Criminological theory.* Upper Saddle River, NJ: Prentice Hall.

Wilson, C., *Computer Attack and Cyberterrorism: Vulnerabilities and policy issues for Congress*, Congressional Research Service Report for Congress, (Congressional Research Service, 2005)

Winstock, A. R. (2014). The global drug survey 2014 findings: Reflections on the results of the world's biggest ever drug survey by dr adam winstock. In *Global Drug Survey*. Retrieved November 1, 2014 from www.globaldrugsurvey.com

Wood, D. M., Greene, S. L. & Dargan, P. I., (2011) Clinical pattern of toxicity associated with the novel synthetic cathinone mephedrone. *Emergency Medicine Journal* 28(4), 280-2

Yar, M. (2005). The novelty of 'cyber crime': An assessment in light of routine activity theory. *European Society of Criminology, 2*, 407-427.

Yoon, H., Yun, M., Freilich, J., Chermak, S., Morris, R. (2012) *Cyberterrorism: Trends and Responses*. Korean Institute of Criminology.

Index